THE EXECUTIVE IN
AFRICAN GOVERNMENTS

The Executive
in African Governments

BEREKET H. SELASSIE

LONDON
HEINEMANN
NAIROBI · IBADAN · LUSAKA

Heinemann Educational Books
48 Charles Street, London w1x 8AH
P.M.B. 5205, Ibadan · P.O. Box 45314, Nairobi
P.O. Box 3966, Lusaka

EDINBURGH MELBOURNE TORONTO AUCKLAND
HONG KONG SINGAPORE KUALA LUMPUR NEW DELHI

ISBN 0 435 83100 3 (cased)
0 435 83101 1 (paper)

Printed in Great Britain by
Cox & Wyman Ltd,
London, Fakenham and Reading

To Koki

For her courage and perseverance in our moments of
trial from Harar to Philadelphia

Prepared with the editorial assistance of Gideon-Cyrus M. Mutiso,
Senior Lecturer in Government, University of Nairobi

Contents

Acknowledgements

My thanks are due to Professor A. N. Allot of the University of London School of Oriental and African Studies, who supervised the research when it was undertaken in the form of a thesis for the degree of Doctor of Philosophy in the University of London, under the title 'The Executive in African Government: A Comparative Constitutional Study'. His keen interest was a source of encouragement, and his criticism stimulating. I must also express my gratitude to Mr. Neville Rubin for his assistance throughout the period of research, and to Dr. Gideon-Cyrus M. Mutiso, who helped me in editing the manuscript and in bringing some parts up to date, especially sections on Kenya.

Many people helped in providing me with material and information relevant to the study. Officials of African embassies in London and Paris spent valuable time in providing such help, discussing some sensitive questions, as a result of which I gained some insight into the actual working of the executive in Africa. I wish to extend my deep gratitude to all these people, who must remain unnamed.

I am also greatly indebted to the following: the library staff of the Institute of Advanced Legal Studies of the University of London; the library staff of the Commonwealth Relations office; the Institut de l'Administration Publique, Paris, the Secrétariat Général du Gouvernement Direction de la Documentation, Paris; the Institut Universitaire de Hautes Études Internationales, Geneva, and for the revision of some of the material, the library staff of the Economic Commission for Africa, Addis Ababa.

This study was made possible through the grant of a research fellowship of the Institute of Advanced Legal Studies (1965–6), and of a British Council scholarship (1966–7), for both of which I am deeply grateful.

Most important, I am grateful to my family who had to suffer a long separation, and who, far from complaining, were a constant source of encouragement from afar.   B. H. S.

Preface

My decision to undertake this study was stimulated in May 1963, during the first meeting of the African Heads of States which established the Organisation of African Unity.

Further enquiries revealed a political phenomenon that has been called neo-presidentialism. The advent of one-party government which was the basis of neo-presidentialism has been complicated by the intervention of the military in politics, or by the threat of such intervention. A comparative study of African constitutions focused on the executive was therefore, I felt, worth undertaking.

This comparative study begins with an introduction and is followed by three parts. Part One, which has three chapters, deals with various relevant constitutional provisions, setting out the constitutional basis of executive power. In the first chapter of this part the single-executive systems are discussed in detail. This chapter is the core of the Part, and indeed of the whole work, as it provides the point of departure for Parts Two and Three. It is therefore more detailed and lengthy than Chapters Two and Three, which deal, respectively, with the dual-executive systems and with two remaining monarchies. In the former case the qualifying phrase 'in historical perspective' is added to the title to indicate that the notion of a dual executive is not of current constitutional significance. The inclusion of this chapter is justified on the grounds that the African single-executive system, called neo-presidentialism, is an outgrowth from it. This historical link goes back to the last decade.

Part Two, entitled the Dynamics of Neo-Presidential Power, contains an account of the relation of the political party and the civil service with the executive. The discussion of the twin pillars of party and bureaucracy on which neo-presidentialism rests, in their relation to the executive, is one of the most important aspects of this study. Inevitably the process of decision-making, from the conception of a given policy to its detailed implementation, figures prominently in this discussion. Here the question of styles of decision-making is taken up, and one of the basic theses is that styles of decision-making in neo-presidentialism were partly determined by colonial and pre-colonial periods.

The basic thesis of Part Three is that neo-presidentialism in Africa has not succeeded in solving the problem of participation in politics and development, with the possible exception of Tanzania. This has mainly contributed to the intervention of the military in politics.

This work is based on a thesis for a Doctorate of Philosophy of the University of London and has been revised in a few parts and reduced in size. It is offered to provide a starting point for the search for institutional devices that our continent will need to secure stability, participation and development.

B. H. S.

Publisher's Note

In between the writing and printing of this book a number of events in Africa have modified in detail the structure of individual governments. The author was able to take account of these changes at the final press stage. As a result a number of new footnotes have been entered and numbered 'a', 'b', etc., as necessary.

General Introduction

The Meaning and Position of the Executive in Africa

The dictionary meaning of the term 'executive' in a political context is (i) that branch of the government charged with the execution of laws; and (ii) the person or persons in whom the high magistracy of the state is vested. The technical description of the term given in modern text-books on constitutional law is as involved as the tasks performed by modern governments. In modern times in the West and Japan there has been a general increase in these tasks, as the so-called 'welfare state' has taken over more and more social and economic functions, formerly performed by private persons or institutions. This increase has been accompanied by an increase in the share of the executive in the initiation of legislation, which according to the doctrine of separation of powers was the province of Parliament. In the socialist bloc the executive has not grown so fast, on account of the preponderant power of the party apparatus.

In Western societies, specialization of function was not limited to the public sector. Thus, economic function has tended to be associated with special social units (firms), the religious with other such units (churches); the advent of government intervention in the regulation and control of social and economic life, therefore, met stiff opposition from some of these social units.

In Africa it has been (and to a great extent still is) common for one social unit such as a lineage group to be concerned with economic, political, and religious functions.[1] The advent, in Africa, of the modern state with an increased share in the planning, regulation, execution, and control, of social and economic matters is thus a development which could not be expected to meet the types of opposition encountered in Western societies. The types of government which have been established, are also sometimes explained in terms of the nature of African community life, and as creatures of or reactions to the colonial experience.[2]

Turning to the definition of the executive in Africa, we may start with the dictionary definition in general, and particularize it to the transitional African situation, by saying that the executive in Africa today is (i) that branch of government charged with the planning, initiation, and execution, of laws; and (ii) the person or persons in whom the high magistracy of the state is vested, who may also have the role of inspiring, guiding, and leading the nation in a period of political, social, and economic transformation.

In African constitutional arrangements the executive has been given, in most states, the right to dissolve Parliament or to refer the subject of conflict to popular judgement in a referendum, which may be so timed and arranged as to produce a desired result. It is true that in the classical cabinet system, the threat of dissolution could be used by the Prime Minister to preserve party discipline and to maintain his government in office. But this assumes the interplay of two rival parties, whereas in Africa the dominance of the executive is made more secure through a one-party state.

The implications of such dominance are immense. The executive, together with the one-party organization, is the most important political factor in Africa, as later pages of this study will show.[3] One school of political science has offered a definition of the political system generous enough to include both systems in transition and revolutionary régimes in the process of acquiring 'legitimacy'. According to this study a political system is:

> That system of interactions to be found in all independent societies which performs the functions of integration and adaptation (both internally and *vis-à-vis* other societies) by means of the employment, or threat of employment, of more or less legitimate physical compulsion.[4]

The political system, not only as the legitimate order maintaining society, but also as a system for transforming it, acquires a dynamic significance and hence becomes of great relevance to societies in transition such as present-day African societies. Political systems in Africa are largely the creations of the modern nationalist leaders who are in charge of the governments. The role of the executive is particularly important in the life of the political system. The role itself is in a large measure created and developed by the leaders themselves, just as the political institutions are shaped by them.

A study of the executive at a crucial period of transition is justified on the ground that it may contribute to an understanding of the character of the nation in transition. In Africa, more than elsewhere, the executive today is very much the centre of network of institutions of the state. And the men who hold executive offices are the central and dominant figures of the society. Most of them led the movements for national independence from colonial rule. They were the central characters during the drama of national birth, and they embodied the hopes and aspirations of their fellow countrymen. It is indeed difficult at times to separate the man from the office, which in many cases was created by or for the man.[5]

It might be said that the executive is a superstructure which merely reflects the character of the society in which it operates, or that the men represent a small group of the educated power-*élite*. This is, of course, true. But Africa is not unique in providing examples which demonstrate the validity of the proposition that people who dominate the seat of government over a certain period leave peculiar marks on their societies. There are many such examples in history. In some of these, in fact, important aspects of the central institutions were worked out with the central figure of the time in mind. The position of the President of the United States of America, for example, would have been made much weaker but for the presence of a public figure like George Washington, who commanded the respect and confidence of all the leaders of the states even though they were jealous of their states' rights and interests. President de Gaulle and the constitution of the Fifth French Republic provide another example.

In the new African states, the executives do not reflect their societies in the evolutionary sense that their positions represent natural outgrowths of the configuration of political forces of the societies. They are new creations superimposed on their societies, which they seek to transform in the sense that nationalists were creatures of the colonial situation.

The term 'nation-building' sums up the political aspect of such attempts at transformation, and chief among the factors in this process is the President, who acts, *inter alia*, as an outward symbol of a new centre of loyalty and national unity. Nor should the titles adopted by some of the African leaders such as 'Mwalimu', 'Mzee', 'El Rais', or 'Osagyefo', be understood as the whimsical creation of power-hungry men. Each has a significance connected with the tradition of the particular society (e.g. Mzee and Osagyefo) or has a definite connection with the personal history of the particular leaders (e.g. Mwalimu). To take Mwalimu, for example, the word means 'teacher' in Swahili, and President Nyerere, who was a teacher by profession, is referred to as 'Mwalimu', the teacher of all his countrymen, in the sense of one who leads. This, however, is so, not merely because of his profession, but because he travelled extensively up and down the country to organize branches of the political party which he had founded in 1954.[6]

Such devices were designed to strengthen the image of the new leaders and with them the nation, which represented a wider loyalty than the tribes to which Africans had hitherto been accustomed.

The question how an ethnic or other loyalty can be replaced by, or transformed into, a wider loyalty, goes hand in hand with the question of national leadership and the successful projection of new ideas and values connected with such leadership. The writ of the colonial power, acting through a network of provincial and district administrators, had treated as a state what had previously been groups of people held together by kingship, kinship, or religion.[7]

Boundaries existed in Africa before the Europeans arrived; but they were cultural boundaries rather than legal dividing lines. The new African leaders inherited from the colonial powers states with arbitrarily fixed boundaries cutting across ethnic and linguistic groups.[8]

It has been said that faced with such a situation the new African executives were:

> far less favourably placed than were the Governments of those 18th century and 19th century states which came into being as a result of the application of organised force, such as the United States of America, Italy, and Germany.[9]

According to this view the 'peaceful' passage to independent statehood of the new African states deprived them of an element of cohesion. Such a view is based on the assumption that the heat of battle and the flow of blood provides a kind of spiritual mortar binding citizens together. If so, and this is by no means certain, then the new nations will have to make do with a political substitute for this 'missing element'. Such a substitute can only be dynamic leadership which can successfully mobilize people, on the basis of ideas that can move people to build a nation.

One result of this can be the replacement of some features of the state apparatus left by the colonial power, and the ideas underlying it, by new institutional forms and patterns. The political awakening of the Africans, which had started slowly, prepared the ground for such new forms and patterns. The term 'neo-presidentialism' summarizes these new forms and patterns. The political awakening, usually called nationalism, in general went through several phases when the ideologies and institutional preferences changed.[10]

Among the most potent ideas which the nationalist leaders used in their claim for independence were those of democracy. They invoked every principle cherished in the politics of the metropolitan world in order to achieve their ends. This started a process of political education among African peoples. 'One man one vote' was a companion of 'Uhuru', 'Umoja', and 'Istiqlal', in the political vocabulary of the ordinary African, just as *négritude* and Pan-Africanism moved African leaders to seek a larger African unity 'transcending ethnic and national difference'.[11] The nationalist movements flowered in the forties and early fifties and started bearing fruit – the fruit of political independence – in the late fifties and early sixties. Morocco, Tunisia, and the Sudan, had all attained independence by the mid-fifties, but the flood-gate was opened in 1957 with the birth of independent Ghana.

The nationalist movements had produced new political and organizational forms. The formation of political parties, the campaigns for election to legislative councils, the rallies and demonstrations, were part of the experience of the latest stage of colonial rule.

The new leaders swept to power on the crest of nationalist waves established their authority in a very short period of time.[12] It all happened so rapidly that some members of the colonial governments did not see the full significance of the events, and continued to refer to the leaders as a band of agitators.[13] Those who realized the seriousness of the situation, however, had to do all they could to remain in power. But their efforts were not very successful. A new era had begun. The leaders were recognized as the legitimate successors to the colonial governors and the stage was set for negotiations for self-rule.

All the while, organized African masses watched with keen expectation – all eyes focused on the new leaders, who personified

B

new hopes, and who commanded the respect and admiration of their peoples, which was translated into authority when the colonial power, hitherto the central and only authority, handed over rule to them. The final phase of this transfer was when the election which put a new African government in office gave it the stamp of legitimacy. The election of the government and later of the President (or Prime Minister, as the case may be) was an event of particular significance in the making of the new legitimate African authority. A whole people's attention was centred on men who were expected to lead the people to a better future. It was no mere ritual, although it was soon to degenerate to this; it was an event in which the people took part, with pride and hope.

Such being the ways in which African peoples sprang into their independent statehood, and the roles played by the leaders and their political parties, in many instances the independent state in the early days came to be associated with the party and the leader. These are the reasons which justified the use of the term neo-presidentialism to describe the system that emerged.

Authority has been advanced as a key concept in understanding the nature and function of the political system, in preference to Max Weber's concept of physical compulsion.[14] According to this approach, authority is established when a general feeling prevails that it must be obeyed. The question how and why such authority comes to be established is not easy to answer, and is perhaps better left to psychologists to grapple with.

If man is a social animal first, and a political animal second, then it would follow that those who have the monopoly of political power should not rest until they capture the old social 'centres of authority' which can refract the light of the new ideas and values which come forth from the new political system. It appears that the monopoly and planned use of the media of communication (propaganda) can in fact achieve this over a short period, provided there is relative order and stability. But the old social order persists and with it some of its values. A dynamic view of politics shows that the notion of stability does not result from the immutability of opposed or balanced forces, but as Jean Buchmann has written:

> dans la capacité d'absorption, dont fait preuve l'ordre social garanti par le régime politique en vigeur, à l'égard des forces qui visent à le transformer.[15]

Where there is inadaptability or incompatibility of structures and 'the margin of tolerance' is passed, then a sudden break or revolution ensues.[16]

In this regard the position of traditional elements is of interest. They are sometimes tolerated in modern societies when they are harmless or helpful. But if they are given representation at high levels, and especially in the person of the Head of State, they can become the centres round which neo-traditional forces can crystallize and thus pose a threat to a new order. The problem has been faced in two ways; either they are suppressed initially by the new political force, as happened in Guinea, or they are tolerated and even given representation at a high level as in Uganda and Lesotho. In the second case the change comes when new forces emerge, rendering the system anachronistic.[17]

Normally a new political leadership establishes its authority over a traditional society not only through the assertion of new principles and the manipulation of symbols and values but *through the effective use of propaganda*. Initially, if the new political power is acquired by an act of revolution, physical force is likely to be visible in the foreground,[18] but eventually the military will withdraw to the background, and physical 'compulsion' will be replaced by a psychological 'compulsion' in the daily life of the community.

The government exerts influence through a massive pressure of information and persuasion which never relaxes its hold on the population. In order to achieve maximum results every medium is used – oral, printed, pictorial, plastic, musical, or dramatic.

The propaganda of the deed is also used, consisting, for example, in symbolic gestures of the leader. Essentially, propaganda is an act of advocacy of a deliberately one-sided nature with certain aims. This is naturally supplemented by instruction and information on a wide range of subjects useful to their recipients. Such instruction and information, apart from its intrinsic worth, can often serve as an incentive for more propaganda. Social revolutions in modern times have developed new techniques of persuasion and propaganda. The party and its auxiliary organizations are used as well as the direct media such as Press, radio, and television, and the latest research in psychology.[19]

In all propaganda there is an inevitable stress on higher principles, socialism for example.[20] In practice, however, personalities and power politics play a large part in the process. Effective use of propaganda machinery may sometimes require glamour and the use of symbols. But too frequent use of such methods tends to draw attention away from principles, which may be replaced by, or confused with, cults. When this happens, ends and means get mixed up and the medium becomes the message. This does not pose a threat to commercial advertising – the 'tiger in the tank' approach has always the same end, namely sales and more sales. The criterion is novelty, and if the 'tiger' is replaced by a 'panther' there will be no public outcry. But in politics the means of social ends may be elevated to the realm of values desirable in themselves, and this complicates the picture.

What of the citizen's part in all this? To some political scientists the citizen is an individual, participating in social life through the medium of groups. He is a citizen 'much more through his productive activity in the economy and in culture than through the expression of his opinion'.[21]

The position of the citizen in transitional African societies today cannot be defined so easily. There are two forces claiming his loyalty: on the one hand the traditional forces of kinship groups from which even the educated *élite* have not escaped completely; on the other, the modern state with all its new attractions.[22]

The modern state makes demands on the citizen just as the lineage group did, so that his place is redefined in a modern setting as a member of a group which acquires a new significance. Where the 'mobilization approach' has been adopted, the demands of society may be greater and the group's activities may be channelled for productive efforts.[23] The individual plays the 'rules of the game' – old and new – for various economic, social, and psychological reasons. The individuals making up the mass of the new African societies often play new roles with enthusiasm. This is a blessing, in that it is needed for new countries in the process of growth. But it can sometimes pose problems connected with the question of authority which, in the newly formed states, is hierarchically organized and concentrated at the top.

The question can be viewed at two levels.

From the point of view of the citizen's creative participation in politics, the system tends to exclude large sections of the population from the exercise of political power, because it is hierarchic and concentrated. This becomes more significant in view of the general absence or underdevelopment of a political infra-structure, including voluntary associations, at the local levels outside the cities. This, as Edward Shils has aptly put it, 'deepens the silence in the countryside in matters of day-to-day political concern'.[24] The political party thus becomes an all-purpose organization supplying the need for an otherwise absent sociopolitical infra-structure. But the danger here is that, where disenchantment with the centre sets in, the party activists may have to deal with the problem of apathy, since the centre and the party are identified. Alternatively, the various peripheries begin to veto the centre, which then concentrates all its resources on controlling the peripheries. This takes resources away from nation building.

Secondly, the problem may be viewed from the point of view of the abuse of power. The power originally held in trust for a definite purpose or cause may be enjoyed for its own sake or held too long and used for time-serving panaceas in the face of unpleasant social and economic realities. More specifically, the one-party state and the strong centralized executive which it entrenches may lead to the emergence of a self-perpetuating ruling *élite* on whose memory the perquisites of office play a trick as to its original mission. The ruling *élite* may in turn start playing a series of 'confidence tricks' on the public, excusing or justifying certain acts or omissions, and, in general, not paying sufficient attention to the public good.

In such circumstances, ideology, socialist or otherwise, can be used as a smoke-screen to conceal reality. Nor is it inconceivable that this may happen when the leader and a few of his closest colleagues are honest and dedicated men, convinced that the best effort is being made by all concerned. For example, Colonel Afrifa, one of the authors of the military coup which deposed President Nkrumah, has written:

> Nkrumah's new class promised to abolish social differences but it increased them by acquiring the products of the nation's workshops and by granting privileges to its adherents. It promised loudly that it was fulfilling the historical mission of the 'final' liberation of the Ghanaian from every misery, but in reality it acted exactly in the opposite direction. Nkrumah's new class led a life of opulence and extravagance in contrast to the growing misery to which the rest of the country was being subjected.[25]

But even Afrifa, a bitter opponent of Nkrumah, nowhere mentions anything hinting that Nkrumah himself was guilty of 'a life of opulence and extravagance.'[26]

The truth is that one-party régimes have an inherent tendency to create a 'new class' in which a handful of 'palace favourites' have control over the access to the executive chief of state and

over government policy and action. The concentrated and centralized power facilitates the emergence of such a 'palace régime' by
laying emphasis on the role of the President as the centre of a new
loyalty and national unity, which in itself is a desirable thing.
The very factor which gives dynamism to such a system may also
be the source of its weakness. An important weakness at critical
times in the life of such a régime is that it makes the office and the
man susceptible to removal along with the system.

Such a situation may create temptations for military adven-
turers, when things go wrong, as can be seen from the series of
coups which have taken place in recent years. The ease with
which a centralized power-structure can be demolished may be
illustrated by these coups. Colonel Afrifa adds poignancy to this
point when he writes:

> On my arrival at the Accra Airport from the Congo in 1962,
> I was to lead the men to Tamale, our destination. I paused
> for a moment and reflected. Should I throw this troop of
> *three hundred men* into Flagstaff House and stop the rot from
> continuing? Should I not by military action stop Kwame
> Nkrumah from leading this country towards communism?...

He hesitated, he tells us, and abandoned the idea, because his
ammunition supply was limited, and because if he failed he feared
he would implicate his commanding officer.[27]

If anything can be learnt from the recent series of military
coups, one imperative is the need to introduce some 'safety valves'
into the one-party state without affecting its dynamism. African
politicians (like all politicians) never tire of making claims that all
is being done in a democratic way. As an illustration we may cite
President Senghor's claim that the successive plans for economic
and social development in Senegal were democratically prepared
'in consultation with all the categories involved and [were] voted
by the elected representatives of the nation.'[28]

It is of interest that Senghor (like the planners in the Republic
of Cameroon), lays due stress on the need to motivate the workers
and '*fill them with a mystique of development*' (italics supplied).[29] But
there is no evidence to show that 'the categories involved' or the
elected representatives of the nation have put much thought into
the task of evolving and refining a system of incentives that is
conducive to change and generally acceptable.

Lastly we must mention the question of mandate and control,
and the relation between these two. When the emphasis is on

effective government the requirement of responsible government pales into insignificance, if it is not completely forgotten. Formal provisions on this need to be backed by extra-constitutional factors if they are to have meaning. The most urgent one is the need to evolve a style which allows meaningful discussion of alternatives by the bulk of the people.

Responsibility should be conceived not in terms of opposition or obstruction, but rather in creative and corrective terms. The need for efficient government and a united nation has motivated constitutional predisposition in favour of parliaments working in co-operation with – indeed dominated by – the executive. The White Paper on the draft Ghana Constitution of 1960 put the matter thus:

> The draft constitution ... has been designed to meet the particular needs of Ghana and to express the realities of Ghana's constitutional position. It is therefore proposed, that the actual Head of the Government should be the President of the Republic. .... It is the Government's view that it is essential in the interests of strong and efficient government that the President and the Assembly should work as one and that this can most effectively be secured by constitutional provisions which link the election of the President to the election of the members of the National Assembly and which provide that if the National Assembly and the President disagree the issue can be decided by a general election.[30]

The chapter on neo-presidential systems will demonstrate that in nearly all cases the presidential mandate and power is so provided for, that it overshadows the supervisory functions of the legislature. But only those who are used to view politics in static terms will dismiss the arrangement as just pure authoritarianism.

The Various Forms of the Executive

No study of forms outside the context of substance (of policy and purpose) can make much sense. The particular form which a government takes should reflect the reality of power relationships. But this may not always be the case. Some governments have traditional forms and progressive aspirations. The reason is that those who wield the power of the state have found that some use could be made of some of the traditional forms. But where the traditional form represents traditional political reality (as it did in Uganda) then there would be conflict between progressive aspirations and traditional interests, or simply between two power blocs. In this connection we may mention the view often advanced that a bicephalous executive is desirable because it makes for varied institutional forms and accommodates more shades of political opinions. It is associated with a parliamentary form of government which is also generally believed to be desirable on the ground that it involves discussion and criticism. It is further claimed that such a system is a sign of political maturity, and that a mature political system is one in which one can feel safe in diversity, in which there is maximum participation of all the different sections of the population.

The major fallacy of such an argument is that it proceeds on an assumption that there is no form of government outside the classical parliamentary form which can guarantee full participation and protection of rights. In fact any form of government which encourages and facilitates mechanisms for thrashing out problems should satisfy the functional test of good government. The parliamentary form can do this, but it can also be obstructive and divisive.

The case for neo-presidentialism has been made on the grounds that it is better suited to the present needs of African countries at a crucial transitional period of their history, when unity and more effective and dynamic state action is required. No one can question the need for unity in a nation. And, while it is not inimical to unity and progress to wish to preserve cultural diversity, a united nation under a strong government will be better placed to guarantee the preservation and development of cultural heritages than a divided nation under an ineffectual government.

In Africa the majority of the states have adopted a unitary (monocephalous) executive presidency, many of them having moved from a classical parliamentary form of government with a dual (bicephalous) executive.

Historically there has been a tendency for Parliaments to gain an ascendancy over absolute monarchs, usually by a gradual process of whittling away of royal prerogatives.[31] Another tendency has been for republics to be established on the ruins of either absolute monarchies or moribund parliamentary régimes. France provides the best example of this. The French experience is instructive, since in France there has been every type of government under different forms since 1789. The attitude of people to the different forms has tended to hinge on their political attitudes, particular forms being associated with certain political positions. It will, therefore, be helpful to outline these attitudes in relation to the executive form advocated.

There have been four attitudes to presidentialism in France. First, there was the traditional extreme left wing view that to have a President in addition to the Prime Minister was an unnecessary duplication and a conservative device to restrain the democratic process.[32] Then there was the traditional extreme right wing (Bonapartist) view that there should be a single chief executive. This curious unity of left and right wing attitudes is explained by the fact that the right wing view stems from the conviction of the need of strong and efficient executive machinery to implement the dictates of the ruler; while on the left there has been a strong statist leaning in socialist thinking, and as socialism replaced liberalism as the ideology of the left, the idea gained ground that the left, once in office, should be in a position to wield strong governmental power in order to carry out its policies.

Thirdly, the radical left-centre generally preferred a dual executive in which an indirectly elected President would be Head of State, but in a weaker position than a Prime Minister, who would be the chief of government. The system under the Third and Fourth Republics represented this attitude. It was so defective, however, that some left wing socialist constitutional lawyers like Professors Duverger and Vedel attacked it, advocating in its place a system under which a President elected universally and directly would be the sole head of the executive.[33]

Lastly there was the conservative right of centre which traditionally wanted to preserve a dual executive in which the President was more powerful than the Prime Minister. The executive of the Fifth Republic of President de Gaulle was based on this idea with an important novelty, namely the fact that after 1962 the presidential mandate was based on universal suffrage. This last factor has given the system under the Fifth Republic a shift of emphasis from parliamentary debates to presidential tours and periodic pronouncements as the focus of political activity. This, as we shall see in Chapter One, has had a definite impact on African neo-presidentialism.[34]

This leaves us with the monarchies and the military executives. All that need be done here is to point out certain anomalies from the point of view of classification; the rest must be left to the appropriate chapters. If we conceive constitutional law in dynamic terms – in terms of change – from absolute monarchy through different forms of parliamentary government to presidentialism – we come up against two remarkable facts: (*a*) the adaptation of some African monarchies, some of which (e.g. in Ethiopia) assumed a modern parliamentary guise, while in reality traditional authority holds sway; and (*b*) the reversal of African neo-presidentialism through military coups, which takes us back to square one, as it were. From the point of view of classification the military régimes may be dismissed as unconstitutional, but they remain part of the reality. To the extent that they do not carry the stamp of legitimacy their 'constitutional' structure does not merit any detailed study in an inquiry such as this. But the advent of military rule, such as it is, and the factors which give rise to it cannot be ignored even by constitutional purists. Nevertheless, these two types – monarchy and 'military executives' – must be given consideration.

NOTES

1. cf. Lloyd A. Fallers, *Bantu Bureaucracy*, Chicago U.P., 1965, pp. 4–5.
2. cf. Julius K. Nyerere, '*Ujamaa*', *The Basis of African Socialism*, Dar-es-Salaam, 1962, p. 3.
3. When reference is made to party organizations, this is to be understood to exclude states ruled by the military.
4. Gabriel A. Almond and James S. Coleman (ed.) in *Politics of the Developing Areas*, Princeton U.P., 1960, p. 7.
5. For a biographical account of some leaders and events *see* Ronald Segal, *African Profiles*, Penguin African Library, Harmondsworth, 1963.
6. cf. R. Segal, op. cit., pp. 123–30.
7. cf. John Fletcher-Cooke, 'Parliament, Executive and Civil Service' in *Parliament as an Export*, Sir Alan Burns (ed.), Allen & Unwin, London, 1966, p. 154.
8. cf. Paul Bohannan, *African Outline*, Penguin African Library, Harmondsworth, 1966, p. 28.
9. John Fletcher-Cooke, ibid.
10. For discussion of these phases and documentation of the thought *see* G-C. M. Mutiso and S. W. Rohio, *Readings in African Political Thought*, Heinemann, 1974.
11. cf. The Preamble of the O.A.U. Charter.
12. By comparison with Gandhi and Nehru, for whom it took decades.
13. cf. Basil Davidson, *Which Way Africa*, Penguin, Harmondsworth, 1964, p. 107.
14. Max Weber, 'Politics as a Vocation', in Gerth and Mills, *From Max Weber*, New York, 1946, p. 7. cf. this with D. Easton, *The Political System; An inquiry into the State of Political Science*, New York, 1953, pp. 130–3; both are quoted and discussed in Almond and Coleman, op. cit., pp. 5 and 6 respectively.

15. J. Buchmann, *L'Afrique Noire Indépendante*, Paris, 1962, p. 13. And again: 'A politically stable society is one which enjoys sufficient vitality to adapt its structure and become amenable to change.' ibid.

16. ibid.

17. cf. Buchmann, ibid.

18. The law is represented by helmeted soldiers bearing arms and placed at strategic positions throughout the land. This is preceded or accompanied by the neutralization of principal leaders of the old order in various ways. A show of force through military parades and civilian demonstrations of support is invariably organized.

19. An enlightened observation of advertising techniques shows that commercial salesmanship owes much to the lessons of political propaganda and vice versa. One salient feature is repetition, another is imitation.

20. Just as the battles for political rights were fought in the seventeenth and eighteenth centuries against 'divine rights', in the name of natural law.

21. cf. J. W. Lapierre, *Le pouvoir politique*, Paris, Presse Universitaire de France, Coll. Initiation Philosophique, 1953.

22. In his traditional setting the African citizen fits in very well with the definition which makes membership of a group the key factor; cf. e.g. I. M. Lewis, *Pastoral Democracy*, O.U.P., 1961, p. 242, in which he explains the practice of collective vengeance in Northern Somalia in terms of self help as 'canalised by lineage affiliation and given structural definition through the complementary principles of clanship and contract'. This is further explained by reference to 'the ecological context of acute competition for sparse resources, and in the abrogation of individual responsibility through group loyalties'.

23. In parts where there is a long history of feuds and wars, latent aggression can thus be usefully channelled for productive purposes; cf. I. M. Lewis, op. cit., pp. 242–65.

24. Edward Shils, 'The Military in the Political Development of the New States' in *The Role of the Military in Underdeveloped Countries*, J. J. Johnson (ed.), Princeton, 1962.

25. Colonel A. A. Afrifa, *The Ghana Coup*, Frank Cass, London, 1966, pp. 84–5.

26. The Ghana *coup* is discussed in Chapter 7. At this stage it must be said that the gap between the new *élite* and the masses which Afrifa describes is not peculiar to Ghana, and Nkrumah's domestic economic and social policy (e.g. industrialization) and the greatly augmented role of the state in this activity is worthy of a closer and more serious analysis by people who are free from a subjective involvement like Afrifa's. Afrifa, who claims to come from a long line of Ashanti chiefs (op. cit., p. 43), believes that chieftaincy should do exactly what Nkrumah was trying to do:

> ... It (chieftaincy) is the embodiment of our souls. The chiefs are traditional focal points of a people's collective activity. They are the rallying-point of our national endeavours. It is in these roles that chieftaincy provides the momentum for our people's advancement.

(op. cit., p. 116).

27. op. cit., pp. 85–6.
28. cf. L. S. Senghor, *African Forum, Vol. 1 No. 3* (1900) pp. 10–16; cf. also Senghor, *On African Socialism*, Pall Mall, London, 1965.
29. Senghor, op. cit., p. 16.
30. White Paper No. 1/60, pp. 5–6.
31. e.g. The British Parliament.
32. cf. J. E. S. Hayward, *Parliamentary Affairs, Winter 1964/65*, p. 23.
33. ibid.
34. The impact of the Westminster (cabinet) model is seen in dual executive parliamentary systems which are discussed in Chapter Four.

PART I

The Constitutional Framework

African Neo-Presidential Systems

Section I Constitutional Basis of the Presidency

A. Colonial Antecedents

Constitutional developments in the majority of African countries in the years of metropolitan government are marked by a good deal of imitation of metropolitan systems. The phenomenon continued to be present in many cases even after the achievement of complete independence. This is perhaps understandable as all new constitutions are more or less inspired by some model or other. The countries of former 'British' Africa began by adopting the Westminster model, those of 'French' Africa followed the French model, and the ex-Belgian territories were influenced by the Belgian system, in each case modifications being made to suit local conditions.

In Anglophone Africa the monarchical system was at first introduced, harnessed to a parliamentary form of government, *à la* Westminster, with Her Britannic Majesty as the Head of State. In Francophone Africa the accession to independence saw the rejection of the classic parliamentary system at the outset. This was fortuitous as far as Africa was concerned. The weight of French constitutional tradition might have fallen on the meagre shoulders of the new African states, had the tradition itself not been subjected to a major change under the Gaullist Constitution of 1958. The time and the political circumstances under which this constitution had been promulgated coincided with, and to a large extent produced, the accession to independence of most of these states. For one of the subjects of the terms of reference of the

Comité-Consultatif Constitutionnel which studied the draft of the 1958 Constitution was 'the solution of the problem in Black Africa'.[1]

There are, of course, states whose constitutions were not modelled on European metropolitan systems – or, at any rate, not directly. Liberia is one example, the United Arab Republic is another. At all events, in all cases institutional inspiration and the reasons for the adoption of certain principles or practices (or, their rejection) are complex. Furthermore, they are not always traceable to a single system. It has been suggested, for example, that the Guinean Presidential régime has borrowed from contemporary constitutional practice of the United States of America.[2]

Nevertheless Guinea's decision to reject the offer of entry into the *Communauté* in 1958 did not mean the rejection of the whole of its French constitutional heritage. The influence of the Gaullist Constitution of 1958 is absent in Guinea because of Guinea's rejection of the framework (the *Communauté*) under which it was proposed. This meant that the provisions limiting the role of the legislature and augmenting that of the executive, present in other Francophone states, are absent in the Constitution of Guinea, even though the system is presidential.

The special significance of the Guinea constitutional system is that it shows what happens when a new state chooses to strike out on its own in search of an institution which will provide a basis for political as well as economic independence. The Constitution combines a presidential system, election of the President, with a parliamentary system, control by Parliament of the government, thus producing a hybrid régime which can only be explained or sustained in the context of the one-party state, as we shall see in Chapter Four.[3]

Ghana's constitutional history under Nkrumah also illustrates the same process. Nkrumah's criticism of the Independence Constitution of 1957 as 'imposed' by the British Government[4] and his subsequent actions to change it drastically did not entail the complete abandonment of the heritage of British Constitutional practices. As an observer has written:

> It is significant that (apart from New Zealand) the country whose constitutional law corresponds the most closely to that of Britain in these matters is Ghana, where the spirit and practices of British institutions are not consciously emulated.[5]

Yet the Nkrumahist Constitution of 1960 is a landmark in constitutional development in several respects, as we shall see later.

The complex nature of the factors governing the relation between the institutional sources and nascent institutions may be further illustrated by the curious fact that while those countries that declared 'rejection' of the colonial heritage did not always do so, those that had started by a slavish imitation in many instances proceeded to use this initial act as a point of departure for bold innovations. Thus many of the Francophone states, having first adopted the Gaullist presidential system, have changed it, giving their own new régimes certain original traits.

It may also be noted that the metropolitan powers were not always solely responsible for the transplantation of their systems at moments of independence. This might not appear to be remarkable in the case of the former British and French states, where the grant of independence had been carried out in most cases under circumstances conducive to institutional emulation. It is remarkable, however, that on the eve of the independence of Zaire, despite all the rancour that accompanied the event, some of the more militant nationalist leaders of that country had insisted at the Round Table Conference in Brussels on the introduction of Belgian parliamentary government, because, it was argued, it was better to copy a system that 'had been tested' than to face the hazards of experimentation. Thus the *loi fondamentale* of Zaire adopted the Belgian parliamentary system including a non-responsible Head of State.[6]

The prime implication of the Westminster model was the fact of dualism in the executive, in which the Head of State is not an effective head of government. The effective executive power resides in a Prime Minister presiding over a cabinet of ministers whose appointment he largely determines. In Africa the dual-executive system did not last very long. Ghana set a trend for a different system by introducing a Republican Constitution in May 1960.

Ghana's example was followed by others – Tanganyika (1962), Nigeria (1963), Uganda (1963), Zambia (1964), Kenya (1965), and Malawi (1966). In the Gambia an attempt to follow the trend did not obtain the required majority until 1970.

In the case of Nigeria and Uganda the dualism of the executive was retained as well as a federal structure of the state; both matters dictated by political factors pertaining to political diversity. It is now clear that the institution of a dual executive in Nigeria was not in itself sufficient to cope with the political problems which plagued that country in the years following independence. Whether a unitary executive can cope with such problems is indeed one of the most important of the questions that need to be answered.

The Westminster model has its counterpart in modified forms in European parliamentary systems. They all have certain common features of which the term classic parliamentary system will be understood to be the referrent. In the case of the French parliamentary system, substantive modification was made by the Constitution of 1958 giving rise to a new term – *parlementarisme rationalisé*, i.e. a régime in which executive and legislature work in co-operation, depending on each other.[7]

The parliamentary system or *régime d'assemblée* which was practised in the Third and Fourth Republics of France, and particularly as seen through the eyes of African leaders, some of whom participated in the life of these institutions, was associated with a weak executive. Now, the main feature of the Gaullist Constitution of 1958 was the reinforced position of the President. This feature was considered to be necessary and more easily adaptable to the needs of developing nations than the classic parliamentary system which, with its *régime d'assemblée*, had meant the domination of the executive by the legislature with perennial crises in government.

The 1958 Constitution was introduced to redress the balance between the two institutions. The leaders of the new Francophone countries of Africa had a good springboard in the Gaullist conception of the position and role of the executive, which suited their needs. But they departed from it in some important aspects. One of these is the creation of a monocephalous (unitary) executive.[8] Five states in Africa have now a bicephalous (dual) executive – Lesotho, the Congo, Swaziland, the Cameroon and the United Arab Republic.[9] In the last there is a peculiar situation in which the federal system has created the office of the Prime Minister of one of the federated states. But the Federal Government has a unitary executive. As will be seen, in both Zaire and the United Arab Republic the President is the executive Head of State with a subordinate Prime Minister and a cabinet.

B. Innovation

Until very recently the study of Public Law divided constitutional systems into three categories, according to whether they belonged to the British, the American, or the French type. We have had a glimpse of the British and French types, and have seen that the constitutions of the new African states have departed from them. The reasons are historical or political or both. The metropolitan models were said to be found inadequate to cover the situation in an African context. Even the new Gaullist model, for example, which was imitated in detail to provide African leaders with an initial cloak of legitimacy, as it were, was later modified substantially.

The American type represents what is otherwise known as a presidential régime, whose main distinguishing feature is a strict separation of powers. The doctrine of separation of powers did not find favour with the new trend. The difficulty of adapting the doctrine to the African reality can be explained chiefly in terms of the prevailing attitude of individual nationalists who dominated the nationalist movements. Also the existence of a single dominant party impinges on the constitutional system.

Even in countries where the party is subordinated to constitutional organs, as for example in the Ivory Coast, and the doctrine of separation of powers is followed, it is more legalistic than real. Power is sought to be unified and concentrated, not diversified and divided. This has been called 'closed power', which does not tolerate plurality of opinions and attitudes.[10] Because this power is 'closed' the political party on which it rests tends to eliminate others and become the only or the dominant party in the state. This fact manifests itself in the structure and functioning of the state apparatus in the executive; and as a novel constitutional phenomenon it deserves to be studied from as many angles as possible.

At first glance, it may appear that some of the unitary executive systems might be traced to the American type. Liberia's constitution, for example, was modelled on that of the United States of America, and in form, still reflects it. Again, Nkrumah's study and long years of stay in the United States of America may have conceivably influenced some of his thinking on this subject. On the other hand his associations with Sékou Touré and Modibo Keita and their radical approach; his concept of the African personality, with its inherent claims for self-expression at all levels; his advocacy of African unity, with its demand for urgent methods at the top level; his attachment to a militant form of socialism, with its intolerance of liberal democracy and economic practice; his preoccupation with and fear of neo-colonialism, may explain some of the novel features of Nkrumah's Republican Constitution.

Whatever influence the American Constitution might have exercised in the mind of Nkrumah, it is clear that it did not find much place in his Republican Constitution.

It is also clear that traditional classification in Western constitutionalism does not embrace the new constitutional systems of Africa, which do not fit into any of its categories. This presents a challenge. One simple response to the challenge is, of course, to dismiss the new systems as authoritarian régimes. But that would not be very helpful. Some useful attempts have been made to discern a general pattern in the new trend crystallized in the African constitutions.[11]

The new trend has been summed up by Jean Buchmann as African 'neo-presidentialism'. The term purports to represent the position, in Africa, where the decline of parliamentarianism is accompanied by the consolidation of executive power which tends to be hierarchical and personalized, with one (or a dominant) party as its base. This tallies with what Burdeau called 'closed' power. At the same time a great deal of the framework of classic systems is preserved. Functional division, if not complete separation, exist between the three organs of state. Parliament is universally elected.

But one of the consequences of African neo-presidentialism has been the emasculation of Parliament and the increase of the legislative power of the executive. Neo-presidentialism grew out of a sort of neo-parliamentarism of the last colonial days which was seen on the African stage in the first exciting days of independence, and then was seen no more. It was characterized by a more vigorous role played by Parliament – even though the executive enjoyed comparatively more power than under classic parliamentary systems. There was, in the early days of independence, more vitality and a sense of purpose displayed by Parliament, spurred on, in many cases, by the presence of a vocal opposition, however small its voice. With the advent of the one-party system, the small voice was silenced and gradually Parliament lost its vigour, if not its usefulness as a medium for legitimizing executive decisions and for creating a national consensus.

An attempt has been made by Jean Buchmann to identify certain salient features of this neo-presidentialism.[12] One trait, as has been observed, is the movement towards a hierarchic structure of power in which an 'irresponsible' Head of State plays a dominant role mostly in a monocephalous system. The Head of State is head of government as well as, in most cases, head of the dominant party. He exercises extensive legislative powers.

This attempt implicitly elevates neo-presidentialism to the level of a new analytical concept. The approach – useful as it is – over-reaches itself when Buchmann proposes certain unique properties of African neo-presidentialism, viz. (1) the designation of the President by Parliament and not election by universal suffrage, (2) the presidential term of office being linked with that of parliament.[12] This was typified by the Ghana model under the Nkrumahist Republican Constitution of 1960. But another variety is exemplified by the Ivory Coast in which the President was elected by universal adult suffrage. This affects the internal consistency of the concept expounded in the first attempt by reference to the Ghana model. For, apart from the variety in the manner of access to office, the nature and extent of the President's powers were almost the same, as we shall see. This difficulty was met by suggesting a new term to describe the Ivory Coast model, viz. *présidentialisme renforcé*, or reinforced presidency.

A great deal of the institutional life of these new countries is in a state of flux; they have been in many respects experimenting. Even some of the central structure and organization is tentative. All this leads us to qualify the concept of 'neo-presidentialism'.

A detailed description and analysis of the organization and structure of the executive will be made below, including the various ways in which the President[13] is elected, some of which bear striking marks of originality. A pattern will emerge in this respect, as well as in the nature of the President's functions, and in the mechanism by which his functions are discharged.

C. The Role of the President

Mention will be made here mainly of the role of the President in his capacity as Head of State and 'Father' of the whole nation. Although it is difficult to say where his function as Head of State ends and his function of chief executive begins – indeed it is unrealistic to make such distinctions in a unitary system – yet an attempt can be made at distinguishing them for purposes of exposition.

All the constitutions of the African states contain the usual provision with regard to the role of the President as symbol and guarantor of the independence, unity and integrity of the nation. He is required to be the guardian of the constitution, to ensure respect for it, to supervise the execution of laws and the proper conduct of public affairs in general. These are no hollow phrases. Manifest and repeated failure in this duty may be attended by resort to unconstitutional means in order to redress grievances. A necessary concomitant of the concentration or personalization of power is the readiness with which blame can be laid at the door of the President. The prospect of this taking place, which events have shown is by no means remote, may exercise a positive influence in causing or enabling the President to discharge his function well.

There is nothing new in the role indicated above. But to the exalted position of the President as Head of State in the traditional sense is added a new emphasis on his role as a nation's 'Father' – a role which has infinitely more dynamic possibilities than that enjoyed by traditional rulers. This is so because of the explosion of human energy and the ever-rising expectation involved in the politics of independence out of which the Presidents of these new states emerged to lead their people.

The general policy has been to canalize the hopes and aspirations aroused in these events for change – for material progress. The President who, in his person or through his office, embodies the hopes and aspirations of a people at crucial moments of its history, has obviously an additional burden added to his task. This is the case in Africa. The nature of this task in regard to the exercise of power will be examined in more detail later.

D. Accession to Office

The constitutions of African states pay due homage to democratic principles. Many of them contain provisions with formulae and slogans expressive of these principles, such as 'government of the people, by the people, for the people' and 'sovereignty emanates from the people', etc. Universal suffrage as the source of legitimate authority is recognized as one of the pillars on which the constitutional system rests. It is universal, equal, and secret, in all cases; and it may be exercised directly or indirectly.

Based on this premise, two types of presidential election exist: (1) direct and (2) indirect. There are, it is true, Presidents who owe their office to modes other than election. But in all of these cases promises are made to legitimize the initial naked power by holding elections.

1. DIRECT ELECTION

The constitutions of most African states provide for the election of the President by direct universal suffrage. The following states belong to this group: Cameroon (Art. 10), Gabon (Art. 13), Guinea (Art. 22), Ivory Coast (Art. 9), Liberia (Art. 3, Sect. 1), Madagascar (Art. 18), Mauritania (Art. 13), Niger (Art. 9), Rwanda (Art. 52), Senegal (Art. 21), Tanzania (Interim Cons. Art. 7 (2), Tunisia (Art. 40). Provision is made in each constitution for regulating candidature, and for the machinery of the elections from nomination to assumption of office. The provisions are detailed in some constitutions, brief in others, detailed regulation of the election being left (in all cases) to subordinate laws.[14]

The qualifications for candidature are on the whole similar to those under the metropolitan systems: the usual requirements of citizenship, minimum age (35 in most, 30 in a few), physical and mental fitness, and enjoyment of civil and political rights at the time of candidature. Some peculiarities may be noted in passing. The Constitution of Rwanda, now suspended by the military government, provided for a maximum age limit (60) and also required that the candidate must be a male citizen who is a local councillor (Art. 54).[15] In Cameroon, because of the federal structure, the candidates for the Presidency and the Vice-Presidency must not come from the same state (Art. 35). In Mauritania and Tunisia the candidate must be a Muslim (Const. Mauritania, Art. 10; Tunisia Art. 38).

The Mechanism of Election

During the First Years of Self-Rule

When the new states gained independence there existed in most of them more than one party. The method of electing the chief executive was therefore invariably designed to ensure the election of a person who was leader of the party commanding a majority in Parliament.

In former French territories there was no uniform procedure. In some, a candidate was required to be supported or nominated by the President of the National Assembly, who would act as an interim Head of State and start consultations. This was the case, for example, in the Ivory Coast and Upper Volta. In other cases the support of a number of deputies of the National Assembly was needed, e.g. in Gabon and Mauritania. Having secured such support the candidate would then present his programmes to the

National Assembly. In Madagascar he was appointed by an electoral college.[16]

Under the Present Constitutions

Most of the constitutions now in force provide that the presidential election should take place at the same time as the general election. The details of election procedure, such as rules on eligibility, nomination, voting, counting votes, supervision, review and publication of results, are left to be regulated by subordinate laws. In most cases there is a marked influence of metropolitan electoral systems. This is particularly so in the Francophone states where the French election procedure is applied with a few variations.

Nomination. A decree is issued by the executive (usually the Council of Ministers), announcing the date of the election. Other particulars are also announced, such as the place where nominations are to be deposited and the person or commission acting as Returning Officer. He is, in some cases, the Registrar of the Supreme Court (e.g. Senegal) and in others the Chairman of an Election Commission (e.g. the Ivory Coast); or again, as in Tunisia, a committee formed of the President of the National Assembly (Chairman), the Mufti (religious head) of Tunisia, the first President of the Court of Appeal, the first President of the Supreme Court of Appeal and the Public Prosecutor. The nomination must be made a certain minimum number of days before the date of the first polling day, the length of time varying from state to state.

When nomination has taken place, a list of candidates is published a certain number of days before polling day. The usual duration of the election campaign is two weeks, and it closes the day before the first voting day. This is quite adequate for vital issues to be crystallized and for people to digest arguments for and against. Long election campaigns are not of value in countries where the election can be costly and choices are limited.

Voting. Under most of the constitutions a system of voting by majority is provided for. A candidate must obtain an absolute majority in order to be declared elected at the first ballot. That is to say, he must obtain half of the votes cast plus one. If he does not obtain an absolute majority at the first ballot, a second ballot takes place within a specified period (normally fifteen days) after the first ballot. At the second ballot only a relative majority is needed for election; in other words the candidate who obtains the maximum number of votes is declared elected.

(iii) *Supervision and Declaration of Elections.* A declaration as to who has been elected is made provisionally. If this is not disputed before the Election Commission the President is elected. If it is disputed, the Election Commission, which in many cases is the Supreme Court, must decide to uphold or annul the provisional declaration. In the case of an annulment an election takes place *de novo.* In several states (Cameroon, Gabon, the Ivory Coast, Mauritania, Niger, Senegal) the Supreme Court supervises the proper conduct of the election. In Madagascar the *Conseil Supérieur des Institutions* did the supervision. In Rwanda a Commission appointed by the bureau of the National Assembly and controlled by the *Conseil d'État* and the Supreme Court had much power of supervision. In Tunisia the Election Committee watches over the conduct of the election. The supervising body is required among other things to ensure equality of treatment of candidates regarding use of the media of communication.[17]

(iv) *Assumption of Office.* The President assumes office after the final declaration has been made and the term of office of his predecessor has expired. He is normally required to take an oath, the form of which varies from state to state.[18]

2. INDIRECT ELECTION

The constitutions of four states (Kenya, Chad, United Arab Republic, and Zambia) and the former constitutions of two other states (Congo and Mali), provide for the election of the President by indirect methods. I have classified these under four different categories: (*a*) cameral, (*b*) collegial, (*c*) preferential and (*d*) plebiscitary.

(a) *Cameral Election – Mali*

In Mali before the *coup d'état* of 1969 the constitution provided that the President be elected camerally in accordance with a strikingly simple procedure. The election was prescribed for the commencement of each legislature, or whenever the government resigned after a vote of censure passed by the National Assembly. (Arts. 7, 34–6.) In either case the President of the National Assembly, after consultations, designated a candidate to the office of *Président du Gouvernement.* The person designated then presented his programme to the National Assembly.

This right to designate the President placed the President of the National Assembly in a position of great influence, and in the context of one-party politics, where he was a member of the same party, he was therefore one of the potential successors to the Presidency. There was no provision requiring the President to be a member of the Assembly. But President Modibo Keita was always a member.

After being thus designated the candidate had to obtain the approval of the National Assembly by a vote of an absolute majority of its members. He was elected for a period not exceeding that of the legislature. His term of office was thus inextricably linked with that of the Assembly. He was elected for five years and was eligible for re-election. (Art. 16.) This is indirect election at its simplest. We have termed it cameral because it is held within (and by) the Assembly.

(b) *Collegial Election – Congo, Chad*

In Congo[18a] and Chad the President is chosen by an electoral college. There is similarity in the two cases in the composition of the electoral college, with some variations. In the Congo it consists of the members of the National Assembly, of the councillors of the prefecturies, sub-prefecturies and municipalities (Art. 24). In Chad it consists of the members of the National Assembly, the mayors and municipal councillors, mayors and councillors of rural communities, and customary chiefs (Art. 6). The inclusion of customary chiefs in Chad, and their exclusion in the Congo, reflects two different policies on the subject: one conservative, the other radical, respectively. Whether the enlarged composition of the electoral college in either of these states makes the position of the President more representative than that of Mali of Modibo Keita is open to question. The procedure for election follows familiar patterns: in the Congo an absolute majority of the members of the electoral college is required at the first ballot. If an absolute majority cannot be obtained a relative majority at the second (and final) ballot decides the election (Art. 24).

In Chad a two-thirds majority is required at the first ballot, and failing this an absolute majority at the second ballot; and, should a third vote be necessary, a relative majority at the ballot (Art. 7).

In the Congo, the election takes place twenty to fifty days before the date of expiry of the existing President's term of office; whereas in Chad it takes place ten to sixty days *after* the expiry of the term of office, which is a rare provision.[19] The President is eligible for re-election in both states; but in the Congo he is eligible once only.

(c) *Preferential Election – Kenya, Zambia*

The Presidents of Kenya and Zambia are elected by what may be called the preferential method, in which every candidate standing for the National Assembly at a general election is required to state his preference in writing in favour of one presidential candidate. The election of the President takes place whenever Parliament is dissolved, or the incumbent dies, resigns, or is incapacitated.

In Kenya, the presidential candidate is also required to be a candidate for the House of Representatives. A candidate must be nominated by not less than 1,000 registered voters. In order to be declared elected as President a presidential candidate in Kenya must (i) be elected to the House of Representatives at a general election, and (ii) obtain the declared support of a number of elected members (including himself) exceeding one half of all the constituencies at the same general election. Failing this, or if a President has to be elected at any other time, he is chosen by the members of the House of Representatives, sitting as an electoral college. There is a maximum of five ballots with intervals for lobbying. If a candidate cannot obtain the votes of an outright majority of all the members in any ballot, another general election takes place, and the whole procedure is repeated.[20]

In Zambia the President is elected by a similar method with differences that must be noted. In the first place the presidential candidate is not required to stand for election as candidate for the National Assembly. His nomination must be supported by 1,000 electors, and if there is one candidate only, he will be declared elected. If the election is contested he is elected by a system of preference. Every parliamentary candidate must declare his preference in favour of a presidential candidate, who may, if so required, endorse a preference declared in his favour. But he does not have to make such an endorsement, and lack of endorsement will not invalidate the candidature of the parliamentary candidate; nor can the presidential candidate prevent any preference made in his favour.[21]

There is similarity in the procedure to be adopted when no presidential candidate obtains more than half of the preferences, in which case in Zambia (as in Kenya) the National Assembly sitting as an electoral college elects the President by an absolute majority in the first ballot. An absolute majority must also be obtained at a second ballot; and failing that, a relative majority at the third and last ballot.[22]

This preferential system is a neat way of securing the election of the President and his supporters to the National Assembly. The election of the President is tied to that of the parliamentary candidates, whose elections are void if they fail to state their preferences. We can see in this an ingenious method of removing the weakness inherent in a system – parliamentary or presidential – where the executive could be fettered by a hostile legislature. For in this new system the fate of the presidential candidate is linked with that of the parliamentary candidate.

The system was first introduced by the Ghana Constitution of 1960 which effected a major breakthrough in constitutional development in this respect.[23] It set a pattern which was taken up by other states: Tanganyika in 1962, Zambia in 1964, and Kenya in 1965. The novel feature of this system is the emphasis and pre-eminence it gave to the constitutional position of the President. In Kenya the constitution makers appear to have been anxious to preserve, along with an executive presidency, traditions of the parliamentary system of government.[24] So the President is required to be an elected Member of Parliament. The 'double mandate' which he must obtain flowed logically from the compromise between a parliamentary and a presidential system. It laid him open to electoral hazards; but once successfully elected, it strengthened his hand.

In Zambia, on the other hand, the position of the President may be weaker in relation to the National Assembly, though stronger in relation to the electorate. Whereas in Kenya, as in Ghana under the Constitution of 1960, it is the preference, and therefore the vote, of the electoral supporters of the presidential candidate that puts him in office, in Zambia every vote cast for a parliamentary candidate is reckoned as a vote for the presidential candidate he supports. In other words, under the system in Kenya, and formerly in Ghana, the President could rely on the support of a majority of the National Assembly though a very small proportion of the electorate actually voted for him. In Zambia, by contrast, the President could conceivably have a hostile majority in the National Assembly, although he has the support of the majority of the electorate.

The President in Zambia is not a member of the National Assembly. In Kenya, the decision to adopt the parliamentary system in part has meant that the President must be a member of the House of Representatives. This fact appears to go against the present trend of placing the President on a more independent basis in relation to Parliament.

Tanzania abolished the preferential system with the introduction of the one-party state. It is of interest to note that the Presidential Commission which studied and reported on the 'Establishment of a Democratic One-Party State' wrote:

> The President of the Republic is the living symbol of national unity, as such he should derive his authority from the people. Their votes should be his mandate. For this reason we have rejected the idea of any form of indirect election. . . .[25]

It is clear, therefore, that 'preferential election' is not necessarily the result of, or related to, the one-party system.

Whether Kenya and Zambia have decided to follow the example of Tanzania no one can say.[26] Among other things, the outcome of the experimentation with 'one-party democracy' will surely have weighed heavily in the minds of the leaders of the two states. The emergence of the Kenya People's Union Opposition party, which was formed early in 1966, presented a temptation to do so in Kenya. The basis of the President's position and with it that of the government, which could have been eroded by members of his party crossing the floor, was reinforced by a provision requiring the members of his party who crossed the floor to seek re-election to Parliament. According to the Attorney-General, this has had the 'effect of reducing substantially the parliamentary strength of the Kenya People's Union Opposition Party. . . .'[27] If the two-party system ever emerges in Kenya, the presence of a hostile opposition could mobilize the government party in Parliament behind the President, thus giving poignancy to the preferential election system.

(d) Plebiscitary Election – United Arab Republic

In the United Arab Republic the constitution provides for the election of the President in a manner which is unique. The National Assembly nominates the presidential candidate and the nomination is then referred to the people for a plebiscite. Nomination at the National Assembly is made upon the proposal of at least one-third of its members. The candidate who wins two-thirds of the votes of the Assembly members is then referred for a plebiscite. If no one obtains the required majority the nomination is repeated two days after the first vote, with the same requirement of a two-thirds majority. At the plebiscite the candidate is considered elected if he obtains an absolute majority of the votes cast. If he fails to obtain an absolute majority, the National Assembly nominates another candidate and the same procedure is repeated (Art. 102).

The procedure for the choice of a new President begins sixty days before expiry of the President's term of office; the election must take place at least one week before the expiry of the term. Should this term expire for any reason before a new President is elected, the former President continues in office until his successor is elected.

The origin of the plebiscite as an electoral concept is connected with the history of the successful transformation of power gained by military means into legitimate political authority. The first time it appeared as such in modern times was in 1852 when it was applied to the ratification of the *coup d'état* of December 1851 and conferred the Imperial Crown on Napoleon III. But the plebiscitary method used in the United Arab Republic as a piece of electoral machinery, after the *fait accompli* of a revolution, has certain marks of novelty. The most important one is that a popularly elected legislature nominates a candidate who is then chosen by the people on a uninominal list.

E. Tenure of Office

The duration of the term of office is long enough to ensure the implementation of policies begun, provided they are diligently applied. The duration is very long in some cases. It is seven years in Gabon, Guinea, and Madagascar; four years in Rwanda and Senegal, and six years in the United Arab Republic. In all the rest it is five years. The President is eligible for re-election in all cases. In Togo he was eligible for re-election only once, and in Rwanda and Tunisia twice.

The absence of any restriction on the right of re-election reveals the need and the desire for leaders with experience and prestige to continue to serve their nations. The first Presidents possessed such qualities when they first assumed office, having ridden on the crest of movements for independence which, in most cases, they helped to start. The risks of personal dictatorship are, however, not excluded even if this is not inevitable.

Normally the President continues in office until the end of his term. In classical presidencies the fixed term of office cannot be ended unless the President is successfully impeached or some natural process intervenes to put an end to it – death, or incapacity through serious physical or mental illness. In a number of African states the President's office may be terminated through the active agency of the Assembly, or he may himself dissolve Parliament and thus bring an end to his own term.[28]

1. VACANCY IN THE OFFICE OF PRESIDENT

Vacancy may result from temporary or permanent absence or disability, resignation, or death, however caused. Such eventualities are naturally provided for in the constitutions of Africa. Where a vacancy is caused by illness a successor is elected according to a variety of procedures. There is the case where the President himself is required to appoint someone to replace him temporarily for the duration of a temporary disability. If he fails to make such an appointment the President of the National Assembly replaces him automatically. Such is the case, for example, in Senegal, where the President of the National Assembly also assumes the office of President in the event of vacancy caused by permanent disability, death, or resignation of the President. The replacement lasts until a new President is elected, which takes place within sixty days after the vacancy has occurred; or if the vacancy occurred less than six months before the end of the term of office the election of a new President takes place within that remaining period. As for its certification, the Supreme Court is empowered to examine the cause of the disability and the National Assembly must then vote on the matter by a two-thirds majority.[29]

In the Congo a similar procedure is adopted. Where a vacancy for any cause is certified by the Supreme Court the President of the National Assembly replaces the President until a new one is elected within twenty to fifty days after the vacancy occurred (Art. 25).

A different procedure exists in other states, such as the Ivory Coast and Niger. There, in cases of permanent disability – death or resignation of the President – the President of the National Assembly appoints a member of the National Assembly for the interim. If the remaining term is less than twelve months, the person so appointed discharges the functions of the President with all the rank, powers and prerogatives attached to the office, for the duration of the remaining period. If the remaining term is more than twelve months a new election must be held. The term of office of the new President ends together with that of the National Assembly.[30]

It will be seen that in such cases the position of the President of the National Assembly is of crucial importance, with provision for potential authority that may be put into effect in the event of a sudden Presidential vacancy. The President of the National Assembly is invariably a man of prestige and political weight. Constitutional provisions which make it possible for the President of the National Assembly, in case of disability, to replace the President, are a measure of the degree to which this fact is recognized.

In Chad and Tunisia, by contrast, the Council of Ministers is given the power to appoint a successor either temporarily (Chad) or in all cases of vacancy (Tunisia). In Chad permanent disability, as determined by a two-thirds majority of the members of the National Assembly and confirmed by the Supreme Court, results in the election of a new President (Art. 9). It is not remarkable that this should be so in Chad, where the election of the President is indirect in the first place. But in Tunisia it seems to be out of tune with the principle of direct popular mandate that the Council of Ministers should exercise the power to appoint a successor in all cases of vacancy. It is convenient, of course, and saves election expenses; but it could conceivably prove to be too convenient and in the long run more costly.

Guinea presents a contrast to this. If a vacancy occurs in Guinea an election for a new President must be held immediately. The Cabinet remains only to expedite outstanding matters (Art. 28).

Mali was a notable exception in the matter of succession to a vacancy, in that the constitution did not make any provision in that respect. This silence of the constitution left a lacuna which made the position of the President of the National Assembly of potential importance. The President of the National Assembly was an *ex-officio* member of the Political Bureau of the party, which in Mali was a supreme body.[31]

In the states whose constitutions provide for the existence of a Vice-President, succession to a vacancy is a simpler and more automatic affair. These are: Cameroon, Gabon, Kenya, Madagascar, Tanzania, United Arab Republic, and Zambia. The Vice-President in Cameroon is elected on the same list as the President, and for the same term.[32] In Gabon there is more than one Vice-President, they are called Vice-Presidents of the government, and are appointed by the President (Art. 8). The President also appoints the Vice-President in Kenya, Madagascar, Rwanda, Tanzania, and the United Arab Republic, subject to the approval of the National Assembly in the case of Rwanda.[33] In Tanzania and the United Arab Republic more than one Vice-President is appointed, one of them being designated First Vice-President.

The Vice-Presidents assist the Presidents in most cases by exercising power delegated to them by the Presidents. Succession takes place in case of a vacancy for whatever cause until a new President is elected. Again the certifying authority is either the Supreme Court (e.g. in Gabon) or the National Assembly (e.g. in the United Arab Republic).[34]

The presence of Vice-Presidents in executive presidencies may appear paradoxical. In some cases, as for example in Gabon and Togo, the office was created to accommodate certain personalities.[35] In other cases, such as Cameroon, territorial readjustment resulting from the federation necessitated some institutional rearrangement, thus creating the office of Vice-President to accommodate the leader of one of the federated units. Not infrequently, tension between the two offices may build up, owing to different political views or different backgrounds. A good example of such tension and its build-up to crisis point was found in Togo.[36]

However, in most cases appointments to the Vice-Presidency are made from among loyal colleagues. The United Arab Republic is a notable example of this. The bold social and economic experiment launched by President Nasser and his team required continuity of application. The history of conspiracies to assassinate the President provided a stimulus for putting in line for succession the closest colleagues who shared the President's policy. The former First Vice-President, the late Marshal Abdel Hakim Amer, was President Nasser's closest friend and erstwhile comrade-at-arms as a 'Free Officer'.[37] Needless to say, the concentration of power on the President creates risks, not the least of which is risk to life and health. Therefore the potential role of the Vice-President cannot be ignored.

2. REMOVAL OF THE PRESIDENT FROM OFFICE

Provision is made for the removal of the President from his office for violation of the law or the constitution. The type of violation or misconduct for which a President may be removed is not defined. The procedure for investigating such violations or misconduct and for fixing responsibility follows a similar pattern in all states. In the Francophone states only the National Assembly has the right to initiate the process.[38] Again, in nearly all these states the High Court of Justice is empowered to try the President for high treason committed in the exercise of his function. The High Court of Justice trying the President is composed of deputies elected by the National Assembly at the beginning of a new Parliament. The Court elects its own President.

In Rwanda the Supreme Court had the exclusive jurisdiction to try the President for high treason. In Madagascar, he could be tried by the Court of Appeal composed of the first President of the Court of Appeal (presiding) and two other members of that Court, and eight Members of Parliament.

In nearly all cases it is provided that the tribunal trying the President is to be guided by the law relating to crimes, and the penalties specified therein apply.[39]

Another type of procedure is provided for in most Anglophone states. In Zambia, for example, if written notice is given by one-third of the members of the National Assembly alleging that the President has committed a violation of the constitution or gross misconduct, and if the National Assembly, by a two-thirds majority vote, supports this allegation, the Chief Justice appoints a tribunal to investigate and report on the matter. The members of the tribunal are selected by the Chief Justice and they consist of a Chairman and not less than two other persons who hold or have held high judicial office. They report to the National Assembly. If the report supports the allegation and the National Assembly resolves by a three-fourths majority that the President is guilty as alleged, the President ceases to hold office, as and when that body so resolves.[40]

A similar procedure is followed in the United Arab Republic, except that a special tribunal tries the President and there is no provision requiring an investigating tribunal to be set up and to study and report on the allegation.[41]

The President enjoys immunity against legal proceedings for criminal or civil acts committed in the exercise of his functions.[42] In the constitution of Francophone states, with the exception of Rwanda, there is no express provision on such immunity. However, since liability to criminal prosecution is limited to high treason, it may be safely presumed that there is immunity against any other legal proceedings.

The provisions on the removal of the President acquire special significance, particularly in view of the advent of an 'irresponsible' executive. Where a President is not subject to the traditional parliamentary pressure such as motions of censure, or is not made answerable on any other public platform, impeachment becomes all the more important. A resort to impeachment would, however, seem to be highly improbable in the context of the one-party state.[43] This would inevitably build up resentment, and like all situations where power is 'closed' would, at critical moments, lead to explosion. It may be recalled that in some countries ministerial responsibility originally started in, and was limited to, criminal matters, at a time when ministers sheltered behind royal prerogatives. A wise President would not allow the slow build-up of presidential prerogatives to shelter malefactors, for this could prove to be his undoing and that of the régime. This is true even in the case of older republics such as the USA, as can be seen from the events arising out of the Watergate scandal.

F. Powers of the President

INTRODUCTORY

As we have already indicated, the new African states were launched upon independence with metropolitan style constitutions. But the leaders of the new states were not satisfied with what they inherited or adopted. From the end of 1960 to the beginning of 1962 thirteen states had in rapid succession either drawn up new constitutions or revised the original ones. Others followed suit to change their Independence Constitutions. In each case the change is marked by the reinforced position of the President. Common historical ties and new associations created the conditions for uniformity of approach and mutual influence. New ideas and attitudes emerging from the experience under independence, and in some cases old ones which had been suppressed for tactical reasons, now persisted in seeking institutional expression. The trend was a movement from traditional parliamentarianism to a new form of presidentialism.

Implicit in this movement towards a reinforced presidentialism, there is a desire for rapid economic and social change. As a corollary to this there is also the will to national unity. The source of the will for change lies in the challenge of two related facts: the impact of the modern industrialized world, and the staggering fact of underdevelopment in the new states made the more urgent by incessant demands for improvement. Social and economic change through education and technological advance is seen as a condition for progress, and even for survival. The source of the will to unity lies in the diversity of social and political life and the threat of security posed by ethnocentrifugal tendencies. In a number of states the leaders may be called leaders more of states than of nations. In contrast to Europe, for example, the institutions of the new states are therefore designed to perform, among other things, the function of creating or cementing new nations.

All this called for discipline – discipline in the individual as in the public life. The instruments chosen to instil, develop and maintain a spirit of discipline, and to carry out the underlying policy, are the President and the party, of which he is head. But while the reinforced position of the President is formally expressed in the constitutional framework, the party, in nearly all cases, is left to operate extra-constitutionally.

The government itself issues out of the party, which is used as a medium of communication to reach down to the roots of society. It was argued that the whole policy depended for its success on a strong government, with clear programmes and an assurance of a reasonably long term of office to carry out the programmes. Such, in outline, is the argument for the new type of executive presidency, and the one-party state stems from it, resulting in the abolition of organized opposition in most states.

The new African constitutions are, then, characterized by enhanced presidential power. The President combines the powers of Head of State and chief executive. This is so whether the executive is bicephalous (dual), as in the United Arab Republic, or monocephalous (unitary). In both types extensive powers are conferred on the President. He represents the state in all public acts and generally exercises powers traditionally associated with a Head of State. At the same time he exercises a variety of important executive powers, and powers in relation to the legislature, some of which bear marks of novelty. The President's powers may be divided into two categories, normal and exceptional.

1. NORMAL POWERS

The powers of the President exercised in normal times may be subdivided into three categories: power in relation to the government; power in relation to the legislature; and power in relation to the judiciary.

(a) Power in Relation to the Government

The President's power under this category is sometimes termed executive power. The majority of the new constitutions provide that executive power is vested in the President, that he is the sole holder of power of this nature, and that he may exercise it directly, or indirectly through officers subordinate to him. This principle, of course, stems from the underlying policy outlined in the introductory part of this section.[44] Or the executive power may be vested, as in Zambia, in the President who exercises it independently, subject to the proviso that Parliament can confer executive functions on persons or authorities other than the President.[45]

(i) Policy-Making Power

From the principle of what might be called the 'exclusive executive power' flows logically the provision that the President shall be the principal policy-making authority, and the new constitutions so provide. But in a few states this power is conferred on the cabinet.[46] Also, in the United Arab Republic the President shares with the government the function of laying down 'the general policy of the State in all political, economic, social and administrative domains' and in the supervision of its implementation.[47]

In all the rest it is provided, with some variation in the wording but with the same effect, that the task of drawing up policy and of defining and promoting general programmes of action belongs to the President. It need hardly be said that in these systems the government, which is the President's government, must have a substantial share in this task. Indeed, it is significant that the constitution of the United Arab Republic should be an exception in entrenching the principle of group decision in an express provision, in view of the military origin of President Nasser's power-base.[48]

(ii) Administrative Power

Having conceived and drawn up policy the President must next have it implemented in programmed action. The two stages do in fact form inseparable links in the same process of government. In order to give a constitutional basis to this matter it is invariably provided that the President shall have the general direction and control of the government.

In the classic cabinet government, the cabinet is the core of the system. As Jennings has written about the cabinet in Britain:

It is the supreme directing authority. It integrates what would otherwise be a heterogeneous collection of authorities exercising a vast variety of functions.[49]

In the presidential systems under consideration here, the President and not the cabinet is the supreme directing authority. The cabinet is his principal organ of co-ordination through which he discharges his functions of directing and supervising the work of government. But he, and not the cabinet, provides the unity to the system of government. In most cases he presides over the cabinet. This fact, in addition to the shift of ministerial responsibility from other institutions to the President, lends practical reality to the pre-eminent position of the President.

Apart from presiding over the cabinet the President can also exercise direction and control through the fact that individual ministerial responsibility is owed to him. There is nothing new in individual contact with the work of each minister. A Prime Minister in traditional cabinet systems can deal with each one of his colleagues. But whereas in that case his power of co-ordination of the machinery of government is subject to the control of the cabinet,[50] in African neo-presidentialism such restriction is rare. In this connection constitutional provisions are generally made which confer on the President regulatory powers, power to ensure the execution of laws and judicial decisions, and power to sign ordinances and decrees.[51] The regulatory power may be exercised by presidential order or decree normally given under his sole authority. Exceptions to this, where such power is given in council, are Congo and Ivory Coast.[52] Some of the constitutions require the presidential acts to be countersigned by the minister in charge of the matter.[53] In some states, for example the Ivory Coast,[54] regulatory ordinances and decrees may be examined by the Supreme Court before they are submitted to the Council of Ministers.

The exercise of executive power cannot, by its nature and purpose, be limited to the President. In practice the President delegates his powers to ministers, even where there is no law requiring him to do so. Such delegation, which can be revoked at any time, is usually signified by an instrument under the hand of the President, or, in matters of temporary duration, orally.[55]

(iii) *Power of Appointment*

Executive authority manifests itself more dramatically in the power of appointment. In all the states under study the President is given extensive powers of appointment. He appoints the members of the government, who are responsible to him, and he determines their powers. With the power of appointment goes the power of dismissal, transfer and reshuffle; and determination of ministerial powers includes the distribution of the portfolios. The totality of these powers places political instruments in the hands of the President which are necessary for him to maintain his position and to carry out his duties by putting the right man in the right job.

Ministers and Deputy Ministers. Key posts which would often require loyalty to the President, apart from ability, are Defence, Interior, Finance, and External Affairs. Sometimes Justice and Economic Planning are considered key posts.[56]

The President also makes all military and (in most cases) civil appointments. This power is linked with his position as the head of the administration which he establishes, organizes and directs; and with his position as Commander-in-Chief of the armed forces.[57] Mali of Modibo Keita marks an exception in this respect, in that the President could make civil and military appointments 'en conseil des ministres'.[58] It must also be noted that the Prime Minister in the Congo appointed civil and military officers by delegation of authority.[59] Also some constitutions contain provisions requiring the Council of Ministers to decide on appointments 'to higher posts of the State'.[60]

The presidential function as Commander-in-Chief of the armed forces implies an important controlling power including operational control. It also includes the control of the term of service through his powers of appointment and dismissal. The dynamics of presidential power obviously involve a special relation with people who man the armed (and security) services, particularly in view of the shadow of the *coup d'état*. The President's powers are thus enhanced by the institutional devices which can be used at his discretion to ensure the security of the state.

(iv) *Diplomatic Powers*

The President appoints ambassadors to foreign states and ambassadors from foreign states are accredited to him. He negotiates, signs, and ratifies, treaties and international agreements, within certain limits. In the majority of the states the limits are set out in the constitution. The approval of Parliament is required for the signing of peace treaties; treaties of commerce; treaties or agreements concerning international organization; treaties which commit the finances of the state, modify provisions of a legislative nature, concern the status of persons, or involve the cession, exchange, or addition, of territory. Moreover, no cession, exchange, or addition, of territory is valid unless approved by the population concerned. The Supreme Court has power to examine international obligations; and if it declares any of them as contrary to the constitution, this can be ratified or approved only after a constitutional amendment.[61]

The Constitution of Cameroon disposes of the matter by providing that treaties which belong to the 'domain of law' must be submitted to the National Assembly for ratification.[62]

In Tunisia, all treaties and international agreements without exception must be submitted for the approval of the National Assembly.

(b) Power in Relation to the Legislature

The increased power of the President in the new states is not limited to the executive sphere. In most of the constitutions the legislative role of the President is enhanced and its scope extended far beyond the traditional position. To begin with, while it is provided that laws are voted by Parliament, the 'domain of law' is defined in most cases. This is the case with nearly all the Francophone states, following in the footsteps of France. What is not covered by the 'domain of law' defined in the constitution is left to the 'regulatory' power of the President – another significant inroad into Parliament's legislative function. A decrease in the legislative power of Parliament has thus meant a proportionate increase in that of the executive. Indeed some constitutions, such as those of Rwanda, before the 1973 *coup d'état*, and Zambia, vest legislative power in the President and the National Assembly.[63]

In the case of Zambia, such power is vested in the President by virtue of the fact that Parliament consists of the President and of the National Assembly.[64] This provision no doubt owes its source to the Republican Constitution of Ghana of 1960, which, with the abolition of the monarchical Parliament (Queen, House of Lords, House of Commons), substituted the President for the Queen in making Parliament consist of President and National Assembly.[65]

Moreover, several constitutions provide that the President may ask the National Assembly to authorize him to pass decrees or ordinances for the execution of his programme in matters falling within the domain of law for a limited period. In the event of such authorization however, the decrees or ordinances cease to have force and effect if they are not submitted for parliamentary approval before the time limit fixed by the enabling law.[66] Also, under the Constitution of the United Arab Republic, where no 'domain of law' is defined, the President is given power to issue 'decisions having the force of law'.[67]

We must now examine some other areas where specific legislative functions are given to the President. They consist in the right to initiate legislation, to give assent to laws and promulgate them, to address Parliament, to dissolve Parliament, and to legislate by referendum.

(i) *Legislative Initiative*

This is a very important power which the President enjoys concurrently with the deputies. It is of crucial importance in the choice and elaboration of proposals for legislation. This is, to be sure, a feature of all modern legislative practices. But in the African constitutions it has acquired a different magnitude: the President is placed in a stronger position than the President of the United States of America, for example, who can only resort to indirect methods to participate in the elaboration of the laws.[68]

The Constitution of Senegal contains a unique provision in this respect: Article 56, after enumerating the subjects falling within the domain of law, provides that the President can 'by reason of their social, economic and financial importance, submit to the vote of the National Assembly draft laws having to do with matters other than those enumerated in the present article' without derogating from the power of the President.

(ii) *Assent to Bills and Promulgation*[69]

It will be seen that this right to send Bills for second deliberation does not amount to complete veto. But the delays which it could entail, plus the influence which the President wields in the National Assembly of these new states, could turn it into a weapon of no mean importance. The period of delay is further extended in some cases, as for example in the Ivory Coast, Niger, and Chad, by a provision which gives the President a right to request that the second deliberation should take place during the session after the one at which the Bill was first adopted. *Again, this request cannot be refused.*

(iii) *Right to Address Parliament*

Allied with legislative initiative, assent to Bills and promulgation of Acts, is the right to address messages to Parliament, directly or through an intermediary. Of primary importance among such messages is the annual address given by the President at the opening (and sometimes at the closing) of Parliament. This is, of course, a traditional right for heads of states in many countries. But it has acquired a special quality in the new constitutions of Africa. Through it the policy-making powers of the President can be brought to bear on the work of Parliament.

The President can determine in advance the issues which are to be debated in Parliament by presenting the outline of the government's legislative programme. He may make this programme the more imperative by laying due stress on certain subjects in a descending order of importance. This he can do as a Head of State and a repository of the national interest. A report on the state of the nation and a programme of action with an array of plans and projects designed to solve problems and to implement policies cannot fail to set the tone and pace of parliamentary activity. The right of address is contributory to the creation of such a state of affairs. It is indeed linked with, and is a vehicle of, the right to legislative initiative. That it is a right with a new quality can be seen in the fact that unlike the Queen's speech in the Parliament of the United Kingdom, for instance, the President's address is not subject to debate or question.[70]

The opening and closing of ordinary sessions of a Parliament are fixed in most cases, but the President has the right to open and close extraordinary sessions. This is subject to a time limit (usually a maximum of thirty days) imposed on the duration of extraordinary sessions.

(iv) *Dissolution of the National Assembly*

The desire to establish and assert executive supremacy over the legislature is perhaps best expressed in the right of the President (*a*) to dissolve the National Assembly, and (*b*) to go over the head of that body, by having resort to referenda – both rights recognized in the constitutions of several African states. We shall first examine the President's power of dissolution.

A number of African constitutions make provision for the dissolution of Parliament.[71] Two (Gabon and Zambia) do not fix conditions for the exercise of the right of dissolution – Article 83 (2) of the Zambian Constitution simply provides: 'Subject to the provisions of the Constitution, the President may at any time dissolve parliament'. Such provision first appeared in the Republican Constitution of Ghana of 1960. Under that Constitution the President's own office fell open to re-election if he dissolved Parliament.

Similarly, the Constitution of Zambia provides that whenever Parliament is dissolved an election shall be held for the office of the President.[72] The provisions of Article 33 (1) and Article 83 (2) taken together mean that what appears to be unlimited power of the President to dissolve Parliament is counterbalanced by the requirement for his re-election consequential on the act of dissolution. In practice such an extreme measure would only be taken in case of serious differences arising between the President and the National Assembly leading to a deadlock. This could conceivably arise, among other reasons, from a refusal of the President to assent to Bills passed by Parliament after a second deliberation and by a two-thirds majority.

In Gabon, the President may dissolve the National Assembly 'in case of necessity', and after consulting the Council of Ministers and the President of the National Assembly. He is not bound by the opinion of anyone. He has also the right to prorogue the National Assembly once, for a maximum period of eighteen months.[73] But dissolution of Parliament does not entail the resignation of the President.

As for the other Francophone states, the circumstances under which the President can dissolve the National Assembly are explicitly stated in four cases, Congo, Madagascar, Rwanda, and Chad. There must be a ministerial crisis resulting from the passing of a motion of censure or the defeat of a vote of confidence. In Mali the relevant provision refered to ministerial crisis without stating the cause. Before dissolution can take place, two ministerial crises must occur in the course of eighteen months in the Congo, and more than two crises in the course of three consecutive years in Rwanda. In Chad a motion of censure or a defeat of a vote of confidence once is sufficient.[74]

Dissolution of the National Assembly automatically resulted in the termination of the President's office in Rwanda, as it does in Zambia. In Madagascar, a two-stage procedure was devised as a condition for dissolution and resignation. In the first place, the President might pledge the responsibility of his government on the strength of a programme embodying general policy. If the

National Assembly rejected this programme or adopted a motion of censure the ministers were required to submit their resignation to the President.

The second stage would begin at this point. The President, after consultation with the President of the Senate, might form a new government and present a new programme to the National Assembly. If the National Assembly rejected this, it would be automatically dissolved and elections for a new National Assembly would be held. If, after the election, the new National Assembly did not accept the programme last rejected, the President was required to resign, and with him the Council of Ministers, and an election for a new President would be held.

This two-stage procedure with its 'shifts' of electoral hazards is a unique device for mutual restraint and persuasion between the President and the National Assembly, involving as it does the fate of both. Still, the President has an advantage over the Assembly in that the latter goes out first to face the hazards.

In Mali, Chad and Gabon, dissolution of the National Assembly would not involve the resignation of the President or his government. It is also interesting to note that in Chad, upon the dissolution of the National Assembly, the President of that body automatically becomes a *Ministre d'État*, which is revealing as to the nature of his position in the legislature–executive nexus.

It will be seen that the constitutional position of the President in Africa in relation to Parliament as regards dissolution is marked by a variety of forms. While some constitutions are silent on the matter, others have a variety of arrangements, in which the President of Gabon stands in the strongest position, followed by those of Zambia, Chad, and Mali, and perhaps Madagascar.[74a]

This lack of uniformity is understandable; it reflects some variation in historical and political backgrounds. The subject of dissolution touches on a sensitive area of political life. No Assembly likes to resolve itself out of existence in normal circumstances. The same may be said of Presidents.

In classical presidential systems, as that of the United States of America, the tenure of office of President and Members of Congress is fixed. In case of deadlock they have to wait to the end of the term. Even in case of hostility, however, the Congress recognizes that government has to go on. The African states that have adopted dissolution as a way out of deadlock could not fail to recognize that government has to go on. If a recalcitrant Parliament and an obdurate President persist in hostility, government will break down, and dissolution would then be a sensible, if not the only way out.[75] Otherwise, it may be safely concluded that resort to dissolution would be rare.

If the experience of the British Parliament is any guide, decisions by the Prime Minister to 'advise' dissolution are rare, centring on crucial events, in circumstances of national division over important issues. The Prime Minister who advises dissolution must nevertheless be presumed to choose a most suitable moment. He does this in the hope of his government's re-election.[76]

(v) *Referendum*

The most important legislative power of the President in the new states is perhaps found in the right to resort to referendum. This is also a dramatic method of overcoming parliamentary opposition to legislative programmes of great public importance.

Referendum has a long history as a political concept for resolving outstanding political issues by referring them to the populace. Referendum as a legislative concept to be used by the executive branch of government to side-track opposition is of recent origin. In its modern context it has a wider scope of meaning and application. Its advent in Africa is post-Gaullist (1958), and Gaullism was its principal source of inspiration. But in its most extreme form it has moved a stage further than under the Constitution of the Fifth Republic. Under that constitution the initiative to use a referendum does not belong to the President. It is decided by the President at the request of the government or of both Houses of Parliament. Also, the subjects which may be settled by resort to referendum are limited to three categories: (1) Bills involving the organization of public powers; (2) Bills involving the approval of an agreement of the *communauté*, and (3) Bills authorizing the ratification of a treaty, *qui sans être contraire à la constitution aurait des incidences sur le fonctionnement des institutions.*[77]

In Africa the referendum has been adopted by the constitutions of a number of the states.[78] The Francophone states used the French Constitution as a model for this, as in many other questions. However, only Madagascar followed the French Constitution in taking the initiative out of the hands of the President. In fact, in Madagascar, only the National Assembly and the Senate could make the proposal for a referendum, voting separately by an absolute majority of their respective members.[79]

In four of the other states (i.e. Gabon, Ivory Coast, Niger, and Senegal), the President may refer all questions which appear to him to require the direct consultation of the people. He may do this after consultation with the bureau of the National Assembly,[80] or with the Council of Ministers and the bureau of the National Assembly;[81] or with the Presidents of the Supreme Court and the National Assembly;[82] in all these four states the consultation is of an advisory nature, and there is no limit to the matters that may be subject to referendum.

In Mauritania, no consultation is required of the President, but the referendum is limited to two matters:

(1) Bills involving the organization of public powers, and
(2) Bills authorizing the ratification of a treaty.[83]

In the Congo, and in Chad, the President may submit any subject to a referendum without the requirement to consult any person or body.[84] It is also interesting to note that the relevant provision in the Constitution of Chad adds that 'all law contrary to the will of the people expressed by way of referendum is automatically void'.[85]

In Rwanda presidential power over referenda as a legislative instrument was non-existent. Referenda could be used to settle institutional disputes between the executive and the legislature in matters not provided for in the constitution, after a question had been submitted for a consultative opinion to the Supreme Court, and if the dispute could not be settled thereby.[86] The novelty of this interesting provision lies in bringing the people to participate in settling institutional disputes between the executive and the legislature. The Rwanda Constitution was a fairly exhaustive one, however, and a constitutional crisis arising out of matters unforeseen by it would be most unusual, although other issues have caused its suspension.

In the United Arab Republic the President may call a referendum 'in important matters affecting the supreme interests of the country'.[87]

In Anglophone Africa the referendum was adopted in Ghana, presumably by way of Nkrumah's contact with some of the Francophone states. The constitution provided that a referendum, for repeal of an entrenched provision of the constitution, could be ordered by the President. But as Rubin and Murray pointed out, there was no provision concerning the means by which the people were required to indicate their desire for such a referendum 'which left the President with an absolute discretion to decide whether the referendum should take place'.[88] Indeed the institution of the referendum, while on the face of it democratic, could be used to defeat democratic ends. The complexity of the issues on which the public are asked to pass judgement in a 'yes-or-no' fashion justifies doubts as to its merits. Presidential régimes, by their very nature, tend to focus attention on the President and away from Parliament as a centre of power, including legislative power. Charismatic leaders can conceivably get the public to accept most of what they wish. This is the logic of the system, and its dependence on a mass-based party underlines the dangers.

(c) Power in Relation to the Judiciary

Where the President is engaged in the exercise of power in relation to the judiciary, three types of situations may be involved. First, there is the power of appointment to judicial posts; second, there is the right of the President to ask for judicial opinion on some questions; third, there is the right to grant pardon.

(i) Judicial Appointment

In Anglophone states, the President appoints the Chief Justice. He also appoints the other judges of the superior courts on the advice of the Judicial Service Commission. The advice of the Commission is mandatory in some (e.g. Zambia) and consultative in other (e.g. Malawi) constitutions. The President can remove the Chief Justice and the other judges of the superior courts on the recommendation of an independent tribunal set up by him. He may remove them only for proved misbehaviour or inability to perform the functions of their office. Otherwise their tenure is secure.[89]

The power of appointment of what are called judicial officers is vested in the President only in the case of Malawi. This includes the power of removal. The President may delegate this power to the Judicial Service Commission. In the other states the judicial officers are appointed and removed by the Judicial Service Commission.

The term 'Judicial Officers' includes the Registrar or Deputy Registrar of the Supreme Court (or High Court), the Chief Magistrates or Magistrates, and such other officers as may be prescribed by Parliament. The Commission consists of the Chief Justice (Chairman), the Chairman of the Public Service Commission or any member of that body designated by its Chairman, a Judge designated by the President (as in Malawi) or the Chief Justice (as in Zambia). One additional member is provided for in Zambia, and he is appointed by the President.

The functions of the Judicial Service Commission include disciplinary matters in regard to judicial officers. In the exercise of such disciplinary function the Commission is not subject to the control of any person or body, except that in Malawi the President may from time to time give general or special directives.

In the Francophone states the President appoints judges of the higher courts – the *magistrats du siège*, who are irremovable, unless they have been proved to have misbehaved or to be unable to perform the duties of their office. The President is assisted by the *Conseil Supérieur de la Magistrature*, which in most states recommends judges (*du siège*) for appointment.

The Conseil usually consists of the Minister of Justice (Chairman), the President of the Supreme Court, and other judges. In some cases, as in the Congo, it is presided over by the President of the Republic himself. Again, the composition varies sometimes, as in Chad, where it includes all the judges of the Supreme Court. In Madagascar the Conseil is known as the *Conseil Supérieur des Institutions*, which also acts as a Constitutional Court. In some states, as for example Ivory Coast, Niger, and Togo, the recommending authority for judicial appointments is the Minister of Justice, who acts on the advice of the *Conseil Supérieur de la Magistrature*. The *Conseil* also exercises disciplinary control over all *magistrats du siège*, which includes the President and the judges of the Supreme Court.

(ii) *The Right to Request Judicial Opinion*

This may perhaps be properly regarded as a limitation on the President's power in as much as it relates more to the power of the Courts in relation to executive (and legislative) authority than vice versa. But even so, in a discussion on the President's power in relation to the judiciary, provisions that derogate from such power are worth noting. Such provisions exist in a number of Constitutions in Africa, where the Courts (normally the Supreme Court, or its constitutional section) may be asked by the President to make a determination as to the legality or constitutionality of any proposal of law or any law already in force.

In the event of a proposal of law being declared unconstitutional by the Court, it can no longer be promulgated.[90] The role of the judiciary in exercising control over the executive in this manner is obviously limited, particularly in view of the fact that the initiative lies elsewhere, and that the Courts have to wait until their opinion is sought. But once opinion is given there is no appeal from it, and it must be followed. Gabon provides a striking exception in that the Supreme Court there may on its own initiative point to legal anomalies and propose corrective measures.[91]

Such provisions are absent from the constitutions of Anglophone Africa.

(iii) *Right to Pardon*

This is a right of the President recognized in all African constitutions. As it is in the nature of a prerogative, the President himself alone makes the decisions, though he would normally take advice from the appropriate authority. The latter in most cases is the Minister of Justice, though he may be assisted or even replaced by a consultative body.[92]

The significant aspect of the executive in relation to the judiciary lies in the controlling part played by the judiciary in the exercise of its function. This has often occasioned conflict and controversy in other systems, and it appears that in Africa efforts have been made in many cases to reduce the areas of potential conflict. Prominent among these are the omission of Bills of Rights from many African constitutions. An eloquent plea for the exclusion of Bills of Rights was made by the Presidential Commission on the establishment of a democratic one-party state of Tanganyika, as it then was, which argued that detailed Bills of Rights would not only involve conflict between the executive and judiciary, but could impair plans for development, which:

> cannot be implemented without revolutionary changes in the social structure. . . . Decisions concerning the extent to which individual rights must give way to the wider considerations of social progress are not properly judicial decisions. They are political decisions best taken by political leaders responsible to the electorate. . . .[93]

For this reason the scope of judicial review of executive action is also restricted, as are legal proceedings against the President while he is in office.[94] Immunity from legal proceedings is, of course, usual in the case of a Head of State. But where he is also the head of the government, it may be justifiably feared that this immunity as a Head of State may make serious inroads on the area of responsibility for the exercise of executive power, particularly where the President wields immense executive powers, as he does in the African states.

For the rest, the judiciary is recognized as 'guarantor of

individual liberty' and its independence is subject to explicit provision in most of the states: in the exercise of their judicial function
the judges are to be subject to no other authority than that of
the law. Equally universal is the provision that the President is
guarantor of this independence.

There are no cases illustrating the way in which this presidential
duty can be carried out. In practice, the President being the head
of the executive, it is from this quarter that any possible threats to
judicial independence may be expected to come, in which case he
would be judge and party in his own cause. In states with radical
parties, the President of the Republic would be expected to protect
the judiciary against measures taken by a party over which he
presides. But in such cases the judge's role is conceived in the
context of the general policy in which the party is supreme. Thus
in Mali the *Bureau politique national* included among its members
the Secretary for Administrative Affairs, who ensured the co-
operation between the political, administrative, and judicial
organs.[95] Again, in Guinea, justice is considered as any ordinary
public service, the officers of which must be from the masses.
Guinea and Zanzibar have thus established People's Courts.

In this connection a commendable step was taken in Tanzania
following the recommendation of the Presidential Commission.
The commission was conscious that in a rapidly developing nation
in which many officials are authorized to exercise wide discre-
tionary powers, there would be abuse of power. It therefore recommended that, in addition to disciplinary committees, a permanent
commission be established with jurisdiction to enquire into allega-
tions of abuse of power of government and party alike. This
commission, which has been established, reports to the President
on its findings. The President's problems as guarantor of judicial
independence as well as chief executive may be obviated through
this institution, which is worth imitation elsewhere.

2. EXTRAORDINARY POWERS

So far, we have discussed the powers of the President in normal
times. The experience of other countries has proved that normal
powers may not cope adequately with matters which need urgent
and draconian measures. Africa is no exception in this respect; the
constitutions have provided for the exercise of presidential power
in periods of emergency. The readiness with which recognition
was given – and later constitutional expression accorded – to this

fact is borne out by the relatively small amount of debate on the subject during the course of African constitution-making.

Perhaps the best foreign example in recent years which was available in support of 'emergency provisions' was that of France, during the debate on what is now Article 16 of the French Constitution of 1958. This article was used as a basis for Francophone African constitutions on the subject. The arguments for it are incontrovertible; denying it would mean creating an opportunity for the disruption of the normal constitutional system.

The use of emergency powers during the colonial period also adds weight to the argument. Thus to take the case of Tanzania as an example, the Republic of Tanganyika (Consequential, Transitional, and Temporary Provisions) Act, 1962 provides that the Emergency Powers Orders-in-Council 1939–61 are to continue in force as part of the law of Tanganyika. The President thus acquired all the powers of making emergency regulations previously vested in the Governor-General.

We may consider two questions in relation to emergency matters: (*a*) what constitutes emergency, and (*b*) what limitation can be imposed on the exercise of emergency powers.

(*a*) *The Nature of a State of Emergency*

Emergency situations, naturally, cannot be predicted with precision, either in terms of the time or the manner of their occurrence. Constitutional provisions in this regard must therefore be laconic. Two varieties of provision have been adopted in Africa to cope with emergency situations. The first simply states that the President may, at any time, by Proclamation published in the Official Gazette, declare that a state of public emergency exists or that a situation exists which may lead to a state of public emergency, if it is allowed to continue. This is the type followed in Anglophone states. The other type of provision, found in the constitutions of Francophone states, is more specific.[96] A representative provision which may be cited is the one contained in the Constitution of the Ivory Coast.[97] It reads:

> When the institutions of the Republic, the independence of the nation, the integrity of its territory, or the fulfilment of its international commitments are threatened by a grave and immediate danger, the President of the Republic shall, after obligatory consultation with the President of the National Assembly, take the exceptional measures required by these

circumstances. He shall inform the Nation of the whole matter in a message. The National Assembly shall meet forthwith.

It will be seen from the foregoing that the first type of provision gives the President full power of decision on an emergency situation; he decides whether and when it exists, and he alone decides to take the measures required. In the second type the situations which give rise to emergency are spelled out, in general terms. Even in this variety, however, the provisions are general and exhaustive enough to give a President a wide scope for decision. He is sole judge of what is 'grave and imminent' danger. And, once the conditions of emergency, as foreseen by the constitutional provision, exist, the power to take the necessary measures lies with the President.

The transition from normal to emergency powers would, of course, involve quantitative as well as qualitative differences in the power exercised by the President. The work normally handled by Parliament would fall on the shoulders of the President, thus adding more work to his office. It would also add a legislative quality to what is normally (chiefly) an executive function.

We may note, in passing, that in the case of the Francophone states, the parallel of Article 16 of the French Constitution is not apt in all respects; it must be remembered that in France the President of the Republic is normally required to exercise an arbitral function, and that he would take complete charge of the government only by virtue of Article 16. In Africa, on the other hand, the notion of an arbiter-President is absent. Presumably this fact would make the transition to the exercise of emergency power less marked in Africa.[98] Nevertheless the provision in emergency, even potentially, is an important source of authority supplementing the normal powers in assuring the primacy of the President.

(b) Limitations on Emergency Powers

One kind of limitation on emergency powers is, of course, the set of conditions, if any, provided by the constitution for its exercise. This includes circumstances such as a threat to the independence or integrity of the nation. The Presidents in Africa are given complete discretion in deciding what type of circumstances require exceptional measures. This must be qualified in the case of the Francophone states where in most cases the President of the National Assembly must be consulted before the declaration of the state of emergency. Yet even in that case the consultation may only result in advice.[99]

The message to the nation and the automatic meeting of Parliament could be potentially an important source of control.[100] There are no specific provisions enabling Parliament to continue, to hold during the period of emergency special meetings which the President cannot close. Such guarantees, which exist in France, would have been an important means of control, as they might have enabled Parliament to impeach the President for any abuse of power. Nor are there provisions regarding the termination of the emergency. A provision, such as under Article 16 of the French Constitution, which requires that the measures taken shall be 'inspired by the will to assure constitutional public bodies the means of accomplishing their mission, within the shortest possible time', would have enabled Parliament to avoid or curtail undue prolongation of the period of emergency. Lavroff and Peiser offer the following comment on the subject:

> Thus, the provisions of Article 16 of the French Constitution have been enlarged in the new constitutions of African states. Rendering easier the application of exceptional powers and the controls that could be exercised less severe, the African constitution-makers have agreed to run the risk of seeing a President of the Republic less favourable to democracy establish a veritable dictatorship by applying the letter of the constitution.[101]

A President bent on dictatorship can lean on the public at large, pointing to the failure of the normal functioning of institutions to justify his continued use of emergency powers. On the other hand, such an excess, like all excesses, contains the seed of its own undoing. When emergency measures are adopted the government usually states that they are adopted 'in order to ensure an early return to peace, order and good government', or words to that effect. This was how such measures were taken in the Western Region of Nigeria in May 1962. These measures, or perhaps the government's resort to them as an easy way out of a problem, contributed to the constitutional crisis of Nigeria.[102]

Section II   Constitutional Basis of Ministerial Power

The central fact of the new African presidency is the preponderant power of the President in relation to the other organs of government. This fact, of course, impinges upon the role of the ministers, whether considered individually or collectively. Individually they are appointed and dismissed by the President, and they exercise their executive function by delegation from him as his assistants. Their collective function as a cabinet or Council of Ministers is discharged subject to the fact that the President is the policy-making, directing and controlling authority, and that he presides over the cabinet. But despite their diminished status and sub-servient role in relation to the President, the role of ministers merits consideration, for, no matter how concentrated the power of any head of government, the exercise of such power is subject to the co-operation of his 'team'. In any given situation power is exer-cised with optimum results when the leader has the good will and support of his 'team', everything else being equal. This lesson could not have been lost on the makers of African constitutions.

The move from a classical cabinet government to neo-presiden-tialism underlined the need for unified, simplified and effective power at the top. But while this reduced the importance of the cabinet by increasing that of the President, it did not remove it. It merely pushed the cabinet to the background – and, even then, not in all matters.

All the same, a detailed examination of the ministerial system is not appropriate in the context of this study. For, apart from the above considerations, ministerial functions in Africa are very much the same as everywhere else. Bearing all this in mind, we may note briefly the position of the ministers in African presiden-tial systems.

A. The Ministers Individually Considered

In the bicephalous systems of the Congo and the United African Republic, the ministry consists of the Prime Minister and other ministers. In both states the Prime Minister and other ministers are appointed by the President. The President also appoints and dismisses ministers in the other (unitary-executive) presidencies; so that there is no apparent difference between the unitary and the dual executive presidencies in regard to the appointment and dismissal of ministers. In the Congo and the United Arab Republic the Prime Minister has no power over ministerial appointment or dismissal, unlike his counterpart in a figurehead presidency. Although he plays an important nominating role, in strict law the President may reject any of his nominees. Nor is there any constitutional provision in executive presidential systems requiring the ministers to submit themselves to parliamentary approval on their accession to office.

Each minister heads a department which is assigned to him by the President. He exercises his ministerial functions within the framework of the general policies laid down by the President either personally or in cabinet. Within that framework the minister in Africa, as elsewhere, has a wide margin of power. He retains his post as long as he holds the confidence of the President, or unless he resigns individually or together with his cabinet colleagues. Some constitutions contain puzzling provisions in respect of dismissal of ministers. An example of this is Article 21 of the Constitution of Gabon which provides that the President puts an end to their (i.e. the ministers') functions by decree, *en conseil des ministres*,[103] so that a minister takes part in a decision about his own dismissal.

INCOMPATIBILITY WITH OTHER FUNCTIONS

Ministerial posts are incompatible with membership of the National Assembly in a number of states. This is exemplified by Article 25 of the Constitution of the Ivory Coast.

This functional incompatibility follows a norm derived from the doctrine of separation of powers, which still exerts its influence, though not as originally formulated in *L'Esprit des Lois*. Some constitutions have departed from the norm by permitting members of the National Assembly to be eligible for ministerial appointments. An example of this is Gabon.[104]

Others follow the Westminster model, making membership of the National Assembly a requirement for such appointment – for example, Article 44 (2) of the Constitution of Zambia, and Article 49 (2) of the Constitution of Malawi. But the President can appoint a limited number of ministers from outside parliament.

The Constitution of the United Arab Republic contains some interesting provisions on the subject. It is provided that no member of the National Assembly may at the same time assume any other public office in the government or in the units of local administration.[105] But it is also provided that members of the National Assembly may be appointed ministerial under-secretaries for National Assembly affairs.[106] The apparent conflict between these two provisions can be resolved if we construe the phrase 'ministerial under-secretary for National Assembly affairs' as referring to a post which falls outside the category of 'public office in the government'. The term 'public office' corresponds to the civil service.[107]

The policy which stresses the incompatibility of a ministerial post with parliamentary mandate is attributable in part to its historical connection with the doctrine of separation of powers, but can also be explained by reference to considerations of government stability. In France, for example, the experience of past republics has shown that the main cause of instability in the government was the ambition of parliamentarians to become ministers.[108] The fear that this might be repeated was one of the reasons for the creation of an executive independent from and preponderant over the legislature. The system also gives the President a wider field of choice of talent and qualification for ministerial appointment. This latter factor seems to have influenced the constitution-makers of some Anglophone African states, where the general rule requiring ministers to be Members of Parliament is modified by provisions empowering the President to appoint a limited number of ministers from outside Parliament.[109]

Other prohibitions also exist which are designed to guard against possible abuses. In most of the constitutions of the Francophone states ministers are explicitly precluded from membership of the 'cadres' of the public service; and in no state may a minister be engaged in any private professional, commercial, or industrial enterprise, though this is left outside the constitution in Anglophone states. This is a subject on which express provisions in the constitution can be very useful, inasmuch as the constitution and the code of conduct that it prescribes are presumed to be known by more people than the organic laws which are passed later pursuant to its provisions.[110]

Again, in most of the Francophone states, ministers are prohibited from acting as representatives of organizations such as trades unions or co-operatives. This prohibition is aimed at preventing economic groups from bringing pressure to bear on the government. It is the counterweight to the provision discussed in the last paragraph.

B. The Government

The ministers considered collectively and grouped round the President are known as the government, though this term is also used in general terms to describe a much wider organization run by the President and his ministers. The government, presided over, directed, and controlled, by the President is the supreme executive and administrative organ of the state.

In the constitutions of Anglophone states there is a body known as the cabinet which forms the core of the government. It consists of the President and the ministers, and is presided over by the President. Membership of the cabinet does not in every case include all ministers automatically. In Malawi, for instance, the cabinet consists of the President and 'such ministers as may from time to time be appointed as members of the Cabinet by the President'.[111] The composition of the government, on the other hand, is wider; it includes ministers and junior ministers (or deputy ministers, as they are called in some states, e.g. the United Arab Republic).[112] The office of minister and junior minister is established by Parliament.

In Francophone states the equivalent of the cabinet is the *Conseil des ministres* (Council of Ministers),[113] which consists of the President and his ministers. The President presides over the council. In some of the constitutions the term 'Council of Ministers' is at times used interchangeably with 'the government'. Also, exceptionally, no mention is made of a Council of Ministers in some constitutions (e.g. Cameroon and Mauritania).

It should be noted that although no difference exists between the dual-executive presidencies of the Congo and the United Arab Republic, and the others, with regard to the composition of the cabinet and its chairmanship, the relevant article of the Constitution of the United Arab Republic provides that the President has the right to call a meeting of the Council of Ministers, to attend, and to preside at the meetings which he attends.[114] The Prime Minister presides at meetings not attended by the President. This arrangement gives the President a free hand, as the need arises, to assert this influence directly. This is one advantage of a dual-executive presidency: the executive President can throw a smoke-screen around himself and thus maintain continuity in the state, while allowing governments to come and go.[115]

THE FUNCTION OF THE CABINET

The exercise of collective responsibility creates an *esprit de corps*, which tends to make a collective organ a little more than the mere total of its members. This is true even in cases where the cabinet is not formally recognized as one of the highest institutions of the state.

In Anglophone Africa the usual formula adopted in describing the function of the cabinet is that it shall be responsible for advising the President with respect to the policies of the government and with respect to such other matters as may be referred to it by the President.[116]

In Francophone states, on the other hand, the cabinet is given a role which is more than advisory, and in many states the constitutional provisions make it an obligation for the cabinet to decide questions of policy. Among the usual questions which the cabinet must deliberate upon are:

> matters concerning the general policy of the state; draft laws to be sent to Parliament; ordinances and executive decrees, appointments to the higher posts of government.[117]

In some states the formula varies but the result is substantially the same; for example, in Madagascar the provision reads, 'In the council of ministers, the President of the Republic determines the general policy of the Republic, etc.'[118]

Among the important functions of the cabinet which must also be mentioned is that of co-ordinating government work often through the device of cabinet and inter-ministerial committees. There is also a cabinet secretariat with a secretary appointed by and responsible to the President. The working relationship of cabinet committees with the cabinet and the various ministries is not subject to written regulations; it operates on an informal basis.

The ministers may be reminded subtly that the President embodies the collective national purpose, in the name of which they all work. It is not difficult for them to read 'orders' in his 'opinions'. It must be remembered that the ministers are responsible to the President.

GOVERNMENT RESPONSIBILITY

In the Westminster type of cabinet government, the cabinet is said to be collectively responsible for the whole policy of government. This means that if a minister's decision is accepted by the cabinet, and the decision is questioned in Parliament, the cabinet will treat the matter as one of confidence in itself. Parliament provides the medium for the discharge of the responsibility. It acts as a forum for deep probings and questions on the issues involved; the rest is left to the Press, radio and television reporters and commentators. Everything takes place in the glare of public opinion, and the public acts as judge every four or five years at general elections.

All this assumes several things. Collective responsibility is inseparable from cabinet government, which goes together with a parliamentary system. A parliamentary system in the classic sense assumes a two-party or multi-party formation in the political life of the nation. In most African states none of these elements are present in the form that they exist, say, in Britain. Where the idea of responsibility has been introduced it has been modified in various ways, for various reasons.

In some Anglophone states the principle of collective responsibility to Parliament is recognized.[119]

In the Francophone states two varieties of arrangement were made. In one type ministers are responsible to the President and the President is responsible to Parliament. We may cite two examples: Mali and Madagascar. In Mali the responsibility of the President was subject to strict conditions; the President might be subjected to a motion of censure in two situations only, (a) where he pledged the responsibility of his government over a general policy declaration, and (b) where not less than a quarter of the members of the National Assembly signed a motion of censure.

In any event, the motion of censure must be positive. [120] The vote of censure would be taken by an absolute majority of the members of the National Assembly. If the motion was passed twice during a period of twenty-four consecutive months, the National Assembly would be dissolved, and with it the government.[121]

Another arrangement, followed in Chad, contains peculiar provisions: there is no presidential responsibility, but the government is responsible to the National Assembly. The President himself may, after deliberation in the Council of Ministers, pose the question of confidence in his government to the National Assembly. The National Assembly may also pass a motion of censure. If a vote of no confidence or a motion of censure is passed by the required majority,[122] then the President can do one of two things: he may either dissolve the Assembly or dismiss the members of the government.[123] This places the President in an arbitral position between the cabinet and Parliament. As his term of office is fixed, dissolution of Parliament would not affect him; on the other hand, he can dismiss his government and form another one. Either way he holds the 'trump card'.

Conclusion

The description and analysis of the constitutional provisions concerning African neo-presidentialism has shown that the constitutions have enshrined a new principle: the dominance of the executive over the other institutions of the state. The discussions here have centred round the constitutions as the basic formal sources of power. The detailed nature of these provisions as well as the wide scope of the study made it imperative to exclude laws other than the constitutions, although a few references to other laws have been made, wherever this was found necessary.

From the constitutions themselves it is clear that both Parliament and the judiciary are in a subordinate position. Every conceivable constitutional mechanism was devised to assure the dominance of the executive. But constitutional provisions alone are not sufficient to guarantee this. Indeed, the structure of the executive and its function cannot be properly understood if it is only looked at in terms of the formal (static) provision of the constitution. The dynamics of the exercise of its power can better be appreciated by reference to other matters. The dominant executive has been dictated by the needs of the times. It has advantages as well as dangers, and it will need a great deal of care, integrity, imagination, and creativity, to devise the necessary means of control, while preserving the dynamism implicit in it at a time of transition and development.

A strong presidential executive system tends to favour (and in general is based on) a single party and the dominance of a single person over others and this in turn creates a tendency for loyalties to single figures rather than to the party structure. This accentuates the problem of succession and may thus disturb whatever institutional structure may have built up, by the time the succession crisis occurs. Some of the constitutional provisions on this question provide an answer, but, there again, they are not in themselves sufficient to avert or resolve a crisis of this sort if it comes. Some states pay due attention to the building of a party structure in which collective leadership is emphasized. This is one solution, but the general trend so far has been more in the direction of the personalization of power, which is given constitutional legitimacy in the strong-executive presidential system. Constitutions can, of course, be changed to suit changing circumstances as the need arises. But once established they tend to acquire an aura of permanence which can affect people's attitudes.

If neo-presidentialism is the dominant form of organization of executive power, the next important form is the dual executive, the historical form with which most states gained independence.

NOTES

1. See *Recueil des Textes relatifs au référendum Constitutionnel*. Paris. Imprimerie de l'Assemblée Nationale, 1958.
2. cf. Léo Hamon, *Les Constitutions des Républiques Africaines et Malgaches d'expression Française*. Introduction. This is difficult to understand or substantiate.
3. cf. M. Lampue, in 'Les Constitutions des États d'expression Française', *Revue juridique et politique d'outre-mer*, 1961, p. 513.
4. K. Nkrumah, *Africa must Unite*, Heinemann, London, 1963, p. 59.
5. S. A. de Smith, *The new Commonwealth and its Constitutions*, Stevens, London, 1964, p. 77.
6. cf. Jean Buchmann, *L'Afrique Noire Indépendante*, Paris, 1962, p. 210.
7. cf. D. G. Lavroff and G. Peiser, *Les Constitutions Africaines*, Vol. I, Paris, 1961, p. 32.
8. On the influence of the 1958 Constitution, *see* Gonidec, *Droit d'outre mer*, Paris, 1959, Vol. II, pp. 396–416.
9. In Tanzania an apparent reversal of the trend has taken place with the introduction of the office of Prime Minister, although there is no constitutional provision for this.
10. cf. G. Burdeau, *Traité de science politique* 1, Paris, 1949, 2nd ed. 1967, p. 464 et seq.
11. cf. Jean Buchmann, (1) op. cit., pp. 214–15; 256–83, and (2) *La Tendance au présidentialisme dans les nouvelles constitutions négro-Africaines*, 12 *Civilisation* 46 (1962). Léo Hamon, 11 *Civilisation* 245 (1961). P. Idenburg, 15 *Rev. Jur. et Pol. d'outre-mer* 195 (1961). A Gandolfi, ibid., p. 369. P. Lampue, ibid., p. 513. de Smith, op. cit., pp. 230–52.
12. cf. Buchmann (1961) 12 *Civilisation* 46, pp. 60, 61.
13. cf. J. C. Juergensmeyer (1964) *J.A.L.*, pp. 157–77, and esp. p. 175. The author of this article starts with Buchmann's thesis on the new concept, and ends with the conclusion that 'reinforced presidency' has replaced 'neo-presidentialism'. Unfortunately, far from clarifying the issues, this has the effect of adding further complications, particularly so, in retrospect, having regard to the emulation of the Ghana model by Tanzania, Zambia, and to a certain extent Kenya, as we shall see.
14. In most cases the party central Executive nominates the candidate; in some cases there is an Electoral College (to nominate a candidate) consisting of the National Executive Committee of the party and of other members of the party such as members of the national committee of party auxiliaries.
15. The Rwanda Constitution provides that men and women are equal in the eyes of the law, but that man is the 'chef naturel' of the family. (Art. 30.)
16. cf. Gonidec, op. cit., p. 405.

17. *See*, for example, constitutions of: Cameroon, Arts. 9, 10; Gabon, Art. 7; Ivory Coast, Art. 10; Madagascar, Loi du 6 juin 1962, which is an integral part of the Constitution of 1961; Mauritania, Art. 13; Niger, Art. 10; Rwanda, Art. 52; Senegal, Arts. 25–35; Tunisia, Art. 391.

18. He either swears or makes a solemn affirmation to perform the duties of his office with honesty and integrity, to defend the constitution and the independence and territorial integrity, etc., or words to that effect. The oath is sworn before the National Assembly or the President of the Supreme Court.

18[a] References are made to the 1963 constitution of Congo. This has now been substituted (June 1973). Under the new constitution the President is elected for 5 years by the Parti Congolais du Travail (Art. 37).

19. But the tenure of a 'lame duck' President does present problems of abuse, which could be perpetrated whether the term is five days or fifty, depending on the integrity of the person involved. An example of such abuse is massive appointment of members of his party or family to lucrative posts.

20. cf. Constitution of Kenya (Amendment) Act, 1964, First Schedule, S. 33. This is usually referred to as the First Amendment Act, Act 28 of 1964. It was published on 24 November 1964. This law was further amended by the Seventh Amendment Act, Act 40 of 1966, which was published on 4 January 1967. It merged the House of Representatives and the Senate into a unicameral National Assembly. The Tenth Amendment Act, Act 45 of 1968, published on 12 July 1968, provides that the President be directly elected by a national electorate during a general election. The presidential candidate is paired with the parliamentary candidate in the ballot of the particular party.

21. In Ghana, the presidential candidate had to give his consent to the preferences stated in his favour; the chances of success of the parliamentary candidate would thus be carefully considered before consent is given.

22. Const. S.33.

23. *See* S.11 of the Ghana Constitution of 1960.

24. *See* 'A Constitutional Triumph over the Division of Regionalism' by Hon. Charles Njonjo, Attorney-General of Kenya, in *The Times*, 20 October 1966, p. 27.

25. *Report of the Presidential Commission on the Establishment of a Democratic One-Party State*, 1965. Dar-es-Salaam, p. 23.

26. Zambia decided to become a one-party state in 1972. Before the election of 1969, Kenya had moved into a form of direct election of the President, tied to the party and local parliamentarians.

27. C. Njonjo, op. cit. Amendments 1–10 brought together in Act 5 of 1969 published 18 April 1969 clearly destroyed the chances of a second party's emerging as predicted by Njonjo in 1966.

28. Dissolution is dealt with on pp. 46–9.

29. Senegal Const. Arts. 26, 33–5.

30. Const. Ivory Coast, Art. 11; Niger, Art. 11.

31. The title *président du gouvernement* is indicative of reduced emphasis on presidentialism.

32. Const. Cameroon, Art. 10; in Togo also the same was the case, cf. Art. 22.
33. Const. Rwanda, Art. 52.
34. Thus in case of unfitness of the President, the cabinet may pass a resolution asking the Chief Justice to inquire into the matter; the latter may appoint a medical tribunal for that purpose (cf. Const. of Kenya (Amendment) Act. Sec. 33.E. Tenth Amendment Act, Act 48 of 1968, provides for the Vice-President to act for three months with some limited powers, if the vacation of the presidency does not coincide with a general election.
35. cf. Lavroff and Peiser, op. cit., Vol. I, p. 25.
36. Ex-President Grunitsky and Vice-President Meatchi were leaders of different political groups and at the time of Olympio's death were both living in exile (in Dahomey and Ghana respectively). On Olympio's death they returned to form the government. On 21 November 1966, while the President was in France undergoing medical treatment, a crisis occurred which nearly ended in a disaster. This basically concerned Vice-President Meatchi and another personality (the Minister of Interior) who had accused Meatchi of having instigated anti-Grunitsky tracts to appear in Lomé. Meatchi denied this and, as acting President, threatened to dismiss the Minister of Interior. It is believed that behind this flare-up lay the basic tension of the Grunitsky Government. It contributed to the *coup*; cf. *West Africa*, 3 December 1966.
37. The line-up in the succession changed radically after the war with Israel of 1967 and the resignation and death of Marshal Amer.
38. The Senegal Constitution requires a three-fifths majority (*see* Art. 87); that of Rwanda requires a three-fourths majority (*see* Art. 10 (6)).
39. For the relevant articles on the foregoing, cf. Const. Cameroon, Art. 36; Congo, Arts. 75, 77; Ivory Coast, Art. 14; Gabon, Arts. 62–3; as amended by Loi No. 23/63; Madagascar, Art. 18; Mali, Art. 46–7; Mauritania, Art. 52; Niger, Arts. 63–4; Senegal, Arts. 86–7; Rwanda, Art. 101 (c); Chad, Arts. 76–8.
40. e.g. Const. Zambia, Art. 36.
41. Art. 112.
42. e.g. Const. Zambia, Art. 43.
43. cf. Chapter 6.
44. Exceptionally, however, the President has been explicitly required to share executive power with members of the government; cf. e.g. Art. 20 Const. of Togo which was in force before the military *coup*.
45. Const. Zambia, Art. 48 (1–3).
46. e.g. Const. Congo, Art. 39; Madagascar, Arts. 11 and 12; and Lois du 28 Juin 1961 and 6 Juin 1962.
47. United Arab Republic Const. Art. 113.
48. It could, of course, be argued that the psychology and practice of 'staff work' in the military facilitates rather than hinders group decision, and that this strengthens the position of the President.
49. Sir Ivor Jennings, *Cabinet Government*, 3rd ed., C.U.P., London, 1969, p. 1.
50. cf. Jennings, op. cit., p. 1.

51. e.g. Const. of Cameroon, Art. 12; Ivory Coast, Art. 15; Gabon, Art. 13; Madagascar, Art. 11; Mali, Art. 11; Guinea, Art. 25; Mauritania, Art. 18; Senegal, Art. 37; Chad, Art. 26; Congo, Art. 29.

52. Const. Arts. 29, 22 respectively.

53. Chad, Art. 6; Congo, Art. 38; Gabon, Art. 21; Guinea, Art. 26; Madagascar, Art. 17; Mali, Art. 12; Mauritania, Art. 19.

54. Const. Ivory Coast, Art. 23.

55. Information based on oral interviews with officials of some African governments. Where such delegation occurs, however, the minister is required to affix the presidential seal or the public seal to the document.

56. On appointment of members of the government, *see* Consts.: Cameroon, Art. 11; Congo, Art. 27; Gabon, Art. 21; Guinea, Art. 23; Liberia, Art. 3, Sect. 5; Mali, Arts. 8, 11; Ivory Coast, Art. 12; Mauritania, Art. 17; Rwanda, Art. 10; Tunisia, Art. 43; United Arab Republic, Art. 114; Zambia, Art. 44 (2); Chad, Art. 8; Kenya, Sect. 77 Constitution of Kenya (Amendment) Act, 1964. The need of giving key portfolios to trusted colleagues (especially Defence and Interior) is understandable in view of the threat or temptation to use unconstitutional means to remove the President and his government, which is born out by the many *coups d'état*, as we shall see in later chapters.

57. Const. Cameroon, Art. 12; Ivory Coast, Arts. 17–18; Gabon, Art. 20; Madagascar, Arts. 11–12; Mauritania, Arts. 18, 20; Senegal, Art. 38; Chad, Art. 12; Rwanda, Art. 56 (8); Congo, Art. 28; Tanzania, Art. 21; Tunisia, Arts. 45–6; United Arab Republic, Arts. 123, 128; Zambia, Arts. 49 and 115; Malawi, Arts. 48 and 87.

58. Const. Art. 9, para. 5.

59. Const. Art. 40, i.e. by authority delegated to him from the President.

60. Const. Ivory Coast, Art. 22; Chad, Art. 10.

61. Const. Gabon, Art. 52; Guinea, Art. 33; Congo, Art. 60; Ivory Coast, Arts. 53–5; Mali, Arts. 38–9; Mauritania, Arts. 44–5; Niger, Arts. 53–5; Rwanda, Art. 56 (h), (i), (j); Senegal, Arts. 76–9; Chad, Arts. 69–71; United Arab Republic, Arts. 124–5.

62. Art. 12. The 'domain of law' is exhaustively defined in the constitution. This detailed provision on the domain of law is a feature of French constitutional law adopted by all Francophone African states. Among other things a state of urgency (*État d'Urgence*) is part of the domain of law.

63. Rwanda, Art. 73; Zambia, Art. 57.

64. Art. 57.

65. The Zambian and Tanzanian Presidents also appoint a limited number of members of the National Assembly. This device enables the President to ensure the presence in Parliament of people representative of special professional or other groups. Nor is it purely representational in purpose; it is partly designed to ensure the presence of people with special experience and expertise, or some other quality.

66. cf. e.g. Const. Ivory Coast, Art. 45; Mali, Art. 28; Mauritania, Art. 36; Senegal, Art. 66; Niger, Art. 45. For example, the Senegalese Parliament passed Loi No. 60–046 of September 1960 for this purpose.

67. Art. 120.

68. cf. e.g. Const. Cameroon, Art. 23; Gabon, Art. 22; Guinea, Art. 14; Mali, Art. 11; Mauritania, Art. 37; Rwanda, Art. 56 (j); Niger, Art. 13; Senegal, Art. 69; Chad, Art. 33; Tunisia, Art. 28; United Arab Republic, Art. 116. In Anglophone states there is executive initiative of legislation in practice, although there is an absence of express provision to that effect.

69. Const. Cameroon, Art. 18; Ivory Coast, Art. 13; Gabon, Art. 12; Mauritania, Art. 41; Madagascar, Art. 13; Mali, Art. 10; Rwanda, Art. 56 (k); Congo, Art. 30; Zambia, Art. 71 (3–7); Chad, Art. 55; Senegal, Art. 62; Tunisia, Art. 44; United Arab Republic, Art. 118.

70. The right of the President to attend and address the National Assembly is exemplified by Article 75 (1) of the Zambian Constitution.

71. e.g. Congo, Art. 32; Gabon, Art. 17; Madagascar, Art. 45; Malawi, Art. 45 (2); Mali, Art. 37; Rwanda, Art. 97; Chad, Arts. 45, 47; Zambia, Art. 83.

72. Art. 33 (1); cf. also Malawi Const., Art. 45 (2), which provides that 'the President may at any time dissolve Parliament'.

73. Art. 17.

74. In Togo, the provision was that after such a crisis, the President had the option of altering the composition of his government, of changing it completely, or of dissolving the National Assembly. In Chad, a majority of two-thirds is required.

74ª The constitution of these two are now suspended by the military government.

75. The events in the Congo in late 1965 demonstrated that this is a fertile ground for military *coups*.

76. On the dissolutions of 1918, 1931, cf. F. W. G. Benemy, *The Elected Monarch*, Harrap, London, 1965, pp. 47–57.

77. Art. 11.

78. Though not in Cameroon, Mali, the former British territories, and Tunisia.

79. Art. 34, para. 4.

80. Const. Ivory Coast, and Niger, Art. 14.

81. Const. Gabon, Art. 16.

82. Const. Senegal, Art. 46.

83. Art. 41.

84. Const. Congo, Art. 33; Chad, Art. 11.

85. Art. 11, para. 3.

86. Art. 72.

87. Art. 129.

88. cf. L. Rubin and P. Murray, *The Constitution and Government of Ghana*, Sweet & Maxwell, London, 1961, 2nd ed. 1964, pp. 97–8.

89. The experience of Ghana has been instructive. There the Chief Justice was removed and put under protective custody for a judgement which he had given, dismissing the case against some former ministers charged with the crime of attempts on the life of the President and on his government. The removal of the Chief Justice, Sir Arku Korsah, set off a wave of comments, mostly hostile. For lawyers it showed the insufficiency of formal provisions of security of tenure, unless other necessary conditions are present.

D

90. cf. e.g. Const. Gabon, Art. 60; Madagascar, Art. 48; Mali, Art. 44. In some states, such as Mali, the President of the National Assembly has also the right to seek the opinion of the court on similar matters.

91. Const. Art. 60.

92. e.g. in Chad the *Conseil Supérieur de la Magistrature* studies the dockets in matters of pardon, and gives its opinions on them. Const. Art. 62.

93. *Report of the Commission*, Dar-es-Salaam, 1965, p. 31.

94. The report of the Commission was implemented.

95. cf. Internal regulations of the U.S.R.D.A. party.

96. The United Arab Republic Constitution simply provides: 'The President proclaims the state of emergency in the manner prescribed by the law.' But it adds that the proclamation must be submitted to the National Assembly for approval within the subsequent thirty days, Art. 126.

97. Art. 19.

98. cf. J. Lamarque, *La théorie de la nécessité et l'article 16 de la Constitution de 1958*, R.D.P., 1961 No. 3, p. 558.

99. In Cameroon the President consults the Prime Ministers of the federated states, Art. 15.

100. In Mauritania, the meeting of the National Assembly is not automatic; the President is required to convoke it.

101. D. K. Lartoff and D. Peiser, *Les Constitutions Africaines, Vol. I*, Paris, 1961, p. 29.

102. cf. O. I. Odumosu, *The Nigerian Constitution*, Sweet & Maxwell, London, 1963, pp. 276–304.

103. Art. 21, para. 3.

104. Art. 21.

105. Art. 96.

106. Art. 143.

107. Such an explicit provision prohibiting the combination of bureaucratic (civil service) power with parliamentary mandate and privilege is rare. But it reflects a radical policy, which stems from a suspicion of the 'mandarins' who are generally considered as opponents of revolutionary programmes.

108. cf. M. Duverger, 'Themis', *Droit Public* (1966), p. 105.

109. cf. for example, Art. 50 of the Constitution of Malawi.

110. Not that this is in itself a guarantee against corrupt practices, but it can act as a higher frame of reference, as an 'educational' code prescribing ministerial behaviour or activity. Such a provision would make it impossible for ministers to hold posts and at the same time use them in furtherance of private gains, in particular through licensing powers, which some former Nigerian and Ghanaian ministers are alleged to have used in this way.

111. Art. 53 (1).

112. The number of ministers in the government is rarely fixed. It is fixed at fourteen in Zambia.

113. In Guinea it is called the cabinet.

114. Art. 115.

115. In the United Arab Republic, where each new Prime Minister has tended to represent differing views from the outgoing Prime Minister

on the crucial question of the policy causing the change, a sort of trial and error process seems to be involved. *See* Chapter 6.

116. cf. Const. Zambia, Art. 51 (1); Const. of Malawi, Art. 52 (2).
117. cf. for example, Const. Ivory Coast, Art. 22; Chad, Art. 10.
118. Art. 12.
119. e.g. Const. Malawi, Art. 53 (3).
120. It must state the principles of a government programme.
121. Art. 37. For a somewhat more involved procedure in Madagascar, *see* pp. 47–8.
122. Two-thirds majority for *projets de loi*; absolute majority for questions of general policy.
123. Art. 45.

2

The Dual-Executive Systems in Historical Perspective

Countries like Gambia, Lesotho, Sierra Leone, Somalia, Nigeria, and Uganda, have had a dual executive. It is probably a mark of the growth of neo-presidentialism that many have turned away from this form, which was basically characterized by a weak Head of State who has lost power to the Prime Minister. In this chapter we discuss the constitutional arrangements there were, as well as the political processes which led to the demise of the figurehead of state. Lesotho will form the central case-study up to the 1970 emergency. The states under consideration here were not the only ones to start with a dual executive. The majority were launched in a similar way. Of the former British colonies, only Botswana and Zambia became republics upon independence. For our present purpose Nigeria and Uganda provide the best examples of the problem. The failure of the system in these two states was caused by a number of factors which cannot be dealt with here in any detail; nor is the question of duality in the executive necessarily a crucial factor. But it is one of the factors, and a discussion of it in connection with circumstances in which it has failed gives poignancy to the study of cases where it has not failed.

By contrast to those in Nigeria and Uganda, the position of the traditional rulers in the Gambia and Sierra Leone is relatively weak. Whatever potential threat they may have constituted at the time of independence or before was neutralized by successful political manoeuvres. In Sierra Leone also the chiefs representing the interior region known as the Protectorate were made part of the new political order by the late Sir Milton Margai through an astute political strategy, formalized in constitutional provisions which required that as many as twelve chiefs must be members of the unicameral legislative body. They were thus incorporated in the representative assembly together with the 'commoners'.

The party in power started as a champion of the cause of the inhabitants of the Protectorate, as against the interests of the creole-dominated[1] *élite* of the coastal region. Even there, however, Margai's political organization was not such as to constitute a threat of extinction to the chiefs, unlike the P.D.G. (*Parti Démocratique de Guinée*) of neighbouring Guinea. Again, in Lesotho they were caught in the wave of modern political movements. Thus Chief Leabua Jonathan, the Prime Minister, heads one of the largest political parties, while the paramount chief (King) was made constitutional head of the state. But unlike the position in Sierra Leone, a bicameral legislature was established in Lesotho, with the Senate comprising chirty-three members, of whom twenty-two are chiefs and the remaining eleven are appointed by the King. They owe this position to their traditional place in society. This may not become an important issue in relation to the dual executive as long as the Prime Minister has himself some close ties with the traditional ruling groups, as Chief Jonathan seemed to have before 1970. But if this should change then the issue would assume a different aspect and perhaps precipitate crisis.[2]

The idea of an upper house comprised of traditional elements helps to entrench these forces and encourage them to foster the sentiments on which neo-traditional parties are nurtured. It could be a meeting ground of traditional rulers to forge a new unity and perhaps constitute an opposition to a strong government whose programmes affect their interests.[3]

In Somalia, the factor of chieftaincy was not of much significance; and in the absence of an ethnic diversity, the problem there was related to multiplicity of political parties, factions, and lineage interests, which had developed during the last few years before independence.

To appreciate the full significance of the factor of diversity as influencing the structure and form of government of a state, it is necessary to give a brief account of cases where the experiment was marked by failure. The changes which shocked Nigeria and Uganda have implications for many other African states where the conflict involved has not been resolved, canalized, or rationalized.

The Uganda case has special significance in the context of the present inquiry, for a number of reasons. In the first place, it provides an object lesson of what can happen when the elements of conflict inherent in the idea of a divided executive are present in an extreme form and built into the constitution. Not only was the status and role of the traditional holders of power fully recognized in the 1963 Uganda Constitution, but the Uganda Parliament was given no power to make any law affecting any aspect of the office of the Kabaka and his government in Buganda. The seed of conflict was thus embedded in the constitution. It created a sharp and mutually contradictory alignment of forces within the government.

In reality, the relationship of the Kabaka as President of Uganda and the Prime Minister was not one between a constitutional Head of State and an executive Prime Minister in all respects. It is truer to say that there were two Prime Ministers.[4] In such a situation disputes inevitably arise setting the two executive 'heads' on a collision course, and one eventually ends by abolishing the other, establishing a unitary executive.

Secondly, the Uganda experience demonstrates that where there are two executives bent on mutual destruction, or competing for supremacy or even parity within one constitutional system, and especially where they represent opposing views on fundamental issues, in the ensuing conflict and attempts at gaining ascendancy traditional forces can be quite adept at mobilizing highly effective support from sections of the population. In Uganda this happened because of the special position of the Kabaka in Buganda society, which was entrenched in the constitution. The conflict took a turn for the worse because this position was activated and projected on to Uganda national politics by the emergence of a neo-traditional party called the Kabaka Yekka (the Kabaka only). This party, which was an ally of Obote's Uganda People's Congress (U.P.C.) began to challenge and attack the central government of Milton Obote, over some issues. In Buganda itself there was a government of the Kabaka which constituted a centre of loyalty and opposition, attracting to it some young educated Baganda. Ironically there was an alliance between Obote's party and the Kabaka Yekka, entered previously in order to defeat another party, the democratic party, also mainly based on Buganda ethnic support. Once Obote's U.P.C. was in power, the Kabaka's party came to constitute the most vocal opposition to Obote's government.

The history of this opposition, however brief, has many sides to it, and one can oversimplify. But the relation of government and opposition, and in particular between Obote and the Kabaka, became strained when Obote's party was joined by recruits from the democratic party – recruits whom he suspected to be Kabaka men with a disguised aim of destroying him and his party and taking over the government. Suspicions of a 'palace coup' led by people from his own party added further fuel to the fire that was smouldering.[5] Then on 4 February 1966 the leader of the Kabaka Yekka, Mr. Daudi Ocheng, accused Obote and his Defence and Information Ministers of receiving looted gold and ivory worth $25,000. From then on it was a matter of time, the question being who would strike first, and how. The rest is history.

Thirdly, in the context of the question why a dual executive is kept or abolished, it is worth remembering in the light of this particular experience, that in the Hobbesian situation of 'war of each against all', with a variety of conflicting claims and threats of division, the effort to keep law and order and to keep the nation going becomes a major consideration. This, of course, is not new; but what makes it new to Africa is that people controlling the apparatus of newly formed states are trying to build nations out of states which are at the moment fragile. This point cannot be overemphasized.[6] The maintenance of unity is a *sine qua non* of all other efforts. Therefore when their control of the state apparatus is threatened the forces which wield weapons of violence must be called upon to play a role. At that stage, the armed forces become decisive elements in the bid for supremacy, just as political parties are crucial at the campaign level of the conflict. This becomes relevant in relation to the distribution of power between the Head of State and the chief of government, and especially as regards the control of the armed forces.

In the case of Uganda the role of the Kabaka as President of Uganda and King of his own Buganda, compounded by his personal propensities for leadership, made the final showdown inevitable. But after Obote struck the decisive blow he could argue that law and order and national unity had to be maintained; and that the Kabaka who, as President, was a symbol of national unity, betrayed his trust in advancing political claims which were disruptive of national unity. This argument seems to have won the day on the face of it, judging by the absence of rebellion in Buganda. In fact, Obote's control of the army was the better argument.

One of the results of a situation where a threat to unity becomes imminent but is met effectively is that it stimulates centralizing tendencies, with the consequential abolition of duality in the executive, as well as perhaps duality in the legislature and in parties. Another result, ironically enough in the case of Uganda, was that it paved the way for a smooth army take-over.

The Nigerian experience is more involved, but the implications are the same. There again – to oversimplify – the position of the Prime Minister of the Northern Region, the late Ahmadu Bello, as the President of the Northern Peoples Congress (N.P.C.) with a majority of seats in Parliament controlled the Federal Government, through the Federal Prime Minister who was his deputy as leader of the N.P.C. Though the position was thus different, in both countries the seed of conflict was present when they were launched upon independence.

The abolition of a dual executive through the overthrow of a government or dismissal of some of its members is not limited to Anglophone Africa. In Senegal, Senghor dismissed (and imprisoned) Mamadou Dia, and later declared a unitary executive. In Zaire, Mobutu abolished the office of Prime Minister about a year after the military coup of November 1965. The crisis which led to a military take-over in Dahomey in December 1965 was centred partly on the conflict between President Apithy and Prime Minister Ahomadegbe. The crisis in Senegal is of interest in at least one important respect. The dual structure in the executive, before the crisis, reflected in terms of the personal power relationships between President Senghor and Prime Minister Mamadou Dia, was also reflected in other institutions. Mamadou Dia had a majority support in the Political bureau of the party (the U.P.S. – *Union Progressiste Sénégalaise*), whereas Senghor had a majority support in the National Assembly. Mamadou Dia claimed that the decision of the bureau should prevail over that of the National Assembly. This Senghor did not accept. Dia tried to prevent the National Assembly by force from passing a vote of non-confidence on his government. The conflict was resolved by the military over which Senghor had control, not only by virtue of his position of being the Head of State and the Commander-in-Chief, but also through special relations.

With these introductory remarks we turn now to a consideration of the constitutional positions of the executive in Lesotho.

A. The Head of State

There were two types of Heads of State in dual-executive systems:
(a) monarchs (The Gambia until 1970, Swaziland, and Lesotho)
and (b) Presidents (Somalia). The monarchical Head of State in
the Gambia was the Queen of the United Kingdom, whereas
those of Swaziland and Lesotho are native kings. The Somali
Presidency had features which are unique in African constitution-
making.

Lesotho is a country styled by its constitution a 'sovereign
democratic kingdom'. The birth of this kingdom on 4 October
1966 brought to Africa the first constitutional monarchy modelled
on the British monarchy but with an African king as the Head of
State.[7] In a certain sense we find in it the position of the British
monarch projected in Africa, but revised and regulated by a
written constitution. The King of Lesotho is enjoined to do all
things 'that belong to his office in accordance with the provisions
of the present constitution and all other laws for the time being in
force'.[8] The first person to be recognized as the holder of the
office of King of Lesotho is the person formerly holding the office
of the Paramount Chief (called Motlotlehi) under the Basutoland
Order, 1965.[9]

On the abdication or death of the King, his successor must be
designated by the College of Chiefs, in accordance with the
customary law of Lesotho, from amongst persons who are entitled
to succeed him; unless a successor has been previously designated,
in which case that person succeeds the King.[10] If any such designation for the succession is disputed by a rival claimant, and an
application is made to the Court of Appeal within six months of
the publication of the designation in the Gazette, the Court of
Appeal is given jurisdiction to hear the matter. But such claim
must be that the claimant is a better candidate, not simply that
the designated successor was not entitled to be so designated.[11]
The College of Chiefs may also designate a person to exercise the
functions of the King in case of his temporary absence or illness.[12]
Every designation must be published in the Gazette.[13] The College
of Chiefs also has power to appoint a regent when the monarch is
a minor (i.e. under 21) or in the event of permanent absence or
disability. Failing this the Court of Appeal has power, on the
application of any person, to appoint a regent in accordance with
the customary law of Lesotho.[14]

The College of Chiefs is composed of the twenty-two principal chiefs and ward chiefs and other members co-opted by them.[15]

FUNCTIONS OF THE KING

The constitution-makers of Lesotho have shown themselves anxious to model the role of the King upon that of the British monarch. This is explicitly stated in respect of the matters on which the King may exercise his functions with his own deliberate judgement under Section 76 (2) of the constitution. The executive authority is vested in him in the same manner as it was vested in the Governor-General in the Gambia or the Queen in Britain. In other words, ultimate executive power lies with the cabinet and the Prime Minister in accordance with the provisions of the constitution.[16] As was the case of the Governor-General of the Gambia, the King of Lesotho acts in accordance with the advice given to him by the cabinet, or a person or authority other than the cabinet in cases where he is required so to act by the constitution or any other law.[17]

However, the King may act in accordance with his deliberate judgement in some cases. Under Section 76 (2) he acts thus in the exercise of the power to appoint or remove the Prime Minister, and in relation to the performance of the Prime Minister's function, in the event of the latter's absence or illness. The same is true in relation to the appointment of the nominated members of the Senate whom he appoints, in relation to his Privy Council and in relation to the dissolution of Parliament; in the appointment of the members of the National Planning Board, as well as his own staff; and lastly in the exercise of disciplinary control over chiefs, save as Parliament may otherwise provide.[18] The proviso to this subsection noted above, states that the King shall refer to United Kingdom conventions in respect of the dissolution of Parliament, the appointment and removal of the Prime Minister, and the exercise of his function in case of absence or illness. In all the rest he shall act in his absolute discretion.

In case of neglect or default of duty by the King, the Prime Minister may inform the King that he will perform the act himself after the expiration of a period which he may specify. If, at the end of that period, the King has not done that act the Prime Minister may do that act himself and report the matter to Parliament. And this is not a justiciable issue.[19] On the other hand the King has the right to be consulted by the Prime Minister and other ministers of the government of Lesotho; and the Prime Minister is required to keep him fully informed.[20] There is also a Privy Council which assists the King in the discharge of his functions; it consists of the Prime Minister, one person nominated by the King, and another appointed by him on the advice of the Prime Minister. The function of the Privy Council is advisory only.[21] There is also a Pardons Committee which advises the King; it consists of persons appointed by the King on the advice of the Judicial Services Commission.[22]

Finally it may be said that the person who fills the office of the King may well find his position restricted and may as a result be tempted to abandon restraint and make vigorous interventions in government. Events in 1967 showed that this is a likely course.

The King of Lesotho (King Moshoeshoe II) announced that he would deliver a speech at a mass meeting on 27 December at Thaba-Bosigo, a small village some twenty kilometres from Maseru, the capital. The Prime Minister thereupon invoked his constitutional powers to forbid the King from proceeding to deliver the public speech. It should be recalled that there had been a conflict going back to pre-independence days. The King (then the Paramount Chief of the Basutos) refused to take part in the constitutional conference held in London in July 1966, presumably because he had come to realize that his powers under the proposed constitution would be limited. He had in fact demanded for himself the control over the armed forces and over foreign affairs; the leader of the majority party, however, opposed these demands and the British Government supported the majority party; and Basutoland became independent on 4 October 1966 as Lesotho.

The masses came to the appointed place at the appointed date to hear the King. Police used tear gas to disperse them, but they would not go. A fight ensued in which eight civilians and one policeman were killed. The Prime Minister announced that there had been plans to overthrow his government and he ordered the King's palace to be put under armed surveillance and the King put under 'house' arrest.[23] The allegation of a planned coup has not been pursued or substantiated. But some people of South African origin were expelled. The Prime Minister had made reference to the support given to the King by the opposition party, the Basutoland Congress Party (B.C.P.). The B.C.P. did not accept the election results of 1965, which gave a small majority to Chief Jonathan's National Party. It is also true that the B.C.P.

condemned the action of the government which, under pretext of realism, had co-operated with the government of South Africa. As it happens the King also condemned such co-operation. This common hostility may have created a temporary alliance between the B.C.P. and the King's party, the Marema T'lou Freedom Party (M.T.F.P.). Thus a decision by a constitutional King to address a public meeting would easily arouse the fears of the government which had in Parliament a small majority which could be undermined by a train of events set in motion by such a speech. This the Prime Minister was not prepared to accept. Hence his refusal to permit the address and his drastic action, which could have easily deteriorated into chaos had the Prime Minister not had the support of interested 'powers', including South Africa.

B. The Cabinet

1. COMPOSITION

The cabinet consists of the Prime Minister and other ministers.[24] There are no provisions specifying the size of the cabinet or the ministers who may be its members. The experience of other countries shows that it is wiser to leave the question of size to the discretion of the Prime Minister to determine according to actual need. On the other hand, a minimum of the cabinet's membership is sometimes fixed, presumably to avoid concentration of power in a few hands. In Lesotho, for example, a minimum of seven is fixed as the number of ministries that may be established, including the office of the Deputy Prime Minister.[25]

2. APPOINTMENT AND TENURE

The power to appoint ministers lies with the Prime Minister. The Prime Minister in Lesotho, as in the metropolitan matrix, is crucial to the formation, life and death of the cabinet. It is of interest to note that in Somalia a different provision existed in regard to the qualification for membership of the cabinet. The cabinet, which was styled the Council of Ministers after the Italian *consiglio dei ministri*, was made up of the Prime Minister and ministers who were required to possess the qualifications to be elected as deputies. This meant that they did not need to be elected members.[26] The political experience of Somalia during the period of the trusteeship of the United Nations, and particularly in the last years before independence, was one of vigorous and multifarious party activities. The opening made in the constitution for non-deputies as members of the cabinet was designed as a safety valve to facilitate the inclusion of different parties in the government. With the fluidity of political life in Africa generally, a rigidly exclusive mechanism for recruitment to an executive may tend to lead to more animosity. A permissive mechanism such as that of Somalia under the 1960 Constitution may induce more consensus.

In Lesotho, the Prime Minister and other ministers must be appointed from among the Members of Parliament. Ministerial appointments may be made from among members of the National Assembly of Senators who are nominated as such by the King (i.e. from among Senators who are not chiefs).[27]

Before assuming office, ministers take an oath of loyalty. In Somalia the ministers took the oath before the President of the Republic, and the ministerial assistants, known as Under-Secretaries of State, took the oath before the Prime Minister.[28]

The tenure of ministerial office had the same duration as the life of Parliaments. Termination of ministerial tenure might take place as a result of dismissal, or suspension following the institution of impeachment proceedings, or as a result of collective resignation following a vote of no-confidence passed by Parliament. As regards dismissal, in Somalia there were no detailed provisions specifying conditions under which the President could remove ministers, as found in the constitution of Lesotho. Experience of cabinet government elsewhere in Africa has shown that, in the absence of explicit provisions for the removal of ministers and in particular of the Prime Minister by the Head of State, the subject can be a source of constitutional crisis. The resort to the conventions of metropolitan systems as a solution where there had been no incorporation of conventions in the constitution has been debated right up to the Judicial Committee of the Privy Council. The case which has become a *cause célèbre* is the Nigerian case of *Akintola* v. *Governor of Western Nigeria*, which was heard by the Federal Supreme Court, and on appeal to the Privy Council as *Adegbenre* v *Akintola*.[29]

The facts were briefly as follows. The then Premier of Western Nigeria, the late Chief Akintola, had been removed from office by the Governor. Akintola brought an action seeking a declaratory judgement against the Governor, and the newly appointed Premier,

Alhaji Adegbenre, ruled that his dismissal was invalid. The Governor was empowered under the constitution of the Western Region to dismiss a Premier if it appeared to him that the Premier no longer commanded the support of a majority of the members of the House of Assembly. Akintola was deputy leader of the Action Group, the party in opposition in the Federal Parliament, and led by Chief Awolowo.

There had been disagreements between Awolowo and Akintola, and Akintola had been asked by the party's federal executive on 20 May 1962 to resign his premiership and his party office. He immediately asked the Governor to dissolve the regional legislature, but the Governor refused to do this. The Speaker of the House of Assembly also refused Akintola's request for the convening of an emergency session of the House to consider a motion of confidence. The Governor received a letter signed by a majority of members of the House of Assembly (including the Speaker) asking him to remove the Premier. He dismissed Akintola on 21 May and appointed Adegbenre (a supporter of Awolowo) in his place.

This created a constitutional crisis. When the House met on 25 May, after Adegbenre's appointment, disorder broke out, and a few days later the Federal Parliament declared a state of emergency, and the Federal Government suspended the new government of the Western Region, placing it in the hands of an administrator.

The Federal Supreme Court of Nigeria held, by a majority, that the Governor's act was invalid on the grounds that his power of dismissal was to be exercisable only when the House of Assembly had formally signified its lack of confidence in the Premier. The Court reached this conclusion on the basis of what it understood to be a convention in Britain applicable in like situations.

The dissenting judgement of Brett, P. J., held that in the absence of an express provision in the constitution limiting the sources of a Governor's information about the strength of a Premier's backing to votes of confidence in the House of Assembly, the Governor was entitled to obtain his information from any other source that was *prima facie* reliable.

The Judicial Committee of the Privy Council preferred this dissenting opinion and accordingly reversed the decision of the Federal Supreme Court, in May 1963. The Privy Council's decision caused a new constitutional crisis which need not be described here.[30]

The Administrator of the Western Region delegated special powers to Akintola to enable him to advise Her Majesty to remove the Governor of the Western Region. This he did, and the Governor was removed in December 1962 and a member of another party, the National Council of Nigeria and the Cameroons (N.C.N.C.), appointed in his place. In the meantime Awolowo and others had been arrested on charges of treason. Akintola formed a new party and, in coalition with the N.C.N.C., formed a government. Now, the effect of the Privy Council decision was to render the formation of Akintola's government illegal; Adegbenre was the Premier *de jure*.

The whole affair is 'an illuminating episode in Nigerian constitutional history in which a political struggle was temporarily transferred to a judicial forum'.[31] The essential point about the whole case for our purpose is that the political realities of each situation dictate the course of events. In the absence of specific incorporation of the constitutional conventions of other countries, their invocation would not help to resist the will of parties or groups determined to follow a course of action contrary to such conventions. Akintola's government would not vacate office. Instead it introduced a Bill for the amendment of the Regional Constitution. This had the effect, with retroactive force, of altering the Governor's power to dismiss a Premier, limiting it to a situation where a vote of no-confidence was passed by the House of Assembly. The Bill was passed by both Houses of the Legislature (Regional and Federal). Its main aim was, of course, to nullify the decision of the Privy Council with retroactive effect. Any controversy that might have arisen on the validity of such steps was put to an end when Nigeria became a Republic in October 1963. The political struggle which gave rise to the case was resolved dramatically in directions not expected by either of the protagonists.

But the problems posed by the case will still remain in regard to dual-executive systems in which the power of the Head of State in relation to the executive head remains unclassified, in the absence of detailed provisions or living conventions regulating such relationship. As long as there is an unregulated power relationship, it will not be the conventions or precedents of other countries, but *real-politik* that will determine disputes.[32] Conventions exert influence only when they are living in the minds of significant groups in the nation.

The Nigerian crisis of 1962–63 demonstrated the difficulty of the judicial role in an atmosphere highly charged with political tension. Even where the law is not uncertain, the participation of judges to decide between conflicting claims on political legitimacy would impair their independent growth.[33]

3. FUNCTION

The function of the cabinet in Lesotho, as in the Gambia, is stated to be to advise the Head of State in whom executive power is vested in strict law; to advise him, that is to say, on the government of the state. Subject to this and to what has been explained already in this regard, the cabinet has the general direction and control of the government in both countries.[34] The general nature of the provision in respect of the function of the cabinet follows the British example. It has advantages of flexibility, but it assumes that the constitutional conventions of Britain will be followed. Its disadvantages are obvious: it invites a possible resort to arbitrariness, and could lead to crisis.

In Somalia, following a continental variation on the Westminster theme, the cabinet's functions were spelt out in detail. All important appointments were made by the President of the Republic in accordance with provisions which required that high officials of the state and commanders of the military forces should be appointed by the President on the proposal of the competent minister after approval by the Council of Ministers.[35] The same procedure for appointment also governed the posting, promotion, transfer, and termination of service.[36]

Such apparent limitation of the Prime Minister's power was misleading. In fact the Prime Minister was in a much more dominant position. He was expressly empowered to direct the general policy of the government. He was responsible for this policy and maintained its unity by co-ordinating and promoting the activity of the ministers.[37] The effect of the explicit delineation of the cabinet's function in Somalia was also to leave anything not covered therein to the Prime Minister's determination.

As if to put the matter of his predominance beyond question the law of 3 June 1962 provided that the Prime Minister was 'directly in charge of the presidency of the council of ministers, which shall provide for the execution of his decisions'.[38] The presidency of the Council of Ministers was an equivalent to what is elsewhere known as the cabinet secretariat. The Prime Minister not only presided at cabinet meetings but decided in advance what was to be discussed there and in what order of priority. He did this through his direct control of the secretariat, which also transmitted decisions to all the appropriate persons and departments, and maintained records. This is a fairly common practice elsewhere, of course, but one function peculiar to the Somali cabinet secretariat was that it was required by law to deal with 'matters affecting the government in general, all administrative acts relating to personnel employed by the State, which are not expressly reserved by law to individual ministers, planning statistical services and drafting of legislation.'[39]

In a cabinet system where the ministers must be Members of Parliament, some of the more significant under-currents of strain and conflict usually appear before or during elections. The reason is that the fate of the Prime Minister is tied to the return of his supporters at the election. An important weapon in the hands of a Prime Minister at such times (as at all times) is patronage. He may buttress his position by holding out promises of the perquisities of office in such a manner that if there is a likelihood of his party's success at the election, even members of an opposition party may join his bandwagon. In this way he may inject new support into his parliamentary group, which would act as a stick for beating conspiratorial colleagues within the cabinet. The experience of Sierra Leone serves as an interesting lesson.

The Prime Minister of Sierra Leone, Sir Albert Margai, inherited a parliamentary party in 1964, which was divided about his succession to the premiership. He did not succeed in building up strong support within his parliamentary party. In the contest for nominations for the last fateful election, many of his supporters within his party failed, including his Minister of Works. It is of great interest to recall that the Prime Minister tried to strengthen his party organization as a vehicle for power in the manner of the P.D.G. (*Parti démocratique de Guinée*),[40] and that it was when this attempt failed that he announced his intention to form a one-party state. This is logical enough, for as his power base within his parliamentary party began to disintegrate, and in the absence of a strong party organization outside the parliamentary party which he could control, the threat to his position became painfully obvious.

Finally, with the announcement of the intention to establish a republican constitution (and the apparent abandonment of the one-party idea) a new method was thought out for the reinforcement of the Prime Minister's position. The draft constitution included a provision allowing the Prime Minister six cabinet appointments of persons not Members of Parliament. This power, added to the obvious power of patronage, would no doubt have reinforced his position had he survived the storm. Sierra Leone was thus poised half-way between the cabinet systems of the Gambia and Lesotho at one end, and that of Somalia at the other. Developments there before the military coup must have been watched with great interest, especially by the leaders in the Gambia and Lesotho.

4. MINISTERIAL ASSISTANTS

Ministers direct the affairs within the competence of their respective ministries for which they are individually responsible. They are assisted in the performance of their duties by political subordinates who are styled Parliamentary Secretaries in the Gambia, Assistant Ministers in Lesotho and Under-Secretaries of State in Somalia. In Somalia the cabinet dealt with appointments.[41] In the Gambia and in Lesotho they are appointed from among the Members of Parliament, excluding (in Lesotho) chiefs and their substitutes. Provision is also made in the Gambia for the office of Permanent Secretaries – a public service office – under whose supervision every department of government is placed, subject to the general direction and control of the appropriate minister. Two or more departments may be placed under the supervision of a Permanent Secretary.[42] This is the familiar language of British administration, and its equivalent also exists in the other states even if not provided for under the constitution.

The cabinet is assisted by a Cabinet Secretary who in all cases acts under the general direction and supervision of the Prime Minister. His office is the counterpart of a Permanent Secretary and in the Gambia it is stated to be a public service office, as indeed it is in the others.[43] In Somalia he was appointed by the President of the Republic on the proposal of the Prime Minister, after receiving the advice of the Council of Ministers.

5. CABINET RESPONSIBILITY

In Lesotho the cabinet is collectively responsible to Parliament for any policy decision made or action taken by or under its general authority and for all things done by or under the authority of any minister in the execution of his ministerial function.[44] This formula seems to exclude the possibility of disowning a minister for reasons of expediency, as it imperatively enjoins collective responsibility for all things done in the execution of ministerial duty. In thus being fixed with written certainty the principle becomes much more rigid than under the British Constitution which can be applied flexibly. There has been no case in either the Gambia or Lesotho in which the question has arisen. But a Nigerian experience under a similar provision may serve to illustrate a problem. During the 1964–65 session of the United Nations, where the question of South Africa's expulsion from the United Nations was debated, the then Minister for External Affairs of Nigeria, Mr. Jaja Wachuku, made a statement which opposed the move. The Nigerian cabinet, though opposed to Mr. Wachuku's statement, felt compelled to back him up when the matter was later raised in Parliament, because under the formula they were legally obliged to do so.

A necessary precaution has been taken by excluding the application of the principle of collective responsibility to cases of appointment and removal from office of ministers and their assistants. It is also excluded in respect of the assignment of responsibility or the authorization of a minister to perform the duties of the Prime Minister in the latter's absence.[45] Again, dissolution of Parliament and questions of prerogative of mercy are not subject to the principle. All these questions are regarded as properly belonging to the realm of executive discretion. There would indeed be confusion if it were to be otherwise.

In Somalia the Prime Minister and the other ministers were 'jointly responsible' for the acts and decisions of the Council of Ministers.[46] There was no explicit provision such as that found in the constitutions of the other two states, on collective responsibility for the acts of an individual minister. It is particularly hazardous, in the absence of cases, to attempt any conclusion. But it may be said that the absence of such a provision would have meant that there was no (legal) obligation on the cabinet not to disown a minister should that be necessary.

The hallmark of collective responsibility is collective resignation following defeat on a motion of confidence, and this was provided for in detail in Somalia. Within thirty days of its formation, the government was required to obtain the confidence of the National Assembly. The government might also request the confidence of the National Assembly at any subsequent time. The National Assembly expressed its confidence or lack of confidence in an open vote of an absolute majority of its members. A motion of no-confidence might also be tabled at the request of ten members of the Assembly. A vote of no-confidence resulted in the collective resignation of the government.[47]

There have been a few government crises in Somalia. The gravest crisis was one which lasted several months and which resulted from the defeat of the government of the late Abdi Rashid Ali Shimarke on a vote of no-confidence in 1964. The then President, Aden Abdulla Osman, nominated the then Minister of the Interior, Abdi Rajak Haji Hussein, after several consultations. But Abdi Rajak was also forced to resign soon afterwards because Parliament passed a vote of no-confidence in his government. This time, the President would not accept the resignation and instead nominated again Abdi Rajak, who became Prime Minister. This example shows that even a non-executive President can wield authority through his influence in the face of the pressure of parliamentary power. This can be explained in this instance in terms of the social structure of the country, as already indicated, and also in terms of the personal history of the President and the prestige he doubtless enjoyed.[48]

The National Assembly could also bring ministers, including the Prime Minister, to trial for the commission of any offence. Such a decision could be taken on the initiative of one-fifth of the members of the Assembly, approved in a secret vote by a majority of two-thirds. For any trial of ministers on an initiative coming from outside the National Assembly, the Assembly had to give its approval in secret vote by a two-thirds majority. If ministers were brought to trial on the initiative of the National Assembly, they were automatically suspended from their duties.[49]

C. Conclusion

This chapter opened with a discussion on the reasons for the adoption and maintenance of a parliamentary form of government, and an attempt has been made to answer the question. What of the future? Prediction is not especially wise in the African circumstances. But what adds a new dimension to the difficulty in several cases is the peculiar geopolitical position of the states in questions. In this respect the Gambia and Somalia also provide similar factors of geopolitics.

The Gambia is the most artificial of nation states. Its very existence tells a story of the scramble for Africa which left the entire continent a patchwork of states with frontiers drawn arbitrarily for political and administrative reasons of the former colonial powers. The Gambia is approximately 4,000 square miles in area and has a population approaching 400,000, the smallest in Africa. The only exportable crop is ground-nuts and this cannot meet the cost of maintaining the Gambia as a viable state. Its budget is balanced by an annual grant-in-aid from Britain. The vast majority of its inhabitants form part of the Senegalese people and the future is best considered to lie in some form of union with Senegal, although the possibility of this has been doubted by a former Governor of the Gambia, on the grounds that the British tradition of parliamentary democracy in the Gambia is strong and widely supported.[50]

Lesotho is an enclave within South Africa. It has an area of 11,716 square miles and the census of 1966 gave the population as 970,000, of whom 117,000, mostly males, were absent, for the greater part across the South African border, working in the gold and diamond mines, and on farms. Only 1,500 square miles out of the total area is cultivated, owing to the hilly nature of the country, though much of the remainder is grassland suitable for grazing. The main exports (wool, mohair, wheat, sorghum, and cattle) do not meet required imports. Ninety-five per cent of these exports goes to South Africa, which also supplies forty per cent of the territory's revenue from its share of South Africa's custom and excise tax payable under a 1910 agreement. In the face of these staggering facts 'independence' and 'government' have a hollow ring, and they would have no meaning but for another fact: the determination of the Basutos against incorporation into white-supremacist South Africa. This fact unites all parties despite their factional or ideological differences, and it may prove to be the one fact which will help the preservation of the Lesotho state and affect the nature of internal politics, keeping all internal conflicts within controllable bounds. But, of course, this will depend on forces outside the control of Lesotho, and on the political development in the whole of Southern Africa.

Somalia's geopolitical position is of a different order. In a certain sense it is the opposite of Lesotho's. The Republic is bordered by Ethiopia, Kenya, the Indian Ocean, and the Gulf of Aden, and shares some forty miles of common frontier with French Somaliland (the territory of the Afars and Issas). Somalia claims parts of Ethiopia and Kenya, and the whole of the French territory, as belonging to her. Ethiopia and Kenya, on the other hand, are determined to maintain their territorial integrity. Tension had built up along the borders of the Ogaden province of Ethiopia and the north-eastern province of Kenya, and several outbreaks of violence have taken place in the past few years. Short of an agreement towards some form of unity of the whole region, the Horn of Africa threatens to be an area of continuing conflict, and this will no doubt affect not only the relations of the states concerned, but their internal politics as well.[51]

Finally it may be concluded that the system of government with a divided executive power does not seem to have much appeal in Africa. There does not appear to be any evidence that it existed in any past African political systems. The dual-executive structure introduced in post-colonial days, which was partly designed to distribute power and contain power conflicts, has not worked in many cases. Indeed, in some the existence of two executives exacerbated the conflict, leading to the abolition of the system. In this sense, although the problem is many-sided, the form of government seems to have contributed to constitutional crises. The root cause of such crises is an internal contradiction of a sociopolitical and economic nature which manifests itself in personality feuds and power struggles. In freezing such contradictions in the constitution, the institutional form may contribute to crises rather than resolving them.

Whether the system will be revived in Lesotho is a matter of conjecture. If the attitude of the people in this state are attuned to the system, and provided the system can in fact serve a useful purpose, the answer may be positive. At the moment all that can be said by way of conclusion is that it does not seem possible in the African situation to find a person who has the appearance of power but who does not exercise it, and a person who exercises power but does not have the appearance of it. Two monarchies have had the executive power concentrated in the monarchy and have escaped the vagaries of a dual executive. These are Ethiopia and Morocco, which are the main subject of the next chapter.

NOTES

1. In this connection 'creoles' are the descendants of freed slaves.
2. *See* pp. 77–80 for the functions of the King of Lesotho, and for the crisis of 22 December 1966.
3. In Ghana the House of Chiefs was adopted by the Convention People's Party only as a temporary compromise for tactical reasons, and at no

time did the C.P.P. lose its grip and allow the chiefs to control the political process. The same is true in Tanzania and Malawi. In Nigeria the size and power of the traditional and conservative north was a factor, among others, that determined the establishment of a bicameral legislature and a dual executive. In Uganda the 'Kabaka Yekka', was organized by the late King Freddie as a countervailing force to check the then growing powers of Obote's Uganda People's Congress.

4. cf. H. F. Morris and J. S. Read, *Uganda, The Development of its Laws and Constitution*, Stevens, London, 1966, pp. 87–201.

5. Mr. Grace Ibingira, the Secretary General of Obote's party and a minister in his government, and other ministers, were later arrested.

6. In Chapter 4 this will be taken up as the point of reference of African constitutional (and political) development.

7. Const., Sect. 32 (1). Strictly speaking the first was in Zanzibar, but the powers of the Sultan were greater there.

8. Sect. 32 (2).

9. Sect. 32 (3).

10. Sect. 33 (1).

11. Sect. 33 (5).

12. Sect. 33 (3).

13. Sect. 33 (4).

14. Sect. 34 (1) (3).

15. Sect. 89.

16. Sect. 71 (1 and 2).

17. Sect. 76 (1).

18. Sect. 76 (2) (a–j).

19. Sect. 76 (4) (6).

20. Sect. 77.

21. Sect. 80 (1) (4).

22. Sect. 86.

23. He was later allowed to leave Lesotho to complete his studies abroad.

24. Art. 73, Lesotho.

25. Sect. 72 (2).

26. cf. Const. Part. 80 (1).

27. cf. Const. Sect. 72 (3).

28. Art. 78 (5). In both cases there was no provision for non-believers.

29. F.S.C. 187/1962; and (1963) 3 W.L.R. 63.

30. For a discussion of the case cf. S. G. Davis 'Nigeria – Some recent decisions in the constitution', *International and Comparative Law Quarterly*, 11, 1962, p. 919; O. I. Odumosa, *The Nigerian Constitution*, Sweet & Maxwell, London, 1963, Chap. 9; J. P. Mackintosh, 'Politics in Nigeria: The Action Group Crisis of 1962' (1963), 11, *Political Studies*, 126 at pp. 137–55.

31. cf. S. A. de Smith, *The New Commonwealth and its Constitutions*, Stevens, London, 1964, p. 90.

32. For a discussion on the relative merits and demerits of incorporating certain conventions by reference, cf. de Smith, op. cit., pp. 82–6.

33. The report of the constitutional commission of Tanganyika must have had the Nigerian crisis in mind when it commented to the same effect.

34. Const. the Gambia, Sect. 65; Lesotho, Sect. 73.

35. Const. Art. 87, and Law of 3 June 1962, Art. 7 (2).
36. Law of 3 June 1962, Art. 7 (3).
37. Const. Art. 83 (1); Law of 3 June 1962, Art. 3 (1).
38. Art. 9 (1).
39. ibid. Art. 9 (3).
40. *See* Chapter 6.
41. Const. the Gambia, Sect. 71; Lesotho, Sect. 78; Somalia, Art. 79 (1).
42. Sect. 73.
43. Const. Gambia, Sect. 74.
44. Const. Sect. 73 (2).
45. cf. Const. Lesotho, Sect. 73 (3). In the event of the Prime Minister's absence his function is temporarily exercised by the Deputy Prime Minister, or in his absence, by a member of the cabinet, appointed by the King. (Sect. 75.)
46. Law of 3 June 1962, Art. 4 (4).
47. Const. Art. 82 (1) (2) (3) (4).
48. President Aden Abdulla Osman was defeated in a presidential election on 10 June 1967. It is of interest to note that his rival and successful candidate was Abdi Rashid Ali Shimarke. The 123 strong Parliament voted 73–50 for Shimarke; cf. *The Times*, 11 June 1967.
49. Const. Art. 84 (1) (2) (3) (4).
50. cf. Hilary Blood, 'Parliament in Small Territories' in *Parliament as an Export* (ed. A. Burns), Allen & Unwin, London, 1966, pp. 247–63, especially pp. 260–1.
51. The present military government, which has made significant strides in the socio-economic field, has not contributed to the easing of tension. If anything there are signs of more ambitious territorial aggrandizement.

3

The Monarchical Systems

A. The Monarchy

The monarchies which are the main subject of this chapter are those of Ethiopia and Morocco.[1] The character of the executive in each monarchy has been determined by the peculiar history of each state. Islam is a factor in Morocco, and has also historically affected the development of Ethiopian political institutions.[2] The constitutional structure of the monarchy in Morocco was influenced by Islam, so that in spite of its 'constitutional' form the type of government created was autocratic. Similarly, in Ethiopia, the monarchy became autocratic and hierarchically organized principally as a response to the continued threat of external forces, chiefly under the impetus of Islamic states.[3]

The Ethiopian monarchy bases its legitimacy on the claim to an uninterrupted line of descent from a union between King Solomon of Jerusalem and the Queen of Sheba. Some writers have argued that this has been a key factor in the maintenance and survival of the Ethiopian empire-state.[4] The revised Ethiopian Constitution of 1955 also makes specific reference to Solomonic descent as the source of legitimacy of the present dynasty.[5] But the relevance of the claim is not necessarily dependent on its historical validity, though everything possible is done to demonstrate this. The main point about the claim is the religious ideology implicit in it, which is supposed to invest its successful claimants with some sanctity.[6] The present revised constitution (1955) is based on the first constitution of 1931. They have both emanated from the top, being granted by the Emperor.

The monarchy in Libya was of relatively recent origin, as a

(national) kingdom, although there have been emirates in Libya over a long period of time.[7] The monarchy of the United Kingdom of Libya came into existence on 27 December 1951, when the Emir of Cyrenaica became King of Libya as Idris I. The Libyan State of modern times was formed on 1 January 1934 by the union of Cyrenaica and Tripolitania under Italian rule. With the defeat of Italy in 1942–43, Cyrenaica and Tripolitania passed under separate British military administrations, and the Fezzan under French. On 21 November 1949, the General Assembly of the United Nations decided that an independent and sovereign state of Libya should be constituted by 1 January 1952: the inhabitants, through a National Assembly, were to determine its form of government and constitution. The National Assembly of inhabitants, comprising representatives in equal numbers from Cyrenaica, Tripolitania, and the Fezzan, met in Tripoli on 2 December 1950 and decided that Libya should be a constitutional monarchy under Mohammed Idris el-Sanussi, whose emirate of Cyrenaica had been recognized by the British since 1946. The first constitution which gave expression to this decision came into force on 7 October 1951.[8] This is shown in the preamble to the constitution, where the Constituent Assembly declared:

> . . . having agreed and determined to form a union between us (i.e. the people of Cyrenaica, Tripolitania and Fezzan) under the Crown of King Mohammed Idris el Mahdi el Sanussi (As-Sanussi), to whom the nation has offered the crown and who was declared constitutional King of Libya by this, the national constituent assembly. . . .[9]

In Morocco, the present Alawite dynasty was established by Mawlay Rashid in 1660. When France established a protectorate in Morocco in 1912, the institution of the monarchy was preserved. It provided the centre of identification for Moroccan nationalist aspirations, and in the inter-war period and after the war, up to 1955, King Mohammed V provided the dominant national image. Although he was less absolute than might be expected, owing to the emergence of political parties in Morocco since the 1930s, he became the centre of political life and controversy – so much so that the French exiled him in 1953. Upon his return from exile on 18 November 1955, he reaffirmed his pledge to 'establish democratic institutions which will spring out of free elections . . . within the framework of a constitutional monarchy'.[10] Once in power again, the monarch was reluctant to fulfil the pledge too soon, chiefly because power would pass from his hand to a dominant political party – the Istiqlal – despite the fact that this party supported the monarchy.[11]

After the death of King Mohammed V (on 28 February 1961) his son, the new King Hassan II, set out to introduce changes which purported to give his rule a broader basis of power. On 7 December 1962 Morocco went to the polls to approve its first written constitution in a Gaullist style of referendum. The question put to the people required a simple acceptance or rejection of the constitution (as in France), presented to them from above by King Hassan II. The results showed a landslide in favour of the constitution. This has been explained (1) in terms of Istiqlal's position (a Yes vote) and its rural organization of religious conservative forces; and (2) because King Hassan II was able to choose the terrain, had the monopoly of radio and television, and had taken the initiative on timing from the left-wing opposition party. When he announced the constitutional referendum the opposition were caught by surprise before they had time to develop a practicable campaign strategy.

It will be seen from the foregoing that each constitution was given in a different way: the Ethiopian Constitution was 'granted' by the Emperor and promulgated after it was passed by the legislative body; the Libyan Constitution was enacted by a constituent assembly representing the people; the Moroccan Constitution was proposed by the King and voted on at a referendum (*see* note 1).

This diversity in the method of establishing the constitutions may give an idea of the nature of power-relations between the King and other political forces in the country concerned. But it is not in itself a sufficient guide as to whether the monarchy is 'constitutional' or not. Nor is the system necessarily 'constitutional' because it is declared to be so by the constitution. In Libya, by the words of the preamble quoted above, and in Morocco under Article 1 of the Constitution, the Kings were declared to be constitutional monarchs. But while it is true that this may tend to impose a certain amount of restraint it does not render the monarch one who reigns rather than one who rules. None the less, by virtue of the fact that the Libyan and Moroccan monarchies were said by their constitutions to be 'constitutional' it would be better to call them quasi-constitutional.

It should be remembered that although classifications are helpful as tools of analysis, in a comparative study of this kind they could get out of hand and mislead. Accordingly, while bearing the two different categories in mind, the monarchies are examined together through some of their characteristic features and then some conclusions are drawn.

1. SOURCE OF SOVEREIGN POWER

In Ethiopia sovereignty is vested in the Emperor, who exercises supreme authority over all the affairs of his empire.[12] His person is declared to be sacred, his dignity inviolable and his powers indisputable – all by virtue of 'His Imperial blood as well as by the anointing which He has received'.[13]

In Libya sovereignty belonged to God alone, and was given by His will as a sacred trust to the state 'which was the source of power'.[14] Saving this provision, sovereignty was vested in the King.[15]

In Morocco sovereignty is declared to belong to the nation which is to exercise it directly by referendum and indirectly through the institutions established by the constitution.[16]

2. SUCCESSION TO THE THRONE

A common feature of the monarchies under review, in regard to succession to the throne, is the hereditary principle, together with the doctrine of primogeniture, only male succeeding male.[17]

But differences appear especially concerning provisions about situations where there is no legitimate heir to the Throne. The Ethiopian Constitution, having provided that succession shall remain perpetually attached to the line of the present Emperor, leaves it to a future special law to determine the order of, and qualifications for, the succession. No such law has been issued in the seventeen years that have followed the promulgation of the Revised Constitution on 4 November 1955. Furthermore, in the absence of a male descendant, or where one is not capable of meeting the requirements of succession to the Throne, the Emperor, after consulting the Crown Council, can designate an Heir Presumptive from among his nearest male relatives in the line of succession[18] meeting the necessary requirements. And the Emperor determines the qualifications for succession to the Throne after consultation with the Crown Council.[19]

The Crown Prince, eldest son of the Emperor and successor to the Throne, has lived as such in the shadow of his father for forty-one years. The provisions which leave to a 'special law' of the future, and to the Emperor, to decide on the qualifications for succession had given rise to a wave of speculations on the successor to the present Emperor. However, the question of succession appears to be settled now, making the constitutional position of the Crown Prince more secure, everything else being equal.[20]

The Libyan Constitution required that if the throne remained vacant after the King's death, owing to the lack of a successor, the two chambers of Parliament should hold a joint meeting to appoint a successor within ten days. A decision had to be reached by at least three-quarters of the members of the two chambers, voting openly by a majority of not less than two-thirds of the members present. If the choice could not take place within the time specified, the two chambers had jointly to proceed to make the choice on the eleventh day, in the presence of an absolute majority of the members of each of the two chambers and by a proportionate majority. If the House of Representatives had been dissolved the old House had to meet until the King was chosen.[21]

During the period when the Throne was vacant, the Council of Ministers was empowered to exercise the constitutional functions of the King in the name of the Libyan people.[22] If the King was a minor or if any circumstance prevented or delayed him from the performance of his functions, the Council of Ministers had, with the consent of Parliament, to appoint a Regent or a Council of Regency to take his place.[23]

In Morocco there are no detailed provisions covering situations where the Throne is vacant. When the constitution came into operation in 1962 the present King Hassan had only just acceded to the Throne, while he was in his early thirties. This may explain the absence of a preoccupation with succession problems. But curiously enough there is a provision on Regency. While the King is a minor, a Regency Council is empowered to exercise the constitutional powers and rights of the Crown during his minority. The Regency Council should be presided over by the King's nearest male relative in the collateral male line who is over 21 years of age, the other members being the President of the Supreme Court, the Dean of Rectors of the University, and the President of the Chamber of Counsellors.[24]

3. NATURE AND SCOPE OF FUNCTION

(a) Head of State

Functions commonly entrusted to Heads of States in other systems are performed, needless to say, by the African monarchs. Such functions are, for example, the accrediting and receiving of diplomatic representatives, conferring honours and titles, remitting penalties, promulgating laws, opening and closing parliamentary sessions, and so forth. Each has the duty, as Head of State, of defending the unity and integrity of his Nation and ensuring the protection and welfare of his subjects.

(b) Chief Executive

The constitutions of the countries under examination entrust executive power to the monarchs whose traditional position is thus reaffirmed in a modern guise, albeit with modification and with varying degrees of limitation and entrenchment.[25]

Power of Appointment

To start with the least-limited monarchy – Ethiopia – we find that the Emperor's power of appointment is unlimited. He can appoint and dismiss the Prime Minister and other ministers and vice-ministers on his own initiative. He also appoints on his own initiative the members of the Senate as well as their President and two Vice-Presidents, governors, judges, mayors, diplomatic representatives, officers of the military and the police, managers and board directors of state undertakings. This power of appointment, which has been used skilfully to advantage over the years, carries with it the power to determine and control the progress and termination of office of government officials including junior civil servants.[26] The Emperor determines the organization, powers and duties of all ministries and executive departments, and administers the whole government.[27] Under this power he can also establish new departments and make financial provision for such departments, which was done for some years after 1955 by Imperial Decrees under the 'emergency legislation' provision of Article 92 of the Constitution. Last but not least, he approves the election and appointment of the Archbishop and Bishops of the Ethiopian Orthodox Church.[28]

Curiously enough, Morocco and not Libya came next in the King's freedom to appoint ministers. For, in Morocco, the King appoints the Prime Minister and other ministers on his own initiative and can terminate their office or accept their resignation. Furthermore the King presides over the Council of Ministers.[29] Judges are appointed by Royal Decree upon the proposal of the High Council of the Judiciary over which the King presides,[30] and civil and military appointments are made by him, though he

may delegate his power.[31] On the other hand, the members of
the Senate (Chamber of Counsellors) were elected.[32]

Under the 1952 Constitution of Libya, by contrast, the King
appointed and removed the Prime Minister, but the appointment
or dismissal of other ministers was to be made by him on the
proposal of the Prime Minister.[33] Again, diplomatic representatives were appointed by him on the proposal of the Minister of
Foreign Affairs.[34] He had the right to establish the public services
and to appoint and dismiss senior officials but was required to do
so 'in accordance with the provisions of the law'.[35] He appointed
the members of the Senate and their President, but not the two
Vice-Presidents who were elected, though subject to his approval.[36]
Judges were appointed by Royal Decree.[37]

(c) Legislative Power

The power to legislate is one of the crucial tests by which the
nature and scope of political power may be assessed. The point
at which constitutionalism ends and absolutism begins may not
be easy to find, but where plenary power is enjoyed by a Head of
State this is hardly a problem, whether the Head of State is an
imperial autocrat or a military dictator.

In African monarchies some constitutional limit appears to have
been placed on the traditional legislative power but the primacy
of the executive can still be asserted by various devices. In the
first place, there is the right to initiate legislation and introduce
resolutions in Parliament and the right to address Parliament in
person, or through messages. Then there is the power to veto
legislation passed by Parliament; and here the difference in the
provisions of the various monarchical constitutions is striking. In
Ethiopia the Emperor can send back a Bill with his observations
or with an alternative proposal.[38] No provision is made to deal
with the event where Parliament persists in its original position,
but in practice this point is only of theoretical interest. In Libya
Bills had to be approved by the King, who also made the necessary
regulations for carrying out the laws without modifying or sus-
pending them or dispensing with their execution.[39] He could refer
the Bill back to Parliament for reconsideration. If the proposal
was passed again by a two-thirds majority of the members of each
of the two chambers he had to assent to it and promulgate it as
law. Even if the two-thirds majority was not secured, if Parliament
in another session could pass the Bill again by a simple majority

of all the members of each of the two chambers the King had to give his assent and promulgate it.[40]

An interesting innovation is found in this respect in the Moroccan constitution which introduces a 'presidential' practice, i.e. a referendum. The King may either give his assent to a Bill or send it back to Parliament for a second reading in a message countersigned by the Prime Minister.[41] Or he may submit it to a referendum, the result of which will be binding on all. And if a government bill that had been rejected by Parliament is approved by a referendum the Chamber of Representatives is dissolved and a new one elected in its place.[42] This shows that the hand of the Moroccan King is much stronger in this field than was that of the Libyan King. It will be seen in later chapters that the practice of resorting to referenda gives the executive great advantage where a deadlock occurs. But the dissolution of Parliament as a consequence of the approval of a referendum is a feature peculiar to the Moroccan Constitution, and has no equivalent place in African neo-presidential régimes.

Another feature of legislative power is the right to legislate in emergency situations in two ways. First, in a national emergency, when the constitutional basis of the state is threatened, the Head of State takes full powers. But this is not peculiar to these systems.[43] Secondly, there is the right to legislate by decree when Parliament is not in session. The frequency of resort to this type of legislation by decree may give a clue to the real powers of the Head of State. In Ethiopia this right has been exercised all too frequently, mainly in respect of financial matters and in situations which can be defined as 'emergency' only by a great stretch of the imagination.[44] A similar provision existed in the Libyan constitution[45] and in both cases the constitutions provided that the decree must be submitted to Parliament at its first meeting following the recess. In Morocco, Parliament must authorize the government, for a specified period and purpose, to take measures which normally fall within the domain of law, by decree after deliberation in the Council of Ministers, subject to ratification by Parliament at the end of the time limit. The variation which is noteworthy here is that it is the Council of Ministers and not the King in person that is empowered to legislate by decree. The explanation may be that the King presides over the Council.

Again there are the King's powers in connection with international agreements and declaration of war, which are expressly provided for in all three constitutions. But some variations must be noted. In Ethiopia the Emperor, who exercises supreme direction over foreign relations, has the right to settle disputes with foreign powers. He alone has the right to ratify treaties and to determine which treaties and other international agreements shall be subject to ratification before becoming binding upon the nation.[46]

But Parliament must approve all agreements which involve the modification of Ethiopian territory or sovereignty or jurisdiction over such territory; or which lay a burden on Ethiopian subjects, modify existing legislation, require expenditures of state funds, or invoke loans or monopolies.[47] Declaration of war can be made only with the advice and consent of Parliament.

In Libya the King had the right to declare war and conclude peace and ratify treaties with prior parliamentary approval.[48] In Morocco, the King signs and ratifies treaties. However, treaties which imply commitment of the finances of the state may not be ratified without prior approval by Parliament.

This, paradoxically enough, appears to place less limit on the power of the King of Morocco than the equivalent provision in the Ethiopian constitution. On the other hand there was no provision enabling the King of Morocco to declare war or to conclude peace, which is no less paradoxical.[49]

(d) Judicial Power

Only the Emperor of Ethiopia exercises judicial power. His traditional court (Yezufan Chillot) continues to function, despite the fact that the constitution vests judicial power in the Supreme Imperial Court and 'such other Courts as may be established by law'. The law in question established the High Court and other Courts of inferior jurisdiction, without making mention of the jurisdiction of the Imperial Chillot. Unwritten tradition has therefore been allowed to prevail over the express provision of the constitution, though the matter has never been disputed in court.[50]

4. RESPONSIBILITY OF THE MONARCHS

The doctrine of British Constitutional Law that the Queen can do no wrong finds a rough equivalent in at least one African monarchy. Article 62 (a) of the Ethiopian Constitution provides: 'In accordance with tradition and the provisions of Article 4 of this constitution, no one shall have the right to bring suit against the Emperor.'[51] This immunity from legal suit, which is provided

E

in general terms, may be given the widest possible scope, covering criminal and civil liability, particularly in view of the reference to tradition. Personal immunity from legal suit was not specifically made the subject of constitutional provision in Libya and Morocco, although in both countries, as in Ethiopia, the constitutions provided that the Monarch shall be inviolable.[52] The position of the Libyan Monarch approximated to that of his Ethiopian counterpart in this respect, as it was provided that he was to be exempt from all responsibility.[53] In another respect the position of the King of Morocco resembles that of the Emperor of Ethiopia, in that both their persons are declared to be sacred.[54]

The personal immunity under Article 62 (a) of the Ethiopian Constitution does not extend to the properties held in the name of the Emperor, which are declared to be under the same régime as is applicable to all properties of Ethiopian nationals.[55] No mention is made in this respect in the constitutions of the other monarchies.

In these systems it is not always possible to disentangle the personal responsibility (or its absence) from the political responsibility. Thus in Ethiopia the person of the Emperor is held to be sacred, his dignity inviolable and his power indisputable, all in one breath; and this provision, apart from tradition, is the basis of the immunity from legal suit, noted above. In such a system where the ministers are responsible to the Emperor (as we shall see below) the implications of this doctrine are immense – no one can criticize the government, as this would be disputing indisputable power.

Political responsibility in Libya was more widely distributed. There, the King exercised his power through his ministers and responsibility rested with them.[56] In Morocco, on the other hand, there is no such distribution of responsibility. The Moroccan King plays a wide role, presiding over the Council of Ministers, the High Council of National Promotion and the Plan,[57] and other bodies, which means less distribution of power and therefore of responsibility. This may explain the absence of an express provision exempting him from all responsibility.

Political responsibility does not rest on constitutional principles alone, even where these may be enshrined in the articles of the constitution. It involves a variety of other factors, including the political experience of the nation concerned and of its active social elements, and the inherited social position of the central force (i.e. the monarch), which predates the formal relationships fixed in the constitution, and comes out in the dynamics of power.

B. The Ministers

We have already seen how the ministers in the monarchies are appointed; but we saw this in connection with the powers of the monarchs. We must now shift our focus to the ministers.

A. ETHIOPIA

In Ethiopia, there is a Council of Ministers, first set up in 1943 under Order No. 1, which was later incorporated by the Revised Constitution of 1955. The Council of Ministers has an advisory function, and is responsible to the Emperor for all the advice and recommendation it tenders. It is composed of all the ministers and is presided over by the Prime Minister who submits to the Emperor, for approval, all matters discussed at the Council, including any change in the rules of procedure.

The Prime Minister acts as a go-between, presenting to Parliament draft legislation prepared by the Council and approved by the Emperor; and presenting to the Emperor legislative proposals passed by Parliament.[58] According to the constitution, each minister is also individually responsible to the Emperor for the discharge of the duties in his respective ministry,[59] a provision no doubt designed to ensure the Emperor's complete control over the machinery of government. The ministers have the right of access to Parliament and may be individually summoned by the latter to answer questions. Ministers may not for remuneration, compensation, or benefit, engage in activities in which there is no governmental participation.[60] In case of offences committed by any of them, including the Prime Minister, in connection with their official functions, they may be tried before the Supreme Imperial Court, upon the initiative of a majority vote of both Houses of Parliament or by order of the Emperor. A special prosecutor must be appointed by the Emperor for each case. This clearly does not amount to a right of impeachment so far as the initiative of Parliament is concerned, since its enforcement depends upon Imperial consent to appoint the special prosecutor, which may be postponed indefinitely.

Early in 1961, soon after the abortive *coup d'état* of December

1960, a committee for constitutional amendment was set up, and in November 1961 it recommended that the constitution be amended to provide for the appointment of the Prime Minister by the Emperor, and for the selection by the Prime Minister of his own cabinet of ministers, who would then be presented to the Emperor for formal installation. The same report also suggested a separation of the position and function of the Head of State from that of the head of government, with a corresponding transfer of executive authority to the Prime Minister and his cabinet.

A minority opinion was in favour of making the Prime Minister responsible to Parliament. The report was shelved for five years. Then on 22 March 1966 the Emperor announced that he would appoint a Prime Minister, who would select ministers and present them for appointment by the Emperor. The following day a law (Order No. 44 of 1966) appeared in the Negarit Gazette. The only real change this law introduced[61] was that it gave the Prime Minister a right to propose the other ministers for appointment by the Emperor. The structure and function of the Council of Ministers remained the same, and no change was made in respect of responsibility – collective or individual. While the Prime Minister is appointed and dismissed by the Emperor, the question of the dismissal of ministers is omitted from the new law. In the absence of an amendment to the constitution they must be presumed to be dismissable by the Emperor. Similarly it may be presumed that the Emperor can invoke the concept of the individual responsibility of each minister to him in order to retain the services of ministers when the Prime Minister resigns.

The office of the Prime Minister has acquired an enhanced status in recent years with the gradual eclipse of the ancient office of the Tsahafe Tezaz (Privy Seal). The present Prime Minister combines his office with that of the Tsahafe Tezaz. But, as Ethiopian history amply demonstrates, such consolidation of personal power is not necessarily accompanied by a corresponding growth of the institutions in question.[62] One factor which has inhibited the growth of the cabinet as an independent institution is the policy of concentration of power itself and the dual responsibility of ministers. A strong Prime Minister seeking to institutionalize the cabinet by creating a *de facto* single ministerial loyalty to him could not last long. The conclusion is inescapable: the cabinet will remain essentially what it has been – an advisory body which can be used as an Imperial lightning-rod in the event of a storm.

B. LIBYA

In Libya there was a Council of Ministers consisting of the Prime Minister (who presided) and the other ministers. The Council of Ministers was responsible for the direction of all internal and external affairs of the state,[63] and they were collectively responsible to the House of Representatives for the general policy of the state. Each minister was also individually responsible for the activities of his ministry.[64] Any signature of the King concerning the affairs of the state required his countersignature of the Prime Minister and of the competent minister.

The House of Representatives could, by a majority of all its members, pass a vote of no-confidence in the Council of Ministers. If this happened the Council of Ministers had to resign. A vote of no-confidence could concern one of the ministers, in which case he alone had to resign. The motion of censure had to be presented by no less than fifteen deputies.[65] Ministers had a right to attend Parliament, but could vote only if they were Members of Parliament. They could also be required to attend.[66] In the event of the dismissal or resignation of the Prime Minister the ministers were considered thereby to have been dismissed or to have resigned.[67]

The constitutional position of the Prime Minister and his cabinet in Libya vis-à-vis the King was stronger than in Ethiopia. But palace politics held sway in the government, which was caught in a political tug of war between two forces – the King and Parliament. The dismissal of the Prime Minister by the King on the one hand and a vote of no-confidence by the House of Representatives on the other had the same result – the resignation of the cabinet. The dilemma of the cabinet was highlighted by the issue of legislation by Royal Decree which caused the resignation of the cabinet at least three times. Then, in 1960, the first vote of no-confidence occurred, bringing down the government of Abdulmajid Kubar, as the result of a road construction scandal. Ironically enough, Kubar had been President of the House of Representatives from Independence until his appointment as Prime Minister in May 1957. The next Prime Minister did not fare any better. He resigned in March 1963, two-and-a-half years after he took office. His government, like all the previous governments, was reshuffled at least once a year. This created ministerial instability, with consequent disruption of government business.

C. MOROCCO

In Morocco the constitutional position of the cabinet represents an interesting combination of the presidential and parliamentary system of government, in which the King plays an active role. There is a government consisting of the Prime Minister and the other ministers, who are all members of the Council of Ministers. But the Council of Ministers is presided over by the King,[68] and the government is responsible to the King and to the Chamber of Representatives.[69]

The Chamber of Representatives may question the responsibility of the government by a motion of censure, initiated by at least one-tenth of the members of the chamber. If such a motion of censure is adopted by an absolute majority of the members of the chamber it results in the collective resignation of the government; but no other motion of censure may be adopted for a year after such an event.[70]

After deliberation with the Council of Ministers, the Prime Minister may pledge the responsibility of the government to the Chamber of Representatives. This may be in connection with a declaration of general policy or a vote on the text of particular Bills. In pledging the responsibility of the government he may seek a vote of confidence which, if rejected by an absolute majority of the members of the chamber, must result in the resignation of the government.[71]

The peculiar position of the cabinet, especially in relation to the King, is an ingenious piece of constitutional innovation, and the history behind it is equally remarkable. Indeed it cannot be properly understood without a brief review of the development of the position of the monarchy over the last decade. This period is marked by a reassertion of the King's personal role in government, against the background of a complex political life. Until 1956, the King maintained an arbitral – almost apolitical – position. Leaders of various national organizations such as parties, trade unions, and resistance groups, exercised crucial influence over the King in all important governmental appointments. The cabinet itself was selected from a list of political figures and technocrats submitted by a Premier-elect, after long consultations with various groups. There was a national consensus over public goals in post-independence Morocco, up to 1956. And this fact, plus the King's policy of non-interference in matters of detail, avoided friction between him and his cabinet. Any threats of a major clash were immediately nipped in the bud by the abandonment of the issue or measure which constituted the threat. The result was a policy of compromise with moderate programmes, carried out partially by a government which suffered from ministerial instability.

After October 1956, the government which reflected this national consensus (the government of National Unity) was reorganized, with Istiqlal – the dominant political party – holding a majority of the ministries. Then, demands were made for full powers to be enjoyed by the government, but were compounded by partisan bitterness and resulted in the resignation of the ministers.

The party causing the major crisis – the Istiqlal – next formed a government in May 1958, but incipient rivalries reduced its effectiveness and shortened its life, and in December 1958, soon after its fall, new ministers were chosen in a personal capacity. But the political stagnation continued until 1960 when pressures coming from different directions converged to change the situation. The Crown Prince was young and impatient; the political parties were frustrated by the stalemate and impatient to use state power for programmes along partisan lines. An attempt made to form a government with the Crown Prince as Prime Minister was resisted by the parties. The King overcame this resistance by assuming leadership of the government, with the Crown Prince as Deputy Prime Minister. The King's failing health and the drive for leadership manifested by the Crown Prince combined to transfer actual executive power from the King to the Prince. The Ministers were again appointed not on a party basis but in a personal capacity.

On 26 February 1961, the King (Mohammed V) died and the Crown Prince (Hassan II) ascended the throne. The young King's ideas on government and leadership may help partly to explain the origin and nature of the present position of the cabinet. The cabinet, according to him, is to be 'a team of responsible men grouped together about a chief, capable of giving the powerful impetus necessary to lead the people in their fight for progress and against poverty.'[72]

This view of personalized power in government is crystallized in the constitution, as we have seen. The King's presidency of the cabinet and his right to appeal to the people through the mechanism of referendum gives his rule a modern guise as well as an effective control over government, as was shown in the referendum of 7 December 1962. It also gives him an advantage in that government successes rebound to his credit, whereas failures can be used to weaken parties that may happen to predominate in his cabinet. As for the future, the King has said: 'I cannot, at the present time, make the exercise of power less direct. . . .'[73]

His creation on 17 May 1963 of a Palace Party – the *Front de défense des institutions constitutionnelles* (F.D.I.C.) – the Hassanite equivalent of the Gaullist U.N.R. – was an attempt to consolidate this personal power. His present cabinet is drawn mainly from this party. The result of the constitutional referendum had not only provided him with the state apparatus he wished, but had also given him a sense of self-assurance. In order to offset the influence of the Istiqlal Party, which, while still loyal to the institution of the monarchy, was becoming a bitter critic of the government (which was his), he created the F.D.I.C. This party was essentially a coalition of the Popular Movement Party and the Liberal Independents – 'the King's men'. King Hassan ousted the opposition of the right but, as the tragedy of the Ben Barka affair demonstrated, he did not shatter the opposition of the left.

Conclusion

The history of monarchies in Europe has been characterized by a shift of power from the person of the King to institutions such as Parliament and a cabinet. This, of course, is the result of a long period of evolution. It is open to question whether this is possible in countries with a history and present reality such as those of the states described in this chapter. On the other hand it is doubtful whether personified traditional power can continue to resist the onslaught of change without dire consequences as was illustrated by the case of Libya. It must be recognized, however, that the monarchies have so far demonstrated an innovating capacity which seems to have helped their survival. The institutions of Parliament and cabinet were introduced in all three monarchies, with varying degrees of transfer of power to these institutions, but in no case was the supremacy of the monarch over the cabinet seriously questioned. Even in the two quasi-constitutional monarchies the balance of power was decisively on the side of the monarch. The traditional authority with which monarchs are invested does not simply slough off, even in the presence of a modern constitution. All the constitutional devices which require the acts of the King to conform to certain requirements may appear to be restrictive of the King's power and indicative of ministerial or parliamentary supremacy. But it is fair to generalize that while they tend to reduce arbitrariness by subjecting the exercise of power to a regulated pattern, in reality they cannot be expected to restrain traditional power. For, unless abolished or emasculated (completely constitutionalized), traditional power tends to get the better of modern devices by sheltering behind modernity and maintaining the reality of its power. The King can use his ministers as a smoke-screen for the exercise of his authority, shifting responsibility to them when the going gets rough.

It may be pointed out that this is not necessarily peculiar to Kings, and that executive Presidents can do the same thing in respect to their ministers. None the less, the elective basis of executive Presidents as opposed to royal succession introduced a point of variance in the respective constitutional structures. Again, in ideological terms the monarchs depend on religious sentiments which are inherent in their countries' ideologies. Indeed the Kings are intimately connected with religious institutions. The Islamic Kings have traditionally held positions of religious primacy as Imams which flowed from the doctrine of one God and the paramountcy on earth of his messenger.[74] This has been expressed in the Constitution of Morocco, for example, where the King is styled as *Khalifal Amir al-mu-minine* (the head of the faithful).[75] In a country where conservative and religious sentiments are strong this has deep implications, as could be seen during the constitutional referendum of 1962. A peasant was interviewed on television on the referendum, just before it was held, and he is reported to have replied: '*Il n'ya qu'Allah, le roi, et oui*' (there is only God, the King, and yes).[76] Thus the social position of the King as inherent in Islamic institutions impinges on his constitutional position as expressed in a 'modern' constitution.

The Presidents, by contrast, have tradition and inertia against them, though they have the conviction that history is on their side, in the sense that their offices are based on ideas of progress which have largely come out of the demolition of tradition. To oversimplify the issues: progress stood for equality and popular mandate, among other things, while tradition stood for privilege and heavenly (or inspired) mandate. Now the will of the monarchies to survive has been demonstrated in their capacities to innovate, as we have seen, and this gives them the aura of modernity or even 'progressiveness'. Moreover, African neo-presidentialism is characterized by authority concentrated in the office of the

President. And the devices used to strengthen the office and leader, essential as they are for national integration, lead one to suspect that at bottom they reflect the same approach to the nature of power as is implicit in monarchies. In other words, attempts to incarnate doctrines and sentiments in personalities contain in them the seeds of creating new privileges, if not (always) new dynasties. After all, Abu Bekr succeeded Muhammad after dispute on the succession, in order to carry out his work. But the succeeding Khalifs have created dynasties claiming descent from the Prophet. The crisis of succession to charismatic leaders who have departed poses a real problem in elective systems. Is not this the main reason why dynasties established themselves in the first place? On the other hand, no less an authority than Tom Paine asserted that more civil wars had arisen from dynastic feuds than from elective systems of government.[77]

NOTES

1. The study set out with four monerchies before the *coups d'état* in Burundi and Libya abolished the monarchies. The *coup d'état* in Libya took place after this work was completed. For comparison there will be some references to Libya in this chapter in the past tense. The Moroccan Constitution of 1962, to which references in the notes are made, was amended in 1972. But as the amendments do not affect my analysis and conclusions, I have left the references unchanged. Where the articles have been changed I have noted, in brackets, the articles of the new constitution.
2. cf. Margery Perham, *The Government of Ethiopia*, Faber, London, 1969, pp. 35–6, 69–70.
3. It is realized that it is not possible to trace the origin of such traits in a political system to one cause only. The point here is that Islam has been the constant factor.
4. M. Perham, op. cit.; cf. also Donald Levine, 'Legitimacy in Ethiopia', paper presented at the annual meeting of the American Political Science Association, Chicago, Illinois, 9–12 September 1964.
5. Art. 2.
6. cf. The Kibre Nagast (Glory of Kings); cf. also Art. 2 of the Revised Constitution.
7. cf. R. Oliver and J. D. Fage, *A Short History of Africa*, Penguin, Harmondsworth, 1962, pp. 66–85.
8. Some amendments were made on 8 December 1962 and 25 April 1963.
9. Preamble to the Libyan Constitution.
10. cf. Ziadeh, Nicola A., *Whither North Africa?* Aligarh Muslim University, Institute of Islamic Studies, Aligarh, India, 1957, p. 72, quoted in Willard A. Beling, 'Some Implications of the New Constitutional Monarchy in Morocco', *Middle East Journal*, Vol. 18/64, p. 163.
11. cf. Beling, op. cit. The opposition was the U.N.F.P. (*Union Nationale des Forces Populaires*) led by the late Mehdi Ben Barka. The opposition

put up a fight by claiming that the Palace had chosen the referendum because it could not trust an elected constituent assembly made up of Moroccans to draft a constitution; and they questioned the right of the King to arrogate this power to impose a condition from the top.

12. Const. Art. 26.
13. Const. Art. 4.
14. Const. Art. 40.
15. Const. Art. 44.
16. Const. Art. 2.
17. Const. Ethiopia, Art. 5; Libya, Art. 44; Morocco, Art. 20.
18. Art. 13 (a).
19. Art. 13 (b).
20. cf. Emperor Haile Selassie's remarks made in answer to a question posed at a Press conference on the eve of the thirty-ninth Coronation anniversary. The Emperor declared that the constitution provides on the succession to the Throne and that succession to the Throne shall be determined accordingly. *Addis Zemen* (daily) 31 October 1969. The health of the Crown Prince, who suffered a stroke in late January 1973, has created another crisis of confidence – still unresolved.
21. Art. 45.
22. Art. 52.
23. Art. 50.
24. Art. 21. The age of majority is set as eighteen years in all three constitutions, and similar provisions on regency were provided in Ethiopia and Libya.
25. cf. Const. Ethiopia, Arts. 26, 27; Libya, Arts. 42, 44; Morocco, Arts. 24, 25 and 29.
26. The division between the civil service and 'political' service is theoretical only and not based on analysis of functions.
27. Const. Art. 27, cf., however, Order No. 44 of 1966, which is an attempt to share power of appointment of ministers with the Prime Minister.
28. Const. Art. 127; cf. also Art. 126.
29. Const. Morocco, Arts. 24 and 25 respectively.
30 Art. 84. (Art. 78 of 1972 Constitution).
31. Art. 30.
32. Art. 45. This Chamber of Counsellors seems to have disappeared in the new Constitution.
33. Const. Libya, Art. 72.
34. Art. 73.
35. Art. 74.
36. Arts. 94 and 97.
37. Art. 141.
38. Const. Ethiopia, Arts. 88 and 91.
39. Const. Libya, Art. 62.
40. Art. 136.
41. Arts. 26, 27, 70, 71, 72. (Arts. 66, 67, New Constitution). The counter signature of the Prime Minister is dropped in the new Constitution.
42. Arts. 74, 75. (Arts. 68, 69, New Constitution).
43. This was discussed in detail in Chapter 1.
44. cf. Bereket Habte Selassie, op. cit., p. 86.

45. Art. 64.
46. Art. 30.
47. Const. Ethiopia, Art. 30 proviso.
48. Const. Libya, Art. 69.
49. cf. Const. Morocco, Art. 35, which gives him power to declare martial law. (Art. 73, New Constitution gives the King power over declaration of war after consulting with Parliament.
50. cf. a controversy on this: (1) R. A. Sedler 'The Chillot jurisdiction of the Emperor of Ethiopia, a legal analysis in Historical and Comparative Perspective' (1964 J.A.L. 59 and (2) Bereket Habte Selassie, op. cit., pp. 87–8).
52. Art. 4 provides that the Emperor's person is sacred by virtue of his imperial blood and the anointment which he has received.
52. Const. Libya, Art. 59; Morocco, Art. 22.
53. Art. 59.
54. Const. Ethiopia, Art. 4; Morocco, Art. 22. (Art. 23 of New Constitution).
55. cf. Const. Ethiopia, Art. 19(d).
56. Const. Libya, Art. 60.
57. Const. Morocco, Arts. 32 and 97. (Arts. 32, 91 of New Constitution).
58. Const. Ethiopia, Arts. 71 and 72.
59. Art. 68.   60. Art. 74.   61. Art. 4.
62. cf. Bereket Habte Selassie, 'Constitutional Development in Ethiopia', *Journal of African Law* (Summer 1966), pp. 82–3. On the fall of the former Tsahafe Tezaz.
63. Const. Libya, Art. 84.
64. Art. 86.   65. Art. 87.
66. Art. 88.   67. Art. 89.
68. Const. Morocco, Arts. 64, 25.
69. Art. 65. (Art. 59 of New Constitution).
70. Art. 81. (Arts. 74, 75 of New Constitution).
71. Art. 80. (Arts, 74, 75 of New Constitution).
72. William I. Zartman, *Government and Politics in Northern Africa*, New York, Praeger, 1963.
73. ibid. But recently the King made announcements of a constitutional amendment which would in effect make the exercise of power less direct. The new Constitution does not justify the claim of more direct power.
74. *La ilaha ill'Allah, Mohammadun rasul 'illah*: 'there is no god but God; Muhammad is the Messenger of God.' 'Imam' is the name of the head of a Moslem community whose duty is to be the Khalif (successor) of the Prophet, and as such, to guard the faith and to maintain the government. Abu Bekr, the first successor of Muhammad adopted the title Khalifat rasul-illah (successor of the messenger of God), whence the term Khalif. Succeeding generations of Sultans have claimed direct descent from the Prophet, in order to legitimize their rule.
75. cf. Art. 19.
76. cf. *Jeune Afrique*, 17–23 December 1962. The '*oui*' refers to the affirmative vote to be given to the proposed constitution.
77. Tom Paine, *Rights of Man*, London, 1791, Chapter 3.

PART II

The Dynamics of
Neo-Presidential Power

4

Pre-colonial and Colonial Sources of Style

In Part One we have noted that the African régimes existing in the 1960s evolved a neo-presidential system of ruling whether they had unitary or dual executives, or were monarchies. A central fact of this system is the personalization of power. In other words, whatever the constitutional framework the style of rulership is very personal and authoritarian. How did this come about in these varied constitutional systems? Explanation must be sought in the African 'dual past'.[1]

A. The Traditional System

Historical and anthropological studies have distinguished several types of societies. In Africa, they have been roughly divided into two categories. First, there are the centralized and hierarchically-structured societies, exemplified by the Ashanti of Ghana, the Hausa–Fulani of Nigeria, the Amhara–Tigre of Ethiopia, the Baganda of Uganda and the Zulu of South Africa. Then there are the decentralized egalitarian societies, to which belong the Nuer of the Sudan, the Logoli of Kenya, and the Talensi of Ghana.[2] Fortes and Evans-Pritchard have written that the first group consist of societies which have:

centralised authority, administrative machinery and judicial institutions – in short a government – and in which cleavages of wealth, privilege and status correspond to the distribution of power and authority,

while the other group consists of societies:

which lack centralised authority, administrative machinery and constituted judicial institutions – in short which lack government – and in which there are no sharp divisions of rank, status and wealth.[3]

They go on to remark that those who consider that a state should be defined by the presence of governmental institutions will regard the first group as primitive states and the second as stateless societies.[4]

The classification into types does not, of course, represent empirical reality with exact scientific precision, as human societies cannot be classified in such a manner. Two societies or two types may have similar features in one respect and may differ in another. Nor is the use of concepts like 'primitive' always helpful. But classification of societies with reference to more specific aspects such as political organization does yield useful results.

There are certain dominant features which make comparison and contrast meaningful. Such is, for example, the presence of a chief or king in the first group of African societies, or his absence in the second group, which is the reason for the use of the term 'acephalous' to describe them.

In the first group of societies there is a chief or king who acts as the focus or centre of the whole system. He would invariably have a council to advise him in many matters. An example of this is the Lukiko of the Kabaka of Buganda. The Lukiko was formerly presided over by the Katikiro, who was the Chief Justice and 'Prime Minister'. There is a striking resemblance between the function of the Katikiro of the Kabaka and that of the Afenegus of former Ethiopian kings. The King normally presided over his council in both cases, and the same is true of the Asantehene of the Ashanti as well as of the Sultan of Morocco.

But even in relation to this particular feature of political systems belonging to the same category, comparisons break down owing to differences in history. For example, the Islamic religious influence in the case of Libya and Morocco marks off the Kings of these two countries in some respects, notably in the degree of concentration of power.[5] The spread of Islam in North, East, and West Africa has introduced a distinct influence which can be seen in the political life of people converted to it. Its doctrine of one God and of the paramountcy on earth of his Messenger acted as a unifying factor which transcended the divisions and conflicts among tribes, though its gospel was spread as much by proselytism as by the sword.[6]

The sultans or caliphs have been heads of both the state and of the Maamounin (the community of believers). The Christian Kings of Ethiopia, too, professed the Orthodox Christian faith and as suppliers of temporal aid to the church exercised an influence on the leaders of the church. But they were not heads of the church.

In chiefly societies of sub-Saharan Africa, where power was centralized, the chief was a member of the most ancient established powerful family, or a religious leader. Invariably there were several such independent chiefs within the same ethnic group. Typical examples of this are the Yoruba chieftaincies in Western Nigeria. The essence of the chieftaincy was that it was an extended family grouping clustered round a chief. One of the salient traits of a chieftaincy was the presence of an equilibrium of authority and responsibility. The authority of the chief was modified by the influence of the extended family, particularly the more powerful among them, and often also by that of other groups.

This balance of authority and responsibility has deep social and political implications. The chief exercised his function in trust on behalf of the community. Much of African law bears this out. Perhaps the best illustration of this is the role of the chief as the custodian of rights in land matters. There was no question of absolute ownership of land, and the chief could not at any time alienate land, even though it might be held in his name. A Nigerian chief put this matter in a nutshell when he said to the West African Lands Committee in 1912:

> I conceive that land belongs to a vast family of which many are dead, few are living, and countless members are unborn.[7]

In the second group, there are no traditional rulers or permanent courts. Whenever a matter of importance arose the elders of the community would summon the whole village community to a meeting and there decide the matter. Where an execution of the decision was required this would be delegated by the village council to selected young men. The village council should not be considered, however, as a permanent institution. It was set up as occasion demanded, as for example, when a crime disruptive of social cohesion, such as murder, had been committed. The mechanism of lawsuit and law enforcement followed a common pattern.[8]

The 'government' in such communities was conducted in a more casual fashion, with less precision in the division of function than in chiefly communities. There was less pomp and decorum, but there was an inner order and tenacity of allegiance to imme-morial custom. Nor is there an absence of the equilibrium we noted with regard to chiefly communities.[9]

There can be no question that even the most elementary societies had their own systems of government and law. The original view that in a strict sense the Nuer, for example, had no law suffered from the narrowness of the Austinian jurisprudence which viewed law as a command of a political superior. Law as an expression of desired conduct exists in all these societies, and the value of anthropological studies has derived from their probing into the various factors which make people obey the decrees of unwritten immemorial custom, particularly in the absence of physically identifiable permanent authority and a hierarchy of organization-implementing orders. A clue to the answer comes from anthropological enquiries. Religious cults play an important role, and the presence of religious and ritual symbols more than made up for the absence of the governor and the police.

> Varied ties of friendship in primitive societies were expressed in allegiance to a common ritual symbol. The people partici-pated in ceremonies to secure the good things of social life, food, children, health, success and peace over an area. The congrega-tions which joined in these ceremonies often established yet another set of linkages, since they drew their members from diverse groups. Or the ceremonies were so contructed that every representative of a political group had ritual powers, but these powers were exercised in a cycle of ceremonies in which every group's representative took part. *All had to act if each was to be prosperous.* The ceremonies aimed to achieve communal prosperity.[10]

These religious cults and rituals interpreted in terms of a general theory of religion, and the unwritten laws interpreted in terms of a general theory of law, yield a fruitful result. One feature common to all these societies is that they are based on a family unit which is extended with a strong emphasis on descent from a common ancestor creating a lineage. Authority depended on the lineage, and the group interest and solidarity which it needed.

As for the history of these societies,

> The verdict of modern scholarship is that the past of Africa is both long and interesting and contains the record of a con-tinuous and in some significant ways highly successful develop-ment over several thousand years.[11]

Africa's political and social history is old, and has involved the deployment of 'a considerable fund of common political ideas'.[12]

The debate on the origin, movements, and development of African peoples, the formation of the various states and the advent of ideas on political organization in the continent, is by no means closed. Some tentative conclusions have been drawn, nevertheless, and it is possible to draw upon such conclusions. Oliver and Fage, for example, consider that the advent of the 'common funds' of political ideas has a pre-Christian and pre-Muslim origin and that it can be traced to Meroe.

According to this view the movement has followed interior lines running out in two long arms westwards and southwards from a common point of origin in the Upper Nile Valley. They call the source the 'Sudanic' civilization, and they believe that the ideas of ancient Egypt formed part of this civilization.[13] Meroe, which was at the height of its power during the first two centuries of the Christian era, was conquered by Axum, thus adding further elements to the 'Sudanic' civilization.[14]

On the nature and extent of the influence of this civilization on the formation of African institutions Oliver and Fage have said:

Stretching right across sub-Saharan Africa from the Red Sea to the mouths of the Senegal, and right down the central highland spine of Bantu Africa from the Nile sources to Southern Rhodesia, we find the axis of what we shall call the Sudanic civilisation. The central feature of this civilisation was the incorporation of the various African peoples concerned into states whose institutions were so similar that they must have derived from a common source. At the head of such states there were kings, to whom divine honours were paid and to whom divine powers were attributed. The king led a life sedulously secluded from the common people; he gave public audience from behind a curtain; not even the most intimate of his courtiers might see him eat or drink. Each year the king hoed the first plot of farming land and sowed the first seeds. Upon his physical well-being depended the fertility of the land and the regular flow of rain. . . . The great rituals of these divine kingdoms tended to be associated with the new moon, and sacred fire was almost everywhere kept burning and carefully guarded as the main symbol of the king's life and authority. The divine king's subjects might number anything from a few thousand to a million, or even more. Such kingdoms tended in fact to form in clusters, with one or more large kingdoms at the centre of the cluster, and a host of smaller ones scattered around the peripheries. But on however small and ineffective a scale, such kingdoms would nearly always show at least vestigial traces of a strongly centralised political structure, contrasting sharply with the loose family or lineage institutions of those societies which had never been organised in this way. . . . Around the royal person circled a galaxy of titled office-bearers, as numerous as the economic organisation of each particular state was able to support. . . . At the head of the administration were a few high officials, often four in number. From these depended a descending hierarchy of provincial chiefs, often recruited from the pages, sons, or nephews of the great, who had been educated at the royal court. The main concern of such administration was the raising of tribute for the support of the king and of the semi-urbanised inhabitants of his capital. . . . External trade was always in some sense a royal monopoly. Artists, craftsmen, and other specialists were located at the royal capital. . . . In a very real sense, therefore, *the 'Sudanic' state was a superstructure erected over village communities of peasant cultivators rather than a society which had grown up naturally out of them. In many cases such states are known to have had their origin in conquest; in almost all other cases conquest must be suspected.* (Italics supplied).[15]

Early writers on African history, mostly Arab scholars, have recorded the existence of 'Sudanic' states in at least three geographically widely spread areas of Africa.[16] The origins of the Hausa states, of Songhai, and of many West African kingdoms, are attributed to the 'Sudanic' source.

The historians, indeed, argue that there is sufficient traditional evidence to indicate that with the development of Iron Age archaeology in Africa, with its methods of absolute dating, fresh evidence may be expected to come to light, pointing to other centres of the 'Sudanic' civilization. They point out that in Uganda, Rwanda, Burundi, and the Kivu province of the Congo, where the formation and re-formation of 'Sudanic' states can be traced through some five hundred years of traditional history, fresh evidence has been discovered showing the history of the states of that region to go back to earlier periods, nearer to the period of Zimbabwe and Katanga.

They also speculate on the possible discovery of comparable

evidence from the south-western region of Ethiopia, notably Kaffa and Enarea. In the whole Horn of Africa, pre-Christian Axum is presumed to have had a prototype in a series of 'Sudanic' states established to exploit the gold and ivory of the north-eastern interior, and it was probably from that direction that the first miners and ivory-traders reached the lake regions, Katanga, and Rhodesia.[17]

In the process of state-formation and reformation, some African societies seem to have escaped the centralizing impact of the 'Sudanic' civilization, and remained at a small scale of organization, while others moved into a complex pattern of bureaucratic organization. Many of the latter grew into imperialist powers, such as those of the Songhai, Mali, Ghana, and Hausa–Fulani empires. As Basil Davidson has written, this process

> began most clearly of all in those regions where easy movement by man and horse made military and political enclosure possible, and worthwhile: in North Africa, in the wide grasslands of the Sudan, and, not long after (though seldom with the horse), in the forest fringe of Guinea and later again (but never with the horse), in the vast woods and prairies of the centre and the south.[18]

One common trait of 'Sudanic' kingships is the idea of sanctity, and the belief that the king or chief represents parental authority and is the link between the community and its ancestors. His association with the well-being of the community thus involved certain repercussions. When misfortune befell the community, blame was attributed to him. Misfortune befalling him was thought to affect the crops or cattle or the rain. Such sentiments are psychologically so deeply rooted that even when hereditary monarchs are replaced by elected Presidents some of the aura still remains.

Apart from sanctity, another common trait is hierarchy. But there are varieties in the type and degree of hierarchic organization. In some (e.g. the Yoruba) the administrative hierarchy consisted of men who represented powerful lineage groups in the society. In others (most of the Bantu kingdoms) the hierarchy consisted almost exclusively of relatives of the King. In the third variety, 'commoners' were chosen, presumably because they lacked the independent basis of power which could make them potential rivals.[19]

Where there have been conquests and empires built on the

basis of such conquests, the empire-states comprised large-scale political units. Within the empire-state were kingdoms based on ethnic homogeneity, while the central political structure of the empire had a complex system of techniques of subjugating and administering large and disparate populations. There have been several examples of such empire-states in Africa. The medieval period from the ninth to the sixteenth century produced three famous empire-states: Ghana, Mali, and Songhai, and the nineteenth century gave rise to two others in West Africa, led by El Hadj Omar and Samary Touré.[20] Trade was one of the techniques used by the ruling group of an empire-state to accumulate the necessary wealth for peaceful or enforced preservation and expansion of the empire. Also certain vital commodities were used as a means of control. For example, the control of the distribution of salt was used as a technique for imposing imperial will on recalcitrant populations. The medieval empires owed a debt to Islam for the introduction of such techniques. For example, in the Ghana empire-state non-Muslim Soninke rulers used Muslim experts as counsellors on commercial and administrative matters, and trade was dominated by Muslims. Also, as already mentioned, Islam as a universal religion facilitated the administration of different ethnic groups, by separating the political roles of government from tribal (local) religious offices. The success of the medieval empire-states may also be attributed to their ability to create a bureaucracy for territorial administration without interfering too much in the conduct of local affairs or attempting to force social integration. All this limited causes for revolt.[21]

Variety in the structure of 'Sudanic' kingship is thus a fact which cannot be ignored, and is explicable in terms of the advent of the system at a comparatively later stage in African history and its superimposition over pre-existing non-hierarchically organized societies. Some of the pre-existing societies must have successfully absorbed kingship and fused it with their own culture. This may explain the fact that in some states the general social pattern of the society is so closely related that the kingdom gave an appearance of the village writ large. But the majority of kingships were unrelated to the smaller-scale social pattern.

The variety may also be seen in the function of the King and the ideas and sentiments concerning his responsibility. In the Kingdom of Kanem as described by Al Muhallabi, the King had absolute power over his subjects and could take what he liked of their belongings.[22] This contrasts with Al Masudi's record of the state near the mouth of the Zambezi river, a state governed by an elected king, who could be deposed if he abused his power or failed to use it wisely.[23] This is characteristic of African kingship or chieftaincy among a wide range of African peoples. Rattray has recorded a similar tradition for the Ashanti chiefs. The words of admonition which accompany the occasion of enstoolment (accession to the throne) are highly significant, in this connection, and worth quoting:

> Tell him that
> We do not wish for greediness
> We do not wish that he should curse us
> We do not wish that his ears should be hard of hearing.
> We do not wish that he should call people fools
> We do not wish that he should act in his own initiative.
> We do not wish things done as in Kumasi
> We do not wish that it should ever be said 'I have no time.
>   I have no time'
> We do not wish personal abuse
> We do not wish personal violence.[24]

The ethics behind these words are part of the fabric of traditional African political systems which cannot be ignored. It is a particular answer to the central problem of power and the limitation of the executive.

Even in the extreme cases of autocratic rule peculiar sanctions have been devised as a check on abuse of power, though they are honoured more in the breach than in the observance. A striking illustration is the role of ecclesiastics in Ethiopian history. In a famous religious work entitled *The Vision of Mary*, Mary is taken by her son Jesus round a hellish place where she sees prisoners tied up to a tree of fire. In answer to her query about their identity, Christ tells her that they are kings and noblemen who disobeyed his will on earth; who robbed, abused, maltreated or killed people.[25]

What emerges out of this brief review of the 'Sudanic' states is also the idea that the executive power was to be tempered by institutional or ideological sanctions. Although it is true that the leader enjoyed the right of summary action and therefore potential for influencing decision, when this technique is applied in the neo-presidential situation, e.g. in conducting parliamentary business under closed party meeting it is structurally a different type of power, not tempered by any other institutions. Also given the preponderant influence of the fathers of the nation the chances of checking it are remote. Thus the traditional style contributes to modern abuse of power.

B. The Executive in the Colonial Situation

European contact with Africa was not the first of its kind in the history of the continent. The whole of East Africa was long involved in trade with the eastern world. North and West Africa were also involved in a two-way traffic with each other. The trade routes running from East Africa (from Zula on the Red Sea coast of Ethiopia, through Axum and Meroe) across the Sudan to West Africa are a proof of an earlier continental link. With the advent of Islam in the whole of East, North, and West Africa and the conversion of many chiefs, a new and important factor entered the political life of Africa. One result of this was a radical breakdown of tribal barriers and the formation of states of a new type through the religious ideology of Islam. An example is the Hausa–Fulani state. The readiness with which people accepted this cannot simply be explained by reference to the radical methods of Islam in converting peoples. The acceptance of the Sultans as absolute rulers, by people of Africa used to more democratic systems, is also remarkable. Some writers of African history have argued that the African is more agreeable to monarchy with absolutism and sacredness attached to the ruler.[26] But this is too simplified an explanation. Islamic influence and its spread in Africa can best be explained by the absence of a gap between the ways of the conqueror and the conquered. Islam embraced within it all who accepted it.

The Europe which conquered Africa was technologically far superior to the conquered continent. This technological gap had political and cultural implications. It dealt a crushing blow to much of the traditional society. True, many philanthropic people and organizations worked to avoid or minimize disruption of the social life, but the total effect of colonial rule was one which undermined the basis of the traditional order. From a material point of view, there is no doubt about the importance of the by-product of modernization which it brought to the African. And this is not limited to roads and railways. The effect of the colonial rule is nowhere more striking than in the field of government.

The legal status of the conquered state was changed; it became part of a colonial state. Wherever there were traditional rulers they were turned into agents of the colonial state. The British colonial policy, known as indirect rule, favoured the preservation of this status in traditional jurisdiction. This meant the recognition of a dichotomy of law, one (the English-introduced law) applying to the expatriates living in the area, and the other (the customary law) applying to Africans.[27] The French colonial policy was a direct rule, with the French law extending to apply to the Africans – a process of assimilation.[28] The Belgian policy sought to make use of both methods, but tended to follow the French method, except in Rwanda–Burundi.[29]

The difference between the direct and indirect method has sometimes been exaggerated. A French historian has recently written that the French colonial rule in Africa did not really practise a system of 'direct' administration. They had recourse to the chiefs as intermediaries. The main difference lies in the legal status of the chiefs which, in the French rule, took the form of complete subordination. Also their diminished juridical status had political implications. It paved the way for their eventual over-throw when a well-organized mass party emerged, as did the P.D.G. in Guinea. It must also be remembered that the British practice of indirect rule was not applied consistently.

The establishment of the colonial state marked the beginning of political changes of crucial importance. The traditional holders of authority were required by the colonial state to maintain law and order and general stability among the African population. For this task they were reinforced in their traditional position with the backing of an invincible power.

At a time when there were as yet no modern-style political leaders to challenge their authority, the chiefs gradually developed an element of absolutism in their rule, though in the eyes of some the very fact of their subservience to a foreign and more powerful authority detracted from their own authority.[30] The establishment of colonial rule was not always achieved without resistance. The Ashanti Wars, the Zulu Wars and the heroic resistance of Samary Touré, to mention the more outstanding, are well known in the annals of anti-colonial history.

Where direct administration was introduced the position of traditional rulers was much weakened. Even there, however, the ruling class of the pre-colonial days had not disappeared in all cases. The policy of direct rule, followed by the French, did not mean the complete abolition of traditional rulers who were used as points of contact with the indigenous population whenever occasion demanded. But they were divested of their traditional-based legal status as rulers.

In the ex-British territories the 'native authorities' were given legal power to administer customary law to Africans. This apparent legal recognition of their traditional jurisdiction in customary law gave them sufficient incentive to co-operate as administrative 'transmission centres' and agencies of social control. The source of their legitimacy was the colonial system. This function was primarily political maintenance of order and stability and was crucial during the period of pacification, which may be said to have lasted roughly up to 1920. The mode of inducing traditional rulers to adjust themselves to the new colonial state by rehabilitating them in a new form as agencies of law and order represented a decisive feature of political change in Africa. Law and order are means of achieving certain desired conduct and patterns of relationship, but they are not always considered merely as means. They may be transformed in the minds of their beneficiaries into the realm of values. When that happens those who hold positions of authority will, when the time comes, seek to join the centre of law-making. That, in the colonial situation, was the Governor, and his chief instrument of policy-making – the Legislative Council, and later the Executive Council.

There has been a good deal of scholarly writing on the history of the Legislative Council, and its offspring the Executive Council, in ex-British Africa.[31] The same is also true of the executive in ex-French Africa.[32] We will now give brief accounts of the two.

1. ANGLOPHONE AFRICA

In the ex-British territories of Africa the development of the executive followed the pattern of what was called 'Constitutions of Crown Colony', in contradistinction to the original colonies (in North America, Bermuda, and the West Indies) and the old dominions (i.e. Australia, Canada, New Zealand, and South Africa), although the latter were also colonies at the beginning.

In the government of the Crown Colonies there was the Legislative Council, a unicameral body whose members were originally appointed by the Crown, the majority being civil servants known as official members. The official members were bound to support the policy of the Governor representing the Crown. The Governor, who was the executive in the colonial territory, could thus control the Legislative Council.[33]

The composition of the Legislative Council was altered, gradually leading to a majority of unofficial (i.e. non-civil servant) members. The Governor's control was, nevertheless, preserved by investing him with 'reserve powers' which allowed him to override the Legislative Council, and to enact legislation without the consent of its members. This was in addition to his power to veto legislation proposed by the Council.

The unofficial members of the Council in some territories included members of the European community as well as Africans. The former were appointed to represent various economic interests – banking, mining, planting, shipping, or trade – sometimes on the nomination of the Chambers of Commerce and similar organizations. Africans were not always included in the Legislative Councils.[34]

An important stage in the evolution of the Legislative Council (of Crown Colony) system was reached when some members of the Council entered that body on the basis of election. The next logical stage, with more demands for representation, was when the elected members outnumbered the other members of the Council. At first election was held on a limited franchise and generally only the principal municipalities were represented in each colony. For example, the four Africans elected to the Legislative Council of Nigeria in 1925 (the first to be elected in tropical Africa) represented the towns of Lagos and Calabar.[35] The ultimate phase of the evolution of the Legislative Council was reached when all its members were elected representatives. At that stage the structure and orientation of the Executive Council, its offspring, began to emerge, markedly different from its earlier form.

The Executive Council of the older dominions was an outgrowth of the Legislative Council. It was at first composed of the Governor and the official members (civil servants). The pattern of development was similar to that of the Legislative Council. Unofficial members were added later, from the Legislative Council. This enabled the Governor to bridge the gap between his office and the Legislative Council, and at the same time provided the assembly-men with some share in the formulation of general policy. But the Executive Council remained a purely advisory body.[36]

In the majority of African territories the Executive Council consisted at first of official members only, then official and unofficial members whom the Governor, in his discretion, could appoint if 'suitable candidates' existed among non-European populations.[37] Towards the end of the Crown Colony system, before internal self-government, elected members of the Legislative Council were included in the Executive Council and made responsible for certain departments of government with two or three officials serving with them as advisers to the Governor, who presided over the Executive Council meetings. This was a turning point from the viewpoint of transfer of executive power to Africans. Some of the African leaders were, for the first time, let into the inner council of the executive with access to, and partial control of, government departments. It showed them the problems as well as the possibilities of executive authority. But even at that stage the Executive Council still had an advisory function only.

As regards the procedure of the Executive Council at a stage when its function was purely advisory, normally questions were explained by the departmental head concerned; there would then be a general discussion; the Governor would ask each member for advice in turn. No vote was taken, and members could not themselves raise questions.[38]

The ultimate stage in the evolution of the Executive Council and its transformation into a cabinet system was generally reached when all the members of the legislative body were elected. By that time there would have been a crescendo of growing demand for more rights, for self-rule, for complete transfer of power – demands made under the pressure of organized movements for independence. Every measure of transfer of power only helped to stimulate more demands followed by more concessions, in a series of arrangements which followed a similar pattern with minor variations in all the colonial territories. A typical example is that of Ghana, which was the first to gain internal self-government and, later, complete independence.

In 1952, the Convention Peoples Party (C.P.P.), Dr. Kwame Nkrumah's party, won a clear majority in the election to the Legislative Assembly. The Governor then consulted with Dr. Nkrumah on the choice of representative members for the Executive Council. The Coussey Committee had recommended that the Legislative Assembly should elect a leader and that members of the Executive Council should be appointed by the Governor in consultation with the leader of government business.[39] The Colonial Secretary felt that it would be preferable for the members of the Executive Council to elect a leader of government business in the Legislative Assembly, on the grounds that there was no developed party system.[40] But the clear majority obtained by the C.P.P.

convinced the Governor that the course he took, which approximated to United Kingdom conventions, was more appropriate. An amending Order-in-Council[41] was soon passed to recognize the facts and Dr. Nkrumah was appointed Prime Minister.[42]

The Executive Council continued to have official members until 1954. In 1954, the Executive Council was replaced by a cabinet which became, as in all cabinet systems, the principal instrument of policy. It was the first cabinet in Black Africa, and its birth was no doubt welcomed on all sides, but not cheered by Dr. Nkrumah and his colleagues. It fell short of a proper cabinet in that, contrary to the demands of the C.P.P. leaders, the cabinet was made responsible not to the Legislative Assembly (which the C.P.P. controlled) but to the Governor. They and others were to reverse their preferences and keep cabinets tied to the President. The desire of Whitehall to see British constitutional conventions implanted in Ghana is none the less clear. This was made clear specifically in respect of the appointment and resignation of the Prime Minister and the acceptance of his advice on other ministerial appointments.[43]

2. FRANCOPHONE AFRICA

The French colonies in Africa were grouped in two federations: *Afrique Occidentale Française* (1895) – A.O.F. – and *Afrique Équatoriale Française* (1910) – A.E.F. The organization of the latter was modelled on that of the former group, which was itself modelled on that of French Indo-China (1887).

Each administrative grouping was placed under a Governor-General who acted as intermediary between the central government in France and the colonies coming under his grouping. He took over a substantial part of the function formerly exercised by the Governors of each colony, thus centralizing the whole administrative system of the colonies. Algeria was kept as a separate administrative unit from the start (1834) with the appointment of a civilian Governor-General after a series of crises, lasting some sixty years[44] and involving struggles between civilian officials and military commanders.

The coastal colonies were governed by civilian administrators reporting directly to Paris and assisted in their decisions by an informal council of subordinate administrators, representatives of the local Chamber of Commerce, which had great influence on the government's colonial policy, and local notables whom the

Governor saw fit to include.[45] The first change came in 1895 when a Governor-General was appointed to oversee the organization and administration of all the French West African possessions. Given the difficulty of communications, his presence was not felt at the start. Then the Constitution of French West Africa (A.O.F.) was promulgated, giving the Governor-General the power to raise money for the Federal Government by taxing the imports and exports of the individual territories.[46]

The Constitution of 1904 and decrees issued on 30 March and 20 April 1925 established the basic form of French colonial government. Under this system each individual colony was governed by a Lieutenant-Governor, who administered it according to general administrative rules applicable to all the other colonies under the 'high authority' of the Governor-General, local circumstances being taken into account. The Lieutenant-Governor (who became full-fledged Governor in 1937) was advised by a council known as the *Conseil d'Administration*, except in Senegal. This council was composed of appointed senior civil servants, and, in the Ivory Coast, Dahomey, Guinea, and Sudan, included unofficial members chosen by the colony's Chamber of Commerce and by a restricted African electorate consisting of chiefs, licensed traders, property owners, and administrative officers of five years' standing.[47] It was considered that the Council, although restricted in power, drew some of the significant elements in the African communities who were most likely to exercise influence in a modern setting into some sort of regularized relationship with the government at the territorial level.[48] Some writers have expressed the view that the electorate was more extensive than that of the local government councils in the British territories, although the latter enjoyed more real power of decision.[49]

In Mauritania and Niger the Council was composed entirely of official members, while in Senegal the position was unique. In Senegal, the four coastal regions had been granted self-government in the 1870s. The Council in these regions consisted of popularly elected representatives, and of members chosen by the administration-appointed chiefs of the interior populations. The Council had quasi-legislative powers over financial matters, similar to the *Conseil Général* of a department in France. The Governor had powers of veto. The colonies, with the exception of Senegal, were in no sense self-governing. Their government, like the French *cercles*, was part and parcel of the French administrative system with its headquarters in Paris.

Coming immediately above the Lieutenant-Governor in the colonial hierarchy were the Governors-General of the Federations. Both the Governors-General and the Lieutenant-Governor of each colony were appointed by the French Head of State. They had the status of *hauts fonctionnaires* (equivalent to senior civil servants), and were strictly subordinated to the central government.[50] The Governors-General alone represented the French Republic and had the right to correspond with Paris. The power exercised in the territorial administration was therefore by delegation of their powers. They accordingly had the right to intervene at any level they saw fit. The prestige of the Governor-General counted for much in practice, giving him effective power. The competent minister in Paris issued orders and instructions to the Governor-General in the form of circulars. But no ministerial decree could be put into effect in the colonies without the Governor-General's promulgation of an *arrêté d'application* explaining the circumstances in which it was applicable and indicating how it was to be put into effect. Again, all colonial budgets had to meet with his approval before being submitted to Paris. The power of the Governor-General was further extended *vis-à-vis* the colonies in fiscal matters by a system of taxation which centralized revenues and enhanced his control over the colonies. His power *vis-à-vis* Paris was extended in that he could declare a state of emergency, as occasion demanded.[51]

There was a Governor-General's council called the *Conseil de Gouvernement*, which functioned until 1939. It consisted of a majority of civil servants, who were mostly European. This council's function was purely advisory, and in fact its work was done by its permanent commission composed entirely of the Governor-General's own chosen men.

Above the Governor-General was the Colonial Minister who could rule by decree and who was also assisted by a superior council, the *Conseil Supérieur des Colonies* (after 1937, the *Conseil Supérieur de la France d'Outre-Mer*), with the same advisory power as the Governor's council. This council was composed of representatives elected by the French citizens and a few 'native' notables from each colony, the deputies and senators of the colonies which had parliamentary representation in Paris, and several nominated members representing metropolitan and colonial interests.[52] Commercial interests dominated the Superior Council, since most of the colonial representatives were linked to the major commercial interests, and the Governor-General was the only man with the prestige and access to the minister to act as a counterpoise to their influence, if only in the interests of administrative efficiency.[53] The influence of commercial interests exerted itself even more at times of ministerial instability during the Third Republic.

The French attempt to impose a uniform and efficient administrative structure weakened and in many cases destroyed traditional political authority. France's *mission civilisatrice* implied that African cultures and political systems were inferior and that they must be replaced by a 'higher civilisation' which would make Frenchmen out of Africans. The Governors-General, and the colonial administration over which they presided, did not therefore feel concerned to preserve traditional systems of political authority. There was little preparation of a modern African political order to take the place of the traditional system. As Foltz has pointed out:

> Where tribal or village allegiance remained strong, it represented primarily allegiance to a social, not a political, order. If a focus for political loyalties was open to the Africans, it was that of a 'Greater France', a distant, vague idea unlikely to survive the shock of the increased direct African participation in the political process.[54]

Most Africans had little or no chance to participate in government of the colony, which operated without reference to their wishes or needs. But with the opportunities opened for training (though limited) a new African nationalist *élite* was in the making.[55]

By the end of World War II the political climate was changing; the growth of a hard core of educated Africans, and the anti-colonialists' euphoria of the period following the Atlantic Charter and the United Nations Charter, gave impetus to nationalist demands for self-government. But there was little change in the political and especially executive structure after the War, except in nomenclature – the colonies being re-named *territoires d'outre-mer* – after 1946. The federations of A.O.F. and A.E.F. continued, without any change in the organization and function of the executive in either. The conference of colonial administrators and experts held in Brazzaville in 1944 set a tone for the granting of political rights that was to come during the following decade.[56]

In the debate on the constitution of the Fourth Republic, there was much talk of radical changes in French colonial policy, but the outcome did not match the hopes aroused by those debates. The 1946 Constitution reflected some (but not very marked) changes. All the overseas territories, as they were now called, were given representation in the French representative assemblies, as well as at the inter-territorial and territorial levels.[57] The representatives to the French National Assembly and to the territorial assembly were elected directly. There were separate rolls and separate representation in elections to the National Assembly (with the exception of the eight territories of A.O.F. and French Togoland), to territorial assemblies (with the exception of Senegal), and the provincial assemblies in Madagascar.[58] The separate rolls consisted of citizens of metropolitan and of local status, the former being in practice almost entirely European, the latter entirely African.[59] This arrangement was bitterly attacked by the members of the Second Constituent Assembly elected by 'native' electorates. For tactical as well as 'ideological' reasons overt criticism concentrated on 'second class' citizenship. This in turn added more fuel to the fire of growing nationalist aspirations. The very concept of the French Republic – one and indivisible – was attacked as hypocrisy.[60] Territorial assemblies could also choose members (senators) of the Council of the Republic and councillors of the Assembly of the French Union.

In the federations of the A.O.F. and A.E.F. there were established Grand Councils whose members were chosen by each territorial assembly. This inter-territorial council had powers and functions similar to those of the territorial assemblies.[61] Neither the territorial assemblies (and the provincial assemblies of Madagascar) nor the inter-territorial assemblies had any general legislative power. The meetings of the territorial assemblies had to be attended by the *commissaire du gouvernement* (usually the Secretary-General of the territory) to explain the point of view of the administration, but he was not a member of the assembly, which contained no representatives of the executive as such.[62] The assemblies were consulted on many matters including the draft of local regulations (*arrêtés*). Their functions centred on the discussion of financial matters, but like metropolitan councils (on which they were modelled) they were required to make provision for 'obligatory expenses'.[63] The Grand Council had similar functions over inter-territorial finances, but all general political power still emanated from Paris and was exercised by the Governor-General, and at the territorial level by the Governors.[64]

Despite the continued retention of political power in French hands, the association of Africans with the government at the three levels (local, 'national', and inter-territorial) brought several consequences. One important consequence was the emphasis given to local or territorial politics. This resulted from the dissatisfaction with the government-general or its 'legislative' part, the Grand Council, which had neither the power or prestige of the French Parliament nor direct contact with the African masses at the local level. The Territorial Assemblies had the contact with the local people, and the French Parliament was the source of ultimate decision. The political activities of Africans were thus concentrated in the territories and in Paris. Their participation in the life of the Territorial Assemblies afforded a training ground for most of the emerging political leaders. And in Paris some of the more famous leaders who were sent as delegates capitalized on their presence there and their connection with sympathetic French politicians. Their membership of the French Parliament also gave them an opportunity for direct contribution to an 'open house' of representatives of all France, thus helping to create a climate of opinion receptive to future changes. Indeed those of the African leaders who were present at the constitutional conventions which framed the 1946 Constitution had, by their direct participation, secured some significant concessions for African political rights. One such concession, for example, was that the voting requirement for the African populations should be left to an electoral law and not entrenched in the constitution.[65]

On the whole only minor changes were made during 1946–55, although there was further extension of the franchise to the African populations. In 1947 a new category of local citizens entitled to vote was added; anyone literate in French or Arabic could vote.[66] In 1951 three other categories were added, viz. (1) heads of households (*chefs du ménage*) who had paid tax or were exempted from it; (2) mothers of two children (*vivants ou morts pour la France*); and (3) civil or military pensioners. There was also an increase of the number of deputies returned by Africans from thirty-one to thirty-seven. Of the latter figure, twenty-one were elected on the common roll (in A.O.F. and Togoland), while in the remaining tropical African territories five were elected by electorates of metropolitan citizens and eleven by those of local citizens.[67]

Meanwhile the pressure for changes in French colonial policy was mounting. In Tunisia, M. Mendès-France initiated a new policy aiming at Tunisian independence; while the 'policy of strength' tried in Morocco, which had culminated in the exile of the Moroccan King, had proved to be futile. Then there was the humiliating defeat in Indo-China and the outbreak of the Algerian War of Liberation. It was officially admitted by the government that major constitutional changes must be made in overseas France.[68] But in tropical Africa reforms came at first only in Togoland, where the powers of the assembly were increased and a Council of Government (*conseil de gouvernement*) was established, consisting of an equal number of members elected by the assembly and of members appointed by the Governor. Each member of the Council of Government was to be assigned a particular branch of the administration by the Governor, but he had only a *droit d'information et d'enquête* and was not charged with executive responsibility. The assembly was empowered to decide the detailed application of laws and decrees, on certain matters.[69]

Although this change was limited to Togoland it had an indirect effect in galvanizing political activities at the territorial and metropolitan level. One of the effects could be seen in the gradual weakening of the position of the government-general, which was reflected in the financial sphere.[70] Nevertheless the government-general remained the focal point for co-ordination of central policies, and acted as the primary redistributive agency for major expenditure, particularly in the case of development aid offered by France through the *Fonds d'Investissement pour le Développement Economique et Social* (FIDES). The Grand Council was given the right to decide the distribution of FIDES aid among the territories, subject to advice given to it from the Ministry for Overseas France and the territorial assemblies.

At the Executive level the Governor-General retained most of his powers, and was advised by his *Conseil de Gouvernement* as well as by the Grand Council. The administrative principle on which his office was established was to direct, co-ordinate, and supervise, a bureaucratic structure stretching across a vast territory, and in this it had served its purpose. Now, however, its political basis was being questioned from all quarters.[71] Curiously enough the territorial assertion for autonomy *vis-à-vis* the federal government-general did not meet with as much opposition from Paris as we might have expected given the centralist policy on which the whole system was built. Gonidec remarks that what he called the 'conjoncture politique' dictated the adoption of the anti-federalist line.[72]

When the elections to the French National Assembly in January 1956 brought in their wake a chain of demands for transfer of power, the stage was set for the next major constitutional reforms, and that came in the form of the *Loi-Cadre*.

The Loi-Cadre

The *Loi-Cadre* was passed in June 1956.[73] It introduced changes of a social, economic, administrative, and political nature. In the political field it introduced universal suffrage, which had far-reaching consequences, by enabling Africans to choose what kind of government they could have, when the time came. It also authorized the establishment in each territory of a Council of Government to administer territorial services. The territorial assemblies were granted power, particularly over the organization and management of administrative services of the territory and over the change of existing regulations (but not statute laws) in that respect. The Law also introduced changes in the functions and powers of the governments-general (including the Grand Councils) of the A.O.F. and A.E.F., and in those of government and representative assembly in Madagascar. Finally it authorized the establishment of district and other local councils in rural areas.

The beginning of an African Executive

The *Loi-Cadre* made special provisions for Togoland and Cameroon, in view of their different history and different legal status. In Togo the new arrangements culminated in the Statute of 1957 which established an internal government within the French union, with an Assembly and a Council of Ministers. The Council of Ministers was changed to a 'Togolese Government' at the insistence of the Togolese Assembly.[74] The proposal originated in Paris, with amendments proposed by the Togolese Assembly which were duly accepted by the French government. Finally the whole system was approved by a referendum held on 28 October 1956.

Under this arrangement the Togolese government was presided over by the French High Commissioner, and composed of a Prime Minister, nominated by the High Commissioner after consultation with the Assembly, together with not more than nine ministers appointed by the Prime Minister, after similar consultation. The Prime Minister and the other ministers were to vacate office if the Assembly passed a motion of censure by an absolute majority of all its members. Legislation relating to critical matters such as defence, foreign affairs, currency and foreign exchange, external trade and customs, was reserved to the metropolitan Parliament. Then in March 1957 the Assembly requested and secured an amendment which strengthened the powers of the Prime Minister.

The power of the High Commissioner to dissolve the Assembly was transferred to the Prime Minister.[75]

The situation was different in Cameroon, and the difference is deeply revealing of the motivation behind colonial constitution-making. In effect, the French Government chose to submit the question of the future of Cameroon not to a popular referendum as it did in Togo, but to the Territorial Assembly after that body was elected. The election was boycotted by the radical nationalist party (*the Union des Populations du Cameroun*), which stood for immediate and full independence and which questioned the good faith of the French Government. The election returned an assembly in which a substantial majority of the seats was held by 'moderates' who favoured a continuation of the trusteeship. This was given effect by a Statute which provided, among other things, that the French High Commissioner remained, like any colonial Governor, '*dépositaire des pouvoirs de la République*'. The Assembly was granted legislative power in a limited field similar to that of Togo. The appointment of the Prime Minister and ministers and the formation of the 'Cameroon government', under the Chairmanship of the High Commissioner was the same as in Togo. But the dismissal of the Prime Minister by a censure motion initiated by the Assembly could only take place if it was passed by a two-thirds majority, though a simple majority was enough when he himself put the question of confidence. The powers of the High Commissioners were specifically defined; they extended to defence, security, and external relations. The relations between the Cameroon Government and the French Government were also specifically defined; in particular the High Commissioner was empowered to supervise the institutions of Cameroon in order to provide the French Government with the control required for the exercise of its responsibilities as an Administering Authority of a Trust Territory. All laws and regulations had to be submitted to him before being put into effect, and he could, within ten days, require their reconsideration by the Assembly or the government. The Statute also provided for the creation of provinces and provincial assemblies.[76]

Unlike the new constitutions of the Trust Territories of Togo and Cameroon, which had been granted by separate decrees, those of the Overseas Territories of A.O.F. and A.E.F. were dealt with collectively in a series of decrees, and that of Madagascar in other series.[77] A further series of decrees covering all the Overseas Territories dealt with the definition of state services, reorganizing the civil services. All these decrees were referred not to the Territorial Assemblies but to the French Parliament, and to the Assembly of the French Union as prescribed in the *Loi-Cadre*. This was severely criticized by Senghor who was deputy for Senegal in the French National Assembly. The attack was made on the grounds that consultation with the Territorial Assemblies was required under Article 74 of the 1946 Constitution. The failure to consult was defended on the grounds that Article 74 applied only to decrees in the normal course, not to those expressly authorized by a Statute and submitted to Parliament itself.[78]

The underlying principle of the *Loi-Cadre* was to grant autonomy to each member of the Overseas Territories. Before the *Loi-Cadre* was enacted there were lengthy debates on African representation, in particular their representation in the Councils of Government. Among the final concessions made was one stipulating that the Africans in the Councils of Government should outnumber the official members.[79] The most important debates centred on the composition and function of the Councils of Government, including their responsibility to the Territorial Assemblies. Attempts had been made during the earlier debates to argue that Overseas Territories (unlike the Trust Territories) formed part of the French Republic which was one and indivisible. It was proposed to establish a mixed executive composed equally of nominees of the Governor and members elected by the Assembly to be vested with certain specific rights in the executive field, on the model of Togo. Later concessions were made, providing for a majority of elected members in the Councils, and after further debate and study it was decided that all the members were to be elected representatives bearing the title of minister, in addition to a Vice-President. The accomplished fact of the Togolese situation appears to have influenced the final outcome – the Africans from the Overseas Territories could not accept anything less than what was obtained in Togo.

On the responsibility of the Council of Government it was provided that it could resign 'if it considered that it no longer enjoyed the assembly's confidence', and individual ministers were obliged to answer questions or requests for explanations from members of the Assembly relating to the matters within their competence. Each minister would be charged with the responsibility for the management of one or more territorial service by delegation from the Governor who would act on the advice (*sur avis*) of the Vice-President of the Council. The Governor had also to obtain the signature of the Vice-President to give effect to the *arrêté* defining the minister's function. A minister would be responsible to the Council of Government for administration, and was to be dismissable by the Governor on the proposal of the Vice-President. The Council would be presided over by the Governor, and, in his absence, by the Vice-President. The Vice-President would submit to the Council an annual report on the government's activities and the territorial services which he would then submit to the Assembly. But the Governor retained reserve powers in the legislative as well as in the executive field. If he considered that any decision of the Council exceeded its power or was likely to prejudice national defence, public order, security, or civil liberty, he could report it to the minister, who, after consultation with the *Conseil d'État*, could annul the decision by cabinet within three months of the Governor's report.

This transfer of more executive power was accompanied by provisions for more autonomy and Africanization of the civil service.

The Gaullist Constitution

The final stage in French colonial constitutional reform came in 1958, with the promulgation of General Charles de Gaulle's Constitution of the Fifth Republic. This offered the Overseas Territories an option of complete independence outside the French *Communauté* or membership thereof. Only Guinea opted for independence outside the *communauté*, thus becoming the first independent republic to effect a complete break from French rule. The rest chose the status of member states. This meant that while they were politically independent they were economically and military linked with France. The President of the French Republic was the head of the *communauté*, and he presided over a Council composed of all the chief executives of the new African states whose constitutions were substantially modelled on the Gaullist constitution. Under these constitutions the executive, in all the new states except Madagascar, was monocephalous, and the Parliament consisted of a unicameral body. In Madagascar the chief executive was entitled President from the start, whereas in the other states he was called a Prime Minister or President of the Council of Ministers. But there was no difference in function. It was a parliamentary régime with the executive holding power on the strength of a parliamentary vote.

The functions and powers of the executive under the new

constitutions were those of an independent government, with the
executive power vesting in the new chief executive. His power
was limited in certain matters (notably military) which were
subject to conditions set by the *communauté*.[80] Gonidec made an
interesting comparison with the position in the commonwealth,
as regards his relation to the head of the *communauté*, noting the:

> essential difference that in the case of the latter the English
> monarch is at the same time Queen of Great Britain and of each
> monarchy (Canada, etc.). The governor-general who represents
> her plays the role of a parliamentary head of state, exercising
> all the traditional functions such as appointment of ministers,
> promulgating laws, granting pardon, etc. The president of
> France, on the other hand, is only the head of the communauté,
> and not the head of a state common to all the member states.
> He is in the same position as the English monarch in relation to
> the republics in the commonwealth (India, Pakistan). . . .[81]

A more apt parallel is the position of the new African executives,
particularly as provided for by the later constitutions[82] in relation
to the colonial executive. Indeed, as already explained, one primary reason for a historical account of the colonial executive is to
establish that the present position of the executive has evolved out
of the colonial prototype. It is clear, for example, that the power
of the colonial Governors in both the former British and French
territories was bound to be autocratic by the very nature of the
functions which it was established to discharge. The colonial
executive was essentially an institution which was set up to secure
the basic need of law and order, and to co-ordinate all activities
connected with that end as well as other activities which provided
the necessary administrative infra-structure for the supply of
essential services. Behind all the colonial administrative and
political structure lay the original aim of colonialism: the acquisition, maintenance, and exploitation of the colonial territories.
This explains, for example, the tardiness in the provision of social
services for Africans such as education, and in the transfer of
political power.[83]

If the colonial executive held autocratic powers on behalf, and
in the interest, of a metropolitan power, it was not unnatural for
those African leaders who grew up under such a system to demand
the same kind of power for what they considered to be the advancement of a different interest, the interest of their people. The
experience under the colonial executive no less than some aspects

of the traditional heritage must partly account for the particular forms African executives have taken. The colonial executive was autocratic even in its last phase; the Council merely carried out the decisions or proposals of the Governor. But his position and power in relation to the colonized people may be more aptly compared with that of an absolute monarch. Comparisons with the position of the executive presidencies are illustrative, although the Presidents in the new African states owe their position to a different mandate, that of an African electorate.

They basically manipulate the single party to aggregate absolute political power in the manner of absolute monarchs, an indefensible position in terms of African traditions.

NOTES

1. cf. George Balandier, 'Le Contexte Sociologique de la vie politique en Afrique Noire,' *Revue Française de Science Politique*, IX, 3 1959, pp. 598–609.
2. cf. M. Fortes and E. E. Evans-Pritchard (eds), *African Political Systems* O.U.P., London, 1967.
3. ibid., p. 5.
4. ibid.
5. For a short history of the advent of Islam in Africa, cf. Roland Oliver and J. D. Fage, *A Short History of Africa*, Penguin African Library, Harmondsworth, 1966, pp. 66–91.
6. cf. Oliver and Fage, op. cit., pp. 68–76.
7. Quoted by T. O. Elias in *The Nature of African Customary Law*, Manchester U.P., 1956, p. 162.
8. cf. Gunther Wagner, 'The Political Organisation of the Bantu of Kavirondo' in M. Fortes and E. E. Evans-Pritchard, op. cit., pp. 217–22.
9. ibid.
10. M. Gluckman, 'Political Institutions', in *Institutions of Primitive Society* (ed. E. E. Evans-Pritchard), Blackwell, Oxford, 1956, pp. 72–3.
11. B. Davidson, *Which Way Africa*, Penguin, Harmondsworth, 1964, p. 19.
12. Oliver and Fage, op. cit., p. 49.
13. cf. Oliver and Fage, op. cit., pp. 49–50.
14. ibid.
15. op. cit., pp. 44–6.
16. Oliver and Fage mention the record of the Moorish geographer Al Bakri of Cordoba who describes a pagan kingship ritual of Ghana; and Al Yaqubi who mentions the Kingdom of Kanem, lying to the north-east of Lake Chad, with its Zaghawa rulers, while the tenth-century writer Al Muhallabi made it clear that this was a divine kingdom of the 'Sudanic' type. Also Al Masudi of Baghdad who journeyed to the east coast of Africa to Sofala in today's Mozambique in or about A.D. 922 recorded the existence of a substantial trade in gold and ivory, which was sent from Sofala to Oman and thence to China

and India. The authors presume Masudi was referring to the Zimbabwe State. cf. Oliver and Fage, op. cit., pp. 46–8.

17. ibid., pp. 48–52.

18. op. cit., p. 22.

19. cf. Lucy Mair, *Primitive Government*, Penguin, 1962, Harmondsworth, 1966, pp. 171–80 and generally Lloyd A. Fallers, *Bantu Bureaucracy*, Chicago and London, 1965.

20. cf. William J. Foltz, *From French West Africa to the Mali Federation*, Yale U.P., New Haven and London, 1965, pp. 2–5.

21. ibid.

22. cf. Oliver and Fage, op. cit., p. 47.

23. Cited by B. Davidson, op. cit., p. 22.

24. cf. Rattray, *The Ashanti Law and Constitution*, O.U.P., 1929, p. 82.

25. cf. *Orient*, 1877, f. 549.

26. Cheikh Anta Diop, *L'Afrique noire pré-coloniale*, Paris, n.d., p. 59.

27. cf. A. N. Allott, *Essays in African Law*, Butterworth, London, 1960.

28. P. F. Gonidec, *Droit d'outre-mer*, Paris, 1959.

29. J. Buchmann, *L'Afrique Noire indépendante*, Paris, 1962, p. 74. An interesting debate on this subject is found in Hubert Deschamps' article, 'Et maintenant, Lord Lugard', in *Africa*, XXXIII, 1963, pp. 293–306, and a reply by Michael Crowder, 'Indirect Rule – French and British Style', ibid. XXXIV, 1964, pp. 197–205. Lord Lugard's name is almost synonymous with indirect rule and 'the dual mandate', which was adopted largely as a result of his initiative in Nigeria.

30. cf. P. J. Idenburg, 'Les nouveaux états africains et les normes démo-cratiques occidentales', *Revue juridique et politique d'outre-mer*, 1961, No. 2, p. 198. For a discussion on the interesting view that the chiefs could not be assumed to be traditional since the basis of their authority and power was extra-societal, cf. G. C. M. Mutiso, 'Cleavage and Organisa-tional Base of Politics in Kenya. A Theoretical Framework' in *Journal of East African Research and Development* (Nairobi), June 1973.

31. cf. Martin Wight, *The Development of the Legislative Council 1606–1945*, Faber, London, 1946; Sir Alan Burns (ed); *Parliament as an Export*, Allen & Unwin, London, 1966; H. V. Wiseman, *The Cabinet in the Commonwealth*, Stevens, London, 1958; S. A. de Smith, *The New Commonwealth and its Constitutions*, Stevens, London, 1964, pp. 38–76.

32. cf. P. F. Gonidec, *Droit d'outre-mer*, Paris, 1959, Vol. 1, pp. 143–50, and pp. 453–65. And F. Berge, *Le sous-secrétariat et les sous-secrétariats d'état aux colonies: histoire de l'émancipation de l'administration coloniale*, Paris, 1962; also William J. Foltz, *From French West Africa to the Mali Federation*, New Haven and London, Yale U.P., 1965.

33. The constitutions of the first English colonies of settlement provided for representative government, following the English model, with a restricted franchise; cf. Sir Alan Burns, op. cit., p. 14.

34. In Kenya, for example, there were no African members until 1944: ibid. p. 35.

35. ibid. p. 35.

36. M. Wight, op. cit., p. 126; Wiseman, op. cit., pp. 16–20.

37. Kenya was an exception to this. Unofficial members there were appointed for a fixed period up to 1954; cf. Wiseman, op. cit., p. 19.

38. ibid., p. 21.
39. Coussey Report, Paras. 382 and 411.
40. S.I. 1950, No. 2094, S.15; cf. also Wiseman's comments, op. cit., pp. 29–30.
41. S.I. 1952 No. 455, S.5.
42. cf. de Smith, op. cit., pp. 55–63, for a discussion of the stages of internal government and the gradations thereof.
43. Cmd. 9169, Para. 31; and S.I. 1954 No. 551.
44. cf. Gonidec, op. cit., Vol. II, pp. 180–92. French West Africa at the end of the nineteenth century consisted of four coastal settlements – Senegal, Guinea, the Ivory Coast, and Dahomey. They were separated one from another and the principal link was a coastal steamer. Behind them in the interior lay a vast hinterland initially under military command.
45. W. J. Foltz, op. cit., p. 16.
46. Decree of 18 October 1904. This decree and subsequent decrees established the territory of French West Africa including the interior which became known as French Sudan. Similar measures for French Equatorial Africa were started in 1910.
47. In 1939 this was extended to include veterans of the colonial army and holders of certain licences.
48. ibid.
49. cf. L. G. Cowan, *Local Government in West Africa*, O.U.P., London, 1958, pp. 52–3, quoted by W. J. Foltz, op. cit., p. 12.
50. Under the Third Republic the colonies came under the Minister for the Colonies, and Algeria came under the Minister of Interior.
51. cf. Gonidec, op. cit., pp. 186–92; and W. J. Foltz, op. cit., p. 18.
52. W. J. Foltz, op. cit., p. 19.
53. ibid.
54. op. cit., p. 20.
55. Foltz gives the figure of 71,000 students who were in schools of some sort in French West Africa by 1938, which represented a mere 3·2 per cent of potential students. But the students were concentrated in the urban areas where they were able to acquire new skills. Very few attended university in France before World War II, but many attended the federal École Normale William Ponty, near Dakar. Ponty granted about 2,000 degrees between 1918 and 1945; op. cit., pp. 20–21.
56. cf. La Conférence Africaine-Française, Brazzaville, 30 January–8 February 1944.
57. cf. Arts. 77 and 78 of the 1946 Constitution; cf. also P. F. Gonidec, op. cit., pp. 143–7.
58. In Madagascar the provincial assemblies corresponded to the territorial assemblies elsewhere in tropical Africa.
59. In the trust territories of Cameroon and Togoland, the inhabitants were not French citizens but French-administered persons. In the rest all were technically Frenchmen, and their territories were part of the French Republic.
60. cf. e.g. Léopold S. Senghor, 'L'Avenir de la France dans l'outre-mer', *Politique Étrangere*, No. 4 (Oct. 1954), pp. 419–26.

61. In Madagascar the representative assembly was similarly chosen by the provincial assemblies.

62. This contrasting position as compared to the British Colonial system of the Legislative Council can be partly explained by the underlying centralization in the French colonial policy; cf. generally Kenneth Robinson, 'Constitutional Reform in French Tropical Africa', *Political Studies*, Vol. vi, No. 1 (1958), pp. 45–69.

63. cf. K. Robinson, op. cit., p. 45.

64. On the Territorial Assemblies, cf. P. F. Gonidec, 'Les assemblées locales des territoires d'outre-mer', *Revue juridique et politique de l'union Française*, 6 (1952), pp. 317–55 and 6 (1953), pp. 443–91.

65. cf. Title VIII article 77; cf. also W. J. Foltz, op. cit., p. 24.

66. Law 47–1606 of 27 August 1947, *J. O. Lois et Décrets*, 28 August 1947, p. 8534.

67. Law 51–586 of 23 May 1951; ibid., 24 May 1951, pp. 5323–4, quoted by K. Robinson, op. cit., p. 46. K. Robinson also gives the figures of the electorate, which had been 1,362,763 in 1946, and rose to 5,061,025 for the elections to the National Assembly of 1951.

68. cf. Speech by the Minister for Overseas France, 9 April 1954, *J. O. Débats parlementaires, Assemblée Nationale*, 10 April 1955, pp. 2–24–8.

69. cf. Law 55–426 of 16 April 1955, *J. O. Lois et Décrets*, 17 April 1955, p. 3832,.

70. Statistical studies made for the period 1946–53 show that there was a growing trend towards territorial expenditure at the expense of the federal; cf. W. J. Foltz, op. cit., pp. 25–30.

71. The redistributive principle which was the *raison d'être* of the federal structure, i.e. spreading the wealth of the coastal regions to the less favoured interior regions was questioned by those who contributed most, especially the Ivory Coast. This proved to be the axis of division later between Houphouët-Boigny and Senghor on the subject of African unity.

72. op. cit., p. 435. Expediency might be another word for it.

73. Law 56–619 of 23 June 1956, *J. O. Lois et Décrets*, 24 June 1956, pp. 5782–4.

74. cf. K. Robinson, op. cit., p. 49.

75. cf. Decree 57–359 of 22 March 1957. K. Robinson suggests, with good reason, that these changes in Togo had been facilitated by the British decision to confer on the Gold Coast independence within the Commonwealth, and by the majority vote in favour of integration with Ghana in the referendum for British Togoland; op. cit., p. 50.

76. Decree 57–501 of 16 April 1957, *J. O. Lois et Décrets*, 18 April 1957, pp. 3153–64.

77. K. Robinson, op. cit., pp. 51–3.

78. ibid.

79. This compares interestingly with the latter phase of the Executive Council in the British colonial system.

80. cf. P. F. Gonidec, op. cit., pp. 407–8.

81. cf. P. F. Gonidec, ibid., at p. 183.

82. cf. Chapter 5 *infra.*
83. There is an ironic twist in the fact that the missionary factor in the colonial experience (which provided the main educational service in the early period and up to 1939) contributed largely to the African political awakening by unwittingly preparing most of the leaders.

5

The One Party in Relation to Neo-Presidentialism

A. The Emergence of One-Party Systems

The phenomenon of the one-party state has been widespread in Africa. Even in states where more than one party has been allowed to exist legally, the political reality has been that of a dominant party which has eclipsed the others, if any, or rendered their emergence impossible. For example, in the Ivory Coast, the constitution guarantees freedom of organization and expression to all parties and groups that respect democratic principles and the principles on which the *Communauté* and the Republic are based.[1] But the fact of the dominant party apart, or perhaps because of its dominance, the penal law of the Ivory Coast leaves little room for legitimate criticism and hence effectively discourages any form of political competition or of public debate.[2]

Similarly in Guinea, Article 40 of the Constitution guarantees freedom of association and in strict law parties can be created. But, as President Sékou Touré has said, they must be formed 'with the interest of the nation in view'.[3]

What, then, is the nature of the one-party state? What are its roots and what are its functions?

Several studies have been made which attempt to analyse and explain the origins and character of one-party governments.[4] Some of these studies analyse the social background, organization and function of the parties.[5] Others analyse the causes of one-party systems and discuss some of their implications in more detail.[6] Some authors lay more emphasis on their role as instruments of national unity.[7]

From such studies and from a close observation of the African political scene it can be said that the emergence of the one-party state was inevitable. Moreover, the phenomenon is linked with the emergence of the strong executive. The leaders who founded or helped to found the parties invariably emerged as the figures round whom other personalities revolved. With the accession to independence the party leader became the chief executive and the more prominent among his party brethren became his ministers. The chief executive retained his position as the leader of the party in most states and this gave rise to the party-government dichotomy which characterizes the dynamics of executive power in Africa today and which has been called here as neo-presidentialism. The inevitability of the one-party state can be borne out by the fact that in some states the opposition leaders volunteered or were persuaded to join the government party and dissolve their own party. Thus in Kenya the late Mr. Roland Ngala, the leader of KADU (Kenya African Democratic Union) crossed the floor of the Kenya House of Assembly, and, having dissolved KADU, he and some of his followers became ministers in the KANU (Kenya African National Union) government of Mzee Jomo Kenyatta. Yet, on the eve of Kenya's independence the differences between the two parties were said to be unbridgeable, being rooted, as it was claimed, in tribal differences.[8]

Opposition parties have been dissolved either through administrative or political manoeuvres, as in Kenya, or legally by passing an Act to that effect, as happened in Tanzania. In the latter case, no opposition party can legally exist, whereas in the former it could, and in fact Mr. Oginga Odinga, one of the chief leaders of KANU, resigned from the government and from KANU to form another party which was subsequently banned.

In many states, the existence, or the legal provisions permitting the existence, of 'opposition' parties simply masks the reality of what is in effect a one-party situation, as has been pointed out already in respect of the Ivory Coast. The same is true of many Francophone states.[9]

B. The Raison d'être of the One-Party System

The appearance of one-party systems in Africa has been variously received in various quarters. The Western Press and some academic writers have generally condemned it as authoritarian. Some bodies which have an interest in Africa have received it with cautionary remarks. Thus the Africa Bureau wrote in 1963, as follows:

The formation of one-party states in Africa has been a controversial subject. The dominance by one political party which has been to the fore in the campaign for independence, over weak opposition groups based on regional considerations or formed after independence was to be expected. The question now raised is whether the formal creation of a one-party state is in conflict with the establishment of a free society. One-party states exist in many countries forming the Organisation of African and Malagasy states, and in Ghana, Tanganyika and self-governing Nyasaland. Circumstances differ in each of these territories, and no generalisations are possible. But the Executive (of the Africa Bureau) views with anxiety the tendency in certain countries to put leader and party above law and to regard all criticism as treachery. The government of a developing territory must clearly give priority to economic development, and time cannot be spared for protracted debate about the merits of one scheme over another, but acceptance of any scheme or policy by the people affected is essential to its success. Concentration of energies through one single party may bring good results in certain circumstances but the test of freedom will come when new parties begin to canvass alternative methods and achieve a reasonable measure of support from the people.[10]

These words, in effect, summarized the views of several writers who considered themselves as 'friends' of Africa, and who were puzzled by the one-party system. Some observers who have written about Africa condemned it out of hand, while others defended it. The debate between Professor Arthur Lewis and Mr. Colin Legum exemplifies these respective positions.[11]

Perhaps the most eloquent case which has been made for the one-party state amongst African leaders is that argued by President Nyerere of Tanzania.[12] President Nyerere argued the case for the one-party state in Tanganyika chiefly on logical, rational grounds, and not merely on the basis of need in a developmental context. His arguments led him to the conclusion that the one-party system can be more democratic than two-party or multi-party systems. He began by questioning the value or the democratic nature of bi-party or multi-party systems as practised in Western countries. In a national executive of a party, he explained, it is common practice for the members freely to discuss and criticize the policy of the party. But this freedom is denied them once they enter Parliament. There a party line must be followed – a line which is approved by the party's leaders. The reason is that at the executive meeting of the party board policy is being laid down which not only permits but requires free discussions. There is no party line to follow at that level, because no such line has been agreed upon, as yet, whereas at the parliamentary level there is a line to be followed. Theoretically all that is left open to discussion in Parliament is detail on how, when, and in what order of priority, the policies shall be put into effect.

> Given the two-party system ... some limitation of freedom is essential – both at election time and in debate – in order to enforce party discipline and unity. And we have seen that these restrictions are not necessary where you have only one party. It seems at least open to doubt, therefore, that a system which forces political parties to limit the freedom of their members is a democratic system, and that one which can permit a party to leave its members their freedom is undemocratic. Where there is one party, and that party is identified with the *nation as a whole*, the foundations of democracy are firmer than they can ever be where you have two or more parties, each representing only a section of the community.[13]

Nyerere further argues that a two-party system can be justified only when the parties are divided over some fundamental issue; and that if it is based otherwise it can only lead to factionalism, antagonism, and waste.[14]

To critics of the one-party system he adds:

> Our critics ... should ... remember the historical difference between parties in Africa and those in Europe or America. The European and American parties came into being as the result of existing social and economic divisions – the second party being formed to challenge the monopoly of political power by some aristocratic or capitalist group. Our own parties had a very different origin. They were not formed to challenge any ruling group of our own people; they were formed to challenge the foreigners who ruled over us. They were not, therefore, political 'parties' – i.e. factions – but nationalist movements. And from the outset they represented the interests and aspirations of the whole nation.[15]

Nyerere's ideas on African socialism (a classless African society) provide a theoretical background for his practical conclusions about the one-party state. But these were not on the basis of a Marxist argument.[16] It is interesting to note that some non-Marxists, in the Ivory Coast, for instance, justify the one-party system on the basis of the Marxist notion of a correspondence between party and class. The argument is that since there is as yet no class distinction in Africa, there can only be one movement for the entire country. This is sometimes put in reverse: since parties reflect class divisions, the appearance of an opposition party must be prevented in order to avoid the development of a class struggle.[17]

It must be stated here that one-party government is not peculiar to Africa. Communist countries practise one-party government in the name of the working class. Nor is this a novel phenomenon. As an eminent American academician has written:

> The overwhelming majority of all the organisations of man throughout history have been ruled by one-party governments. Most of the time in most parts of the world all organisations have been under one-party rule. In certain parts of the world at certain times in history there have been a few two-party (or multi-party) organisations; but one-party rule is the standard and wellnigh universal case.[18]

But historical parallels or rational arguments are not always advanced in support of one-party governments in Africa. Even in some cases where this is done, it may be rather in the nature of rationalization of steps already taken under the pressure of immediate problems. The leaders who had led independence movements were faced with growing disillusionment on the part of sections of their populations. The removal of the former enemy, the colonial power, left them facing a diversity of problems, some of them created by the colonial experience. There was a tendency to reassert sectional or regional interests which made political parties the hot-bed of ethno-centrifugal forces. The opposition parties in Ghana, for instance, were based mainly on regional allegiances, though this was by no means limited to Ghana. President Kenyatta, on the other hand, had this to say when facing an opposition which grew as a splinter group out of his KANU party on policy grounds:

> ... Perhaps the gravest danger for us and for all other developing countries is the tendency for some people to exploit the

known problems of our people for personal political reasons. We sometimes hear of people who go about telling the general public that government has done very little to improve the conditions of the masses . . . they wish to exploit the fact that we cannot achieve everything overnight. They play upon the emotions of our people although they know that they have no alternatives to offer.[19]

With the passage of time, as the 'independence leaders' found that their natural authority became tarnished, and in the face of the challenge of the post-independence reality, they were driven to take drastic measures to regain their former popularity and to maintain their authority. Some became defensive and hypersensitive to criticism. Some of the measures they took tended to create tension and hostility and in some cases some leaders of suppressed opposition parties replied by desperate attempts on the life of the chief executive.[20]

This in turn heightened the tension and sense of insecurity of the government leaders. It also confirmed the arguments for one-party government.

Colonialism produced the framework of a central government, and in reaction to itself, it also (later) produced a nationalist movement. But, as one observer has written, 'it failed to integrate the tribal, regional, and sectional interests into a coherent national unit with an overriding single loyalty'[21] which was not personalistic.

African governments of all newly independent countries have thus been faced with the double task of (i) establishing their own authority, and (ii) achieving a rate of economic growth commensurate with the expectations which they themselves helped to create. This was often accompanied by the emergence of assertive pressure groups which led to struggle for power, and to diversion of energy, and waste. Where governments faced such situations at times when their own positions were precarious, the idea of the one-party state had an irresistible attraction, and all the arguments in its favour acquired greater significance as against any contrary arguments.

C. The Party and Neo-Presidentialism

The history and organization of the party in most African countries is such that it is the executive which dominates the party. Before independence, the popular movements were organized for the purpose of mobilizing the masses in order to remove colonial rule and attain independence. With the attainment of political independence, the focus shifted to the consolidation of power, to attempts to create national unity and economic development. For this purpose the executive concentrated in its hands the political force, and this in turn chiefly determined the nature of the 'party' and the constitutional structure. The 'party' leaders and stalwarts, who were originally almost always a combat group struggling for independence, became the leaders of government in the new independent states. They now had to govern and, for this purpose, had taken over the state apparatus of governing. As regards the party, this could mean either that it would be left in limbo, or alternatively, that it would be organized for a new purpose. The latter course was followed, of necessity.

The ideal role of the 'party' in such a situation would be, primarily to express the aims of the government to the people, and only secondarily to remind the government of the needs of the people and to that end to participate in the preparation and appraisal of policy. The first is justified because of the fragile nature of the new state. The party is indispensable in the task of government-directed national integration and modernization.

The second task is also necessary, particularly in view of the weakness of parliamentary and other constitutional organs of control. The structure and organization of the party in most newly independent states reflects these considerations. The role of the party and its relation to the government is a subject on which there are patterns of similarity in most of the states. The discussion that follows will, therefore, be limited to a few selected but representative cases.

The examination of the party structure and the organizational principles underlying this will, it is hoped, emphasize the role of the party and its impact on the government. The party has replaced Parliament as the real focus of political activity, in the sense that it is in the party that attempts are made to secure a consensus of opinion. The leaders keep in touch with the grass roots through the party organization, practically every day of the year, whether Parliament is in session or not. Messages pass up and down the organizational network conveying the orders, ideas, and opinions of the government to the population, and the reactions of the country to the government's measures. This mechanism does not require the literacy of the members, for communication can be carried out by the party branches, in various other ways in the vernacular.[22] The party congress itself is an event surrounded by great ceremony. Apart from its function as a policy-making body, it has a ritual function, ritual in the larger sense of the word – as in any general election or party convention in America, for example.[23]

The discussion that follows will be limited to a few representative cases.

In some studies attempts have been made to classify African one-party systems on the basis of the formal nature of their relationship to the government.[24] Three types of relationships are discerned: (i) dominance of the executive over the party, as exemplified, for example, in the Ivory Coast; (ii) collaborative relationship between the executive and the party as found in Guinea and (iii) subordination of the executive to the party, as was the case in Mali before the 1969 coup. It is maintained that in spite of the identity of the principles of organization of the parties in the three states other differences are none the less evident. The structure of the parties in all three states was said to be hierarchically organized, but, it is maintained, the internal functioning of the Parti Démocratique de la Côte d'Ivoire (P.D.C.I.) is relatively more flexible than that of the corresponding parties in Guinea, and in Mali under Modibo Keita. The reason given for this is historical, i.e. the fact that the P.D.C.I. still retains close links with the Rassemblement Démocratique Africain (R.D.A.).[25] The reason given for the predominance of the executive over the party is the personal position of President Houphouët-Boigny.

Personalities can affect the character and function of parties. As founder of the P.D.C.I., Houphouët-Boigny has been a dominant figure, as were Sékou Touré and Modibo Keita in their respective parties. But unlike these two, Houphouët-Boigny did not have to contest with the French neo-colonial power in the years immediately before independence and afterwards.[26] His dependence on the party was therefore less marked, with the consequent diminished role and status of the party in formulation and control of policy. The P.D.C.I. does not govern or legislate, but rather plays a minor advisory role in the higher institutions of the state, acting as a medium of communication from government to people.

The party in the Ivory Coast is completely subordinate to the executive; in Guinea, executive predominance is qualified by the unity of party and government at the level of chief executive and is tempered by other factors. But the predominance of the executive by controlling the highest governmental and party institutions is ensured.

1. FORMAL STRUCTURE

The formal structure of the parties – the P.D.C.I. (Parti Démocratique de la Côte d'Ivoire) of the Ivory Coast; and P.D.G. (Parti Démocratique de Guinée) – owes much to the fact that they were based on the organization of the French Communist Party, unlike the Union Progressiste Sénégalaise (U.P.S.) which was influenced by French Socialist Parties.[27] In both parties the organizational principles of 'democratic centralism' and of party discipline operate.

The first means that all the personnel of the directing organs of the party are chosen by a democratic process of election from the top to the bottom. All party branches are accountable periodically to the organ which elected them and to that which is immediately above them. The branches in theory can ask for information or make propositions on party programmes and activities to any party organ which elected them, and to that which is immediately above them. The branches' decisions are taken by the majority of the members present; and once a decision is taken the minority are bound by the decision of the majority.[28] The branches must implement the decisions of the higher organs of the party.

Again, as regards discipline the parties share common principles and practice. The first principle, of democratic centralism, implies the necessity of strict discipline. Members of the party must submit to certain strict obligations which make them party militants. They must participate actively in the political life of the country. Within the framework of the party organization they are expected to offer ideas and criticisms on programmes and activities. There is a set of sanctions applicable to members for breach of party discipline. The overall effect of these sanctions is to make members active and obedient, to curb indiscipline and thus integrate them to the party.

The party machine and its functioning reflect the two organizational principles mentioned above. Democratic centralism implies a pyramidal structure, while discipline ensures the cohesion and regular functioning of the machine. In the theory of the ordinary operation of this machine, the centre must be given, with the greatest accuracy possible, the point of view of the branches so that it can make the right decisions.

At the apex of the party organization there is the Congress, which is the supreme policy-making organ. It issues programmes of action, hears reports, and controls the accounts of the party. It also elects the executive officers (members of the Political Bureau). In the Ivory Coast the Congress meets once a year in ordinary sessions, and in Guinea it meets every four years. The Congress may be convened in extraordinary sessions either at the instance of the Political Bureau or at the request of more than half of its members.

In the Ivory Coast the Congress is composed of delegates from the branches (*sous-sections*), while in Guinea it is composed of the members of the Political Bureau and the members of the federal bureaux (from the regions), who are statutory members.

Next, there is the Political Bureau, which is the supreme executive organ. The decisions of the Congress are executed by this organ, and because of its permanence and size it is, in reality, the most important organ of the party. In the Ivory Coast there is an executive committee (*comité directeur*) consisting of thirty-five members, which delegates the power to the Political Bureau to assume 'the direction of the policy of the party during the intervals between its meetings'. The Political Bureau in turn delegates to the Secretary-General 'the administration of the party and gives him wide powers of convocation and of decisions to that effect'.[29] The Secretary-General's principal function is to control the activities of branch Secretaries-General (*sous-sections*), who exist in every administrative sub-division of the country. The Political Bureau is composed of an honorary president (at the moment Houphouët-Boigny), a Secretary-General, a technical adviser on political matters, an organization secretary, a treasurer-general, assistant treasurer, secretary on administrative affairs, Press secretary, propaganda secretary, secretary for mass education, and one ordinary member. The *comité directeur* consists of the members of the Political Bureau plus branch secretaries-general, deputies, ministers, prefects, councillors (local) and mayors. At the branch level there are a Secretary-General, a treasurer, and six members elected by the branch assembly. The branch Secretaries-General are agents of execution of the policy of the Political Bureau.

In Guinea, the Political Bureau, which is also the supreme executive organ, consists of fifteen members elected for four years by the Congress from among outgoing members (of the Bureau) and members of the Bureau of Federations. The Bureau implements decisions of the Congress and of the 'National Council of the Revolution' – a body which next to the Congress is a high organ and which holds meetings in between the meetings of the Congress. The Bureau meets at least once a month and is convened by the Secretary-General.[30] It has four commissions: (i) the Commission on Political Control and Organization; (ii) the Commission on External Relations, presided over by the Minister of Foreign Affairs; (iii) the Economic Commission, presided over by the Minister for Economic Development; (iv) the Social Commission, presided over by the Minister of Health and Social Affairs. The members of the Commissions are all members of the Bureau. The Commissions are controlled by the Secretary-General, President Sékou Touré, who is assisted in this task by the Permanent Secretary of the Political Bureau. There is also an Executive Commission consisting of the Secretary-General, the Presidents of the Four Commissions, and the Permanent Secretary of the Bureau. The Executive Commission co-ordinates the activities of the Commission and prepares the meetings of the Bureau. The Permanent Secretary of the Bureau acts as the centralizing agent for all information coming from all branches of the party, and he regulates all conflicts arising between branches.

At the next level of organization each federation has a bureau of seven members, of whom six are elected[31] and the seventh is the Governor of the region, and is an *ex officio* member. It is elected for three years, and supervises the implementation in the region of the decision of the higher organ of the party.

A similar organization existed in Mali under Modibo Keita. The Political Bureau, which consisted of eighteen members, was the supreme directive organ. It consisted of the Secretary-General; the political secretary; secretary for organization; secretary for administrative and judicial affairs; secretary for economic, social, and cultural affairs; Press secretary; the treasurer-general and his assistant; and ten commissioners, of whom two were responsible for external relations, two for regulating conflicts, two for accounts, and two for youth, along with one commissioner for women's affairs and one for trade union matters. The President of the Republic and the President of the National Assembly were *ex-officio* members of the Political Bureau.[32] The Bureau, among other functions, directed and controlled the activities of all elected members. Within the framework of the powers of the Bureau, the Secretary-General acted as the guide of the party.[33] He represented the party in all places at all times and acted on its behalf with the agreement of the Bureau. He ensured the respect and the maintenance of the party line and the correct execution of the party programme. He could call meetings of the Bureau and he directed its work. He could delegate his function to the political secretary, who was next in line to the Secretary-General in the Bureau, and who was in charge of the general political education of militants.[34] The other secretaries were in charge of the matters which corresponded to their titles.

2. RELATION TO GOVERNMENT

In spite of the similarities in the principle and organization of the parties it has been suggested, as already mentioned, that the place of the party in the government is not the same. In the Ivory Coast the P.D.C.I. has ceased to define the general guidelines of the party since the party congress of 1959; and the Political Bureau plays the role of counsellor to the President of the Republic. As the Congress does not meet, the President of the Republic (Honorary President of the party) defines the party programme, which becomes the same as the government programme.[35] In effect President Houphouët-Boigny has replaced the Congress of the party in the task of giving general orientation to government policy and action. In spite of claims to the contrary made by the party officials of the P.D.C.I., in fact the primacy of party over government is not the rule in the Ivory Coast. The primacy of politics has been abandoned. Nkrumah's dictum 'seek ye first the political kingdom, and all things else shall be added unto you', has its antithesis in Houphouët-Boigny's philosophy. He has said to his people: 'if you don't want to vegetate in bamboo huts concentrate your efforts on growing good cocoa and good coffee. They will fetch a good price, and you will become rich.'[36]

In practice, of course, both Nkrumah and Houphouët-Boigny departed from their dicta. The former knew that man does not live by politics alone, as the latter knew that man does not live by bread alone. He paid attention to political organization. The P.D.C.I. has become a willing instrument of Houphouët-Boigny's personal power, just as the Convention People's Party in Ghana became an instrument of Nkrumah. This manifests itself at various levels. The Secretary-General of the P.D.C.I. is also the President of the National Assembly of the Ivory Coast. This fact reinforces the predominance of Houphouët-Boigny over the National Assembly through the President of the party.

Again, although in appearance the party nominates the

candidates to the National Assembly, in fact it is Houphouët-Boigny who has the last word after consultation with the Political Bureau.[37] In theory the candidates are chosen by the secretaries of the P.D.C.I. and by such other major groups as participate in the election arrangements. Then the list is submitted to the Political Bureau for final approval. In practice the inner circle controlled by Houphouët-Boigny retains control over the entire process. Local party branches are informed of the number of places their region will have and are asked to draw up a list of candidates for these places in order of preference. In 1960, for example, the general secretaries of the party assembled in Abidjan to prepare the lists, heard Houphouët-Boigny's recommendations, and then approved a motion to give him and the Political Bureau full authority to draw up the slates.[38]

The situation has been aptly summarized thus:

> ... in the representative democracy of the Ivory Coast, the prestige of one man radically transforms the classic theory. It is no longer a question of the electors choosing representatives who are able to decide and act. General elections serve only to show the confidence of the people in one man.[39]

The nature of the relation of the P.D.C.I. to the government in its parliamentary aspect may be seen clearly in the unanimous approval given to the Bureau and the Commissions of the National Assembly, as proposed by the party spokesman on 27 November 1960.[40] Again in matters of arbitrating conflicts between ministers and any parliamentary commission, a minister would normally refer the matter to the President of the Republic who may submit the question to the Political Bureau of the party. If the party spokesman in Parliament announces that the Bureau has decided in such and such a way, all members submit to this decision. But the party does not normally intervene in technical matters, which are worked out between the executive and the bureaucracy, basically under him. The party intervenes only in political matters, or in matters which may have deep political implications.

In Guinea, the party appears to be predominant in practice as well as in formal structure, thereby emphasizing the primacy of politics. A distinction must be made between general questions of policy, in respect of which the party is predominant, and matters of day-to-day administration which are firmly controlled by the government. Once the Congress has established the general policy as guidelines for action it is left to the government to follow these and implement them.

The dynamics of executive action connected with the implementation of the general policy involve questions, the details, volume and technical complexity of which necessarily leaves them to be dealt with by the government bureaucracy. But the chief executive of the government, who is also Secretary-General of his party, supervises the execution of the party policies. The merging of the offices of head of party and government in one man may partly explain the function of the party. One value of such a merger is that it in theory preserves the primacy of the party, making it impossible for the chief executive to emasculate it by subordinating the chief of the party to him. It also avoids conflict, preserves unity, and obviates the problem of succession, which is one of the problems that is critical in personalized systems.

In Guinea, the Political Bureau, which the Secretary-General controls, does not in fact dictate to him or to his government, but rather leaves it to him to see to it that party militants accept the decisions of the government.[41] It is also true that the manner in which the party policy and programme is worked out shows a collaboration between the two.[42] But this is not peculiar to Guinea; other parties follow the same procedure. Also, the content of the Secretary-General's report and the manner of its presentation is not necessarily a sound guide to the nature of the party-executive relationship. In Senegal, for example, the report of the Secretary-General of the U.P.S., Léopold Sédar Senghor, to the Fifth Congress shows the same approach as that of Sékou Touré. The same was true of the report of Idrissa Diarra, the political secretary of the U.S.R.D.A. of Mali, to the Sixth Congress.[43] In each case an exhaustive examination of the past performance of the government and the party is prescribed. Problems are analysed and solutions suggested in outline on economic, social, political, and cultural matters. The report cannot be too critical, as it is presented by the leader of the government. On the other hand, there is a remarkable degree of self-examination. The report of President Senghor to the Fifth Congress of the U.P.S. concentrates its attention on the economic development plan and a reappraisal thereof. Senghor puts it thus: 'the plan is and must be, during the next four years the principal object of our action as well as of our preoccupations. Because *planning is a method of action* which is indispensable to all those who espouse not only socialism but more generally economic effectiveness in social justice. . . .'[44]

The relation of the Political Bureau to the executive in both Guinea and Mali was said to be one of co-operation and understanding. But certain differences emerged which have given rise to the suggestion that whereas in Guinea the relationship is collaborative, in Mali it was one in which the Bureau was predominant.

In Guinea after the Seventh Congress, the role of the Political Bureau seems to have been reduced to that of confirming the decisions prepared or even taken by an executive commission of five members consisting of the Secretary-General (chairman), the Presidents of the technical commissions of the Bureau, and the Permanent Secretary.[45] Moreover, the commissions, it will be remembered, function under the direction and supervision of the Secretary-General who is helped in this task by the Permanent Secretary of the Bureau.[46] Hence the relation between the Bureau and the executive is tightened, through the agency of the executive commission of the Bureau in which both party and government meet. The Political Bureau, which meets once a month, seems to be a permanent organ of control and consultation, rather than an executive organ. In between its meetings the government executes the directives of the Bureau. The President of the Republic, because of his relationship to the Bureau, benefits from the authority of the party, which in the professed revolutionary ideology of Guinea is the motivating force of the political system. The President acts as the organic link between party and government, informing the Bureau of the actions of the government and notifying ministers about the decisions of the Bureau. But the Bureau in no way replaces the Council of Ministers, as an executive organ of state.

The powers of the President of the Republic (and Secretary-General of the party) are exercised in Guinea in a manner which conveys a picture of a much more tightly held governmental and party executive authority. In applying the general guidelines laid down by the Congress, the Secretary-General can in the name of the Bureau push ahead with his ideas unquestioned. Thus on 3 August 1963, the Council of Ministers approved a proposal of President Sékou Touré, concerning measures for controlling financial and commercial transactions entered into abroad. He authorized Mr. Diallo Saifoulaye, who was in charge of administrative and financial matters in the Bureau, to prepare a decree creating an inter-ministerial commission which would study all agreements concluded with foreign countries. This decision was an application of a decision of the Political Bureau which was made in accordance with the economic resolution of the Sixth Congress of December 1962.[47]

In Mali, on the other hand, the party directed all the institutions of the state. The Political Bureau played a vital constitutional and governmental role. It held weekly meetings to supervise the activities of the executive and the legislature. The President of the Republic presided at these meetings of the Bureau. Party and government thus appeared to be more united, but the Bureau preserved a vital and dominant role. It was guided by the general policy laid down by the Congress. A reading of the Sixth Congress of 1962 shows the wide range of such policy. As an illustration we will cite an extract from the economic field. The Congress gave an imperative mandate to the Bureau and to the government on the national plane

> to tackle economic acclimatization immediately and vigorously; to establish new economic institutions rapidly, developing commercial centres in a socialist plan based on African realities; to use every means to create an infrastructure of railways, road, water and air (transportation) in accordance with the needs of the country; to intensify agricultural production; to increase internal consumption and the exploitation potential; to use every means to establish industries; to intensify research on mineral resources in order to make Mali a state fit to be a member of modern Africa; and to direct and control effectively the economy of the country through the state which will take a more active part in it, notably by the creation of a national office of external commerce and the intensification of the co-operative sector.[48]

The activity of the party in Mali, as in Guinea, was guided and directed by the Political Bureau. But there was more massive participation in Mali. At the top the Bureau acted as a counsellor of government. At the base the administrative authorities did nothing without the support of the responsible party officials. The supremacy of political over technical questions was a guiding principle. The membership of the Bureau itself was significant, in this respect. Out of the nineteen members elected by the Sixth Congress, only six were ministers in the government. Although these six occupied an important place in the Bureau, the rest were numerically preponderant and could thus perhaps subordinate the executive to the party.[49] It is of interest to note that the Mali

Government, formed soon after the end of the Sixth Congress on 14 September 1962, was so formed by the Political Bureau, on the proposition of the Secretary-General, who was an outgoing President of the Republic. The investiture by the National Assembly took place three days later. The dual role of the Secretary-General was revealed in his presentation speech made to the national assembly.

> What I can tell you is that we have the feeling that this new cabinet which has just been formed as well as the departments which are more balanced than those of the former government will allow the new cabinet to play its role effectively by implementing the development plan of the Republic of Mali in the best conditions.

Thus far he spoke as the new chief executive. Then he added

> And what I can add, and I say this in the name of the national Political Bureau, is that these measures which we have just taken are the prelude to other courageous, vigorous, and necessary, measures in the policy of readjustment which could not operate in the period between the two congresses.[50]

How did the Secretary-General fulfil his dual role in practice in so closely co-ordinated a working relationship between party and government? The weekly meetings of the Bureau took place on Tuesdays and the Secretary-General informed the Bureau of the work of the Council of Ministers at its previous meeting, which would be on the preceding Thursday. The Secretary-General decided which matters discussed in the council were important enough to be presented to the Bureau. But if the Bureau had made a decision on a subject which then came up in the Council, the latter's debate would centre on technicalities and on details of implementation. The decision of the Bureau had to prevail. In this way the supremacy of the party could be exercised every week. The President of the Republic transmitted the decision of the Bureau to the appropriate department for execution. If a presidential decree was needed, for example, he would (as Secretary-General) ask the secretariat of the Bureau to prepare it. In his absence, the political secretary of the party (who was second in line in the party hierarchy) presided at the Bureau and he worked in co-operation with the acting President of the Republic. All decisions of the Bureau reached in his absence were binding on him when he resumed work. This constant link between the

Bureau and the Council of Ministers was institutionalized. This could be seen clearly in the regular publication of the decisions of the Bureau and the equivalent decision of the Council of Ministers, which regularly appeared side by side in *L'Essor*, the official organ of the party.

As an example of the extent of the Bureau's powers we will cite one decision among many. At its meeting of 22 January 1963, the Bureau, in approving the recommendations of the National Personnel Office, decided to modify the status of the Governor of the Bank of the Mali Republic, raising his rank to that of a minister. The President of the government presented this decision to the Council of Ministers at its next meeting on 24 January, and the proposal became law on 1 February 1963.[51]

The Bureau issued circulars to all the sections of the party, which were binding on all party militants, whether they were party officials or civil servants. The circulars were signed by the Secretary-General who, in this respect, acted in both capacities, as chief executive and as party chief. A typical circular of importance was one dated 13 November 1962, on the subject of 'economic and fiscal fraud' (or evasions). It was published in *L'Essor*, on 19 November in the name of the government and the party. In it the Secretary-General began by saying that while, during colonial times such an offence was understandable because it operated against a foreign oppressor, in a free Mali it was an anti-social, anti-patriotic act and must be punished as such. He then proceeded to announce the establishment of a special administrative organ or a committee in each governorate to administer export controls in a manner stated in the circular. All party militants were also enjoined to be vigilant against 'economic offenders', for 'each militant of the U.S.R.D.A. must consider the denunciation and discovery of offenders as a political task'.[52]

The organization and relationship of party and administrative organs at local levels is also marked by a unity of purpose. In Guinea, the Sixth Congress of the *Parti Démocratique de Guinée* (P.D.G.) condemned the duality of party and administrative organization at the local level as constituting a threat to the unity of the state. Then the Seventh Congress decided to transfer the power of village councils to village party committees and since then there has been a unity of party and administrative function at that level. Again, although the duality exists, at the higher level (*arrondissements* and regions), in practice the administrative officials at these levels consult the party officials on all important questions. The party is thus unified at the local level with administrative organs.[53]

The logic of one-party rule seems to lead to the abolition of duality or plurality not only of this kind but of regional government. This can be further illustrated by the brief post-independence history of the Ghana regional assemblies. They were established in 1958 and abolished in 1959. Nkrumah declared: 'It would be wasteful, cumbersome and thoroughly unsound administratively, to have in the proposed local government structure another tier, in the form of regional assemblies.'[54]

The C.P.P., however, was neither as thoroughgoing in its village mass organization nor, it seems in retrospect, ideologically as firmly based as were other parties elsewhere. It is easy to find faults in a party that has failed, but it seems clear that although the C.P.P. appeared to start as a mass party and continued to present such a front, it was not in reality a genuine mass-party, as events proved. Its 'control' over the local administrative apparatus did not in any way amount to a dominant position for the party over the administration. A close observer of the Ghana political scene saw in the abolition of the power of regional authorities 'measures' taken to 'emphasise and augment the power of the party in the regions'.[55] Others, being wise after the event, claim that these measures were designed to secure Nkrumah's personal control over developments throughout the country. It is further claimed that it mattered very little whether the newly appointed regional commissioners were all members of the C.P.P.[56]

> Aside from the party leader, there existed no centre, no source of power, controlling their conduct. . . . He (Nkrumah) selected and appointed the commissioners, remained personally in touch with them, controlled their emoluments, and decided when and on what grounds they were to be disciplined.[57]

The parties in Guinea and Mali, as in most African states, started as ideological parties, not as parties of specific classes. The movement for independence had involved a general national interest. But this was a far cry from the sort of class interest that motivated many of the historic parties in Europe and America. Some of the African parties seemed to have deviated from the 'ideological' line as sketched in their original aims and objectives. The shift of authority from the Congress of the P.D.C.I. to President Houphouët-Bougny is one example. Why has the P.D.C.I.

not resisted this? One explanation may be that the real power base of Houphouët-Boigny was the Plantation Owners and Workers Union which might be described as an interest group that contributed to a process of 'ideological discharge' of the P.D.C.I. However, one conclusion may be hazarded as being generally applicable: the national leader must earn and retain the confidence of the party organization more than that of the legislature. The party is therefore the institution which must be mainly relied on as providing means of control over the executive.

Turning to other parts of Africa, we find similar patterns of development. For example, to take one pattern, Dr. Hastings Banda, the President of Malawi, has turned the Malawi Congress Party into an instrument of personal power. He is the life chairman of the party, and the central executive of the party is wholly selected by him. The chairman has concentrated the power of dismissal of members entirely in his hands. The party has a highly centralized organization and its branches must remit to the party central office all funds, however collected.[58] Dr. Banda does not rely on the party alone as an instrument of personal power. He has built a private army out of the 'Young Pioneers'.[59] The Young Pioneers have been trained by Israelis on a military basis – drill, modern agricultural methods, homecraft, etc. The military drill is designed to instil implicit obedience to superiors. After completing his training the Young Pioneer goes into the village to work with the rural inhabitants to show them how to improve their standard of living. The Young Pioneers enjoy parity of power with the police and the army. They exercise the power of arrest, for example, while the police have no power of arrest over them. Dr. Banda is their commander-in-chief.[60]

The practical result of all this is that the M.C.P. lost whatever original ideological pretensions were claimed for it and its machinery, and that the Young Pioneers are used as an instrument for suppressing all criticism and for the perpetuation in power of an individual and a clique around him. Nor does Dr. Banda conceal this fact behind 'ideological' pronouncements. In the space of two years he got rid of six of his original cabinet of seven ministers for opposing him on such questions as Africanization of the civil service, and policies towards Rhodesia, Portugal, and South Africa. The clearest evidence of Dr. Banda's personal rule is his decision, in opposition to O.A.U. policy and the opinion of his ministers, to accept help and advice from South Africa. For example, the Sucoma sugar mill project near Blantyre has been financed by the

Industrial Development Corporation of South Africa which stipu-
lated that at least sixty per cent of the material used in the construction of the mill had to be of South African origin.[61]

The M.C.P. was used as the original power base. The concentrated power of the party chairman enabled him to build up a
core of following which mobilized public opinion for him as a
national leader. As soon as the members of his party who (next to
him) were the most important, were removed, Dr. Banda could
no longer rely on the party or the government apparatus alone as
a source of power. Hence the para-military 'Young Pioneers'.

Some aspects of the Ghana experience can be compared with
that of the M.C.P. But Nkrumah never abandoned the original
ideological basis of his party, even though the C.P.P. was further
removed from the masses in 1966 than he was ready to believe.
As two students of the subject have written:

> The most obvious change from the 1950 Positive Action days
> was that the C.P.P. no longer behaved like a mass political
> party. Instead, it combined a preference for 'summit' con-
> ferences with the style of a United States political machine.
> The C.P.P. did not work through the trade unions or involve
> the masses in its battles in any way; . . . Rather than organisa-
> tion, agitation, and political education aimed at generating
> power from below, the C.P.P. preferred or felt forced to try to
> exert influence from the top down by negotiation. And when
> negotiation failed it resorted to administrative repression. The
> C.P.P.'s behaviour during and after the third and last general
> election in 1956 illustrates its increasing isolation from its
> popular base.[62]

The C.P.P. at the outset relied on young men for support. But, as
it tried to form a broad coalition against the colonial administration, it felt unable to organize an attack on traditional and other
forces which later became the centre of disaffection. By 1956, the
C.P.P. no longer based itself on the young men in the rural areas.
It even attempted to outbid the opposition for the favour of the
chiefs, working through them in the rural election campaigns.[63]
It would also adopt American-style 'pork-barrel' campaigning,
often holding out to a local council the promise of a generous
development grant or threats of its withdrawal.[64] Soon after
independence, in March 1957, 'disturbances' broke out in the
Trans–Volta Togoland area, and the new government had to use
troops and police to suppress the disturbances, in which several

people were killed. A few weeks later an anti-C.P.P. movement sprang up in Accra, from among unemployed Ga workers and the small merchant class. They called themselves the Ga Standfast Organisation. They demanded jobs, better housing and lower food prices.[65] The result was depoliticization, signified by the passage of the Avoidance of Discrimination Bill which prohibited all tribal, religious, and regional parties. In these circumstances, shaken by the mass rallies in Accra and the armed revolt in Togo, the C.P.P. government, which was still in command of all levers of power, began to rely primarily on the state apparatus.[66]

Further depoliticization followed in 1958, when the Preventive Detention Act was passed. Under it the executive could 'order the detention of any person who is a citizen of Ghana if satisfied that the order is necessary to prevent that person acting in a manner prejudicial to the security of the state'.[67] The administration of the Preventive Detention Act between 1958 and 1966, which is associated as much with the C.P.P. as with Nkrumah, does no credit to either.[68] In actual fact even some of the bitterest critics of Nkrumah agree that he 'displayed a sense of moderation and humane consideration in the exercise of his ever-growing power'.[69] The Ghana experience has an added significance in that its outcome has been conclusive in one sense, demonstrating the point that a party which has no popular basis, or which has abandoned such basis, could not be relied on to support a government in distress. Whether the Malawi Congress Party will go the way of the C.P.P. is difficult to say. But if the President of Malawi relies more and more on the Young Pioneers for his political military balance, it is doubtful whether the M.C.P. would act differently in the event of an armed challenge.[70]

In Tanzania President Nyerere set up a commission in January 1964, to study and report on the establishment of a democratic one-party state. The Commission's report was later adopted almost in its entirety and the constitution was modified accordingly.[71] It is interesting to note that two members of the Commission were sent abroad – one to Guinea, another to Yugoslavia – to study the systems in these countries.[72]

On the character and role of the party the Commission had this to say:

In a country where any number of political parties are permitted to function the basic character and role of a party can be left to be settled by the party managers. They have no constitutional significance. If the party managers are obtuse or injudicious or intolerant they will suffer the consequences of unpopularity and exclusion from power. In a one-party state, however, the situation is very different. Decisions affecting the basic character of the party have a deep constitutional significance, since they may well determine the extent to which a citizen is able to participate in the process of government. . . . In a one-party state the threat, actual or potential, from an opposition group disappears. This means that the party's survival no longer depends on mass membership or affiliation. From this it is sometimes argued that the party should see itself in the new context as an *élite* group, a minority ideologically dedicated who provide from above the leadership necessary to motivate the inert mass of the community. Whatever practical advantages it may have in terms of dynamic leadership we decisively reject this view of the party and its role. . . . We do not see TANU as an *élite* but as a mass party through which any citizen of goodwill can participate in the process of Government.[73]

The other experiment which is peculiar to the history of the nation concerned is that of the Arab Socialist Union. Egypt is an example of an African state where there were no serious ethnic or regional problems, but where there were class problems. Prior to the Revolution of 1952[74] there was an endemic political malaise which was rooted in the economic and social structure of the country. There was the ever-growing power of the big landlords whose holdings manifested the most serious inequality in the distribution of land-ownership, the increasing impoverishment of farmers, and the declining wages of agricultural workers. There was also the faltering industrial activity which had 'suffered so much from monopolistic pressures, widespread exploitation, lack of qualified entrepreneurs, scarcity of capital and limitation of markets'.[75]

The new régime faced these problems, and the attempts it made to solve them culminated in the National Charter of June 1962 and the Constitution which was based on this. The National Charter provides for the creation of the Arab Socialist Union which, according to the preamble of its statute, 'represents the socialist vanguard which leads the march, expresses their will, directs national action and undertakes effective control of the march of such action, within the framework of the National Charter'. It was envisaged that the peasants, armed forces, workers, intellectuals, and national capitalists, could all join in one alliance.

There is on the face of it a similarity of approach to membership of the party in the post National Charter situation of the United Arab Republic and in Tanzania before the Arusha Declaration of 1967. TANU was considered to be a 'nationalist movement which is open to all – which is identified with the whole nation'.[76] Nevertheless, adherence to the principles of the party is a condition for membership in both cases. Since these principles exemplify the 'ideological' basis of many African parties, we will set them out briefly here:

The aims and objects of TANU as set out in the Arusha Declaration (1967) are:

(a) To consolidate and maintain the independence of this country (Tanzania) and the freedom of its people.

(b) To safeguard the inherent dignity of the individual in accordance with the Universal Declaration of Human Rights.

(c) To ensure that this country shall be governed by a democratic socialist government of the people.

(d) To co-operate with all political parties in Africa engaged in the liberation of all Africa.

(e) To see that the government mobilizes all the resources of this country towards the elimination of poverty, ignorance and disease.

(f) To see that the government actively assists in the formation and maintenance of co-operative organizations.

(g) To see that wherever possible the government itself directly participates in the economic development of this country.

(h) To see that the government gives equal opportunity to all men and women; irrespective of race, religion or status.

(i) To see that the government eradicates all types of exploitation, intimidation, discrimination, bribery, and corruption.

(j) To see that the government exercises effective control over the principal means of production and pursues policies which facilitate the way to collective ownership of the resources of this country.

(k) To see that the government co-operates with other states in Africa in bringing about African unity.

(l) To see that the government works tirelessly towards world peace and security through the U.N.O.

The main objectives of the Arab Socialist Union, as defined by its statute, are to 'realize sound democracy' and to safeguard the following guarantees which have been embodied in the National Charter:

(a) Minimum representation, i.e. fifty per cent, for workers and farmers in all popular political formations at all levels.
(b) The right of criticism and self-criticism.
(c) The principle of collective ownership.
(d) Formation of co-operative and labour unions.
and
(e) The gradual transfer of the authority of the state to elected councils.

In the pursuit of these objectives the Arab Socialist Union is charged with duties which are expressed thus:

To become a positive power behind the revolutionary action.
To protect the principles and objectives of the revolution.
To liquidate the effects of capitalism and feudalism.
To fight against the infiltration of foreign influence.
To fight against the return of reaction which has been eliminated.
To fight against the infiltration of opportunism.
To resist passivity and deviation.
To prevent haphazard work in national action.

These aims of the parties in the two countries reflect the aspirations of their respective people as expressed through the leadership of the parties (and governments). For historical reasons there are differences in some of the declared objectives. For example, in the United Arab Republic special emphasis is laid on the vigilance against the return of reactionary forms which were removed by the revolution; on the other hand the basic aim of constructing a democratic socialist society and maintaining independence are common features in the aims of both parties, as they are of most African parties. These summaries of the aims of TANU and the Arab Socialist Union may serve as a general frame of reference against which to view the aims of other parties which have formed governments charged with the duty of directing the affairs of their states. There are, of course, some differences in approach and execution. In Mali and Guinea, for example, the parties set for themselves the task of radically reconstructing their societies, and the parties proposed to play their role in this reconstruction along Leninist lines. In contrast to this, there were the approaches of

Presidents Nasser, Nyerere, and Senghor. It is worth noting that the U.P.S. of Senegal has the following provision in its statute as one guide to its action:

> The U.P.S. aims at the suppression of all forms of oppression of class or caste through the conquest of political power, the socialization of the means of production and exchange, the establishment of a communal society and of a true democracy to the service of the people. That is to say, the U.P.S. draws its inspiration from the socialist method, but it intends to integrate the cultural values of Black Africa into socialism.[77]

Other objects were espoused by African political parties. President Habib Bourguiba has explained the changed role of the party as its function was altered from the struggle for freedom to the struggle for development:

> The ... difference is that instead of the policeman or the foreign flag that wounds our dignity, it is the spectacle of misery, ignorance and under-development. . . . We are mobilizing ourselves for a struggle more difficult than that for political freedom, because it calls for the combined use of both our material and our human resources. It forces men to master their instincts and their egocentricity, to transcend themselves, raising themselves, raising their vision and their action to the level of the national interest. The battle is first of all a conquest of self; it is impossible to build on hatred of others. Our goal is to enlist the co-operation of every citizen and to build a nation which is neither the game reserve of the bourgeois nor the dictatorship of the proletariat.[78]

He may have spoken for many African political leaders.

As for the structure of the parties, the role outlined for the party to play dictated a hierarchical and centralized party machine differing from the U.S.R.D.A. of Mali and the P.D.G. of Guinea perhaps in emphasis and in symmetry only.

The critical difference is that whereas in the majority of countries the party has been used for purposes of maintaining the executive in power, only in a few countries is a hierarchical and centralized party machine used to reorient the society. It is clear that in Tanzania, for example, the idea of a party as an ideologically unstructured national movement embracing the entire population and expressing its aspirations has been abandoned in favour of greater ideological control and proselytization of the members.

The Arusha Declaration of January 1967 puts the matter succinctly thus:

> Since the founding of the Party greater emphasis has been put on having as large a membership as possible. This was justified during the struggle for independence. Now, however, the national executive committee feels that the time has come for emphasis to shift away from mere size of membership to the quality of membership. Greater consideration must be given to a member's commitment to the beliefs and objectives of the Party, and its policy of socialism.[79]

It is now required of all concerned to observe the membership clause of the party constitution closely. Where it is thought unlikely that an applicant really accepts the beliefs, aims, and objectives of the party, it is required that he should be denied membership. TANU is 'a party of workers and peasants'.[80] The Declaration also recommends that members should receive thorough teaching on party ideology so that they may understand it, and they must always be reminded of the importance of living up to its principles.[81]

Again, the Arusha Declaration requires that every TANU and government leader must be either a peasant or a worker and should in no way be associated with the practices of capitalism or feudalism, should not hold shares in a company or hold a directorship in any privately owned enterprise, or receive two or more salaries or own houses which he rents to others.[82] 'Leaders' in this sense includes members of the TANU national executive committee, ministers, Members of Parliament, senior officials of para-state organizations, all those appointed or elected under any clause of the TANU constitution, councillors and civil servants of the upper and middle cadres.[83] Tanzania is a state of peasants and workers with socialist aims, but is not yet a socialist state. 'It still has elements of capitalism and feudalism and their temptations. These elements could expand and entrench themselves.' A true member of TANU is a socialist,

> and his compatriots, that is fellow believers in this political and economic faith, are all those in Africa and elsewhere in the world who fight for the rights of the peasants and workers. The first duty of a TANU member, and especially of a TANU leader, is to live by these principles in his day-to-day life . . .[84]

The party in Tanzania is a key institution and the relationship of its organs to some of the organs of the state has an important constitutional significance.[85]

The supreme organ of TANU is the National Conference, which meets every two years.[86] The National Conference consists of officers of the party, national, regional, and district, delegates directly elected by the districts; and affiliated organizations, Members of Parliament, and certain nominated persons.[87]

It has general powers of formulating policy and supervising the actions of TANU. It can change any decision made by any other organ of the party or by any officer of the party. It has the power to expel persons from membership and (by a two-thirds majority) to amend the constitution of TANU.

However, the length of the time between the meetings of the National Conference affects its relative importance. In practice, real power lies with the national executive committee of TANU, as it does with the Political Bureau in Guinea. The National Executive Committee (N.E.C.), meeting once every three months, decided on matters of great national importance which the National Conference could not reverse or repudiate even if it had it in mind to do so. Some major decisions of the state have been taken at N.E.C. meetings, for example the decision to establish a democratic one-party state. The N.E.C. consists of some eighty members. The President of the party is elected by the National Conference for six years. The other members include seventeen elected by the conference and an equal number of Regional Commissioners who are *ex-officio* members. The Secretary-General, the Deputy Secretary-General and the National Treasurer are appointed by N.E.C. It is interesting to note that the Presidential Commission, while recognizing the importance of the need to maintain continuity in the day-to-day administration of the party, recommended that the President of the party should be empowered to remove the Secretary-General and National Treasurer, presumably at his discretion. Previously they could only be removed for misconduct. The President is nevertheless required to report on the circumstances to the next meeting of the N.E.C.[88]

The Presidential Commission was at pains to point out the importance of co-ordinating the decisions of the N.E.C. with those of the government. The question of the N.E.C. membership has a bearing on this matter. The N.E.C. needs to be well informed on the details of action already taken or contemplated by government, and to have readily available expert advice on the administrative and legal problems which may be posed by any policy under consideration. The Commission therefore recommended that the principal secretary to the President (of the Republic) and the principal legal adviser to the government should be *ex-officio* members of the N.E.C.[89]

The role of the N.E.C. in relation to the National Assembly is also of interest. Members of the National Assembly are *ex-officio* members of the party National Conference, and their function as members of this conference as well as the National Assembly may enable both institutions to exercise a degree of mutual control over one another. The report of the Commission on this is instructive. The Commission reported:

> The establishment of a one-party state in which the position of the party is formally recognised in the constitution itself must necessarily destroy the distinction which exists at present between the institutions of the party and those of the government. We welcome this. The distinction between government and party has never been understood by the people. For the ordinary man uninterested in constitutional theory TANU is the government and the government is TANU. This does not mean, of course, that in a one-party state the institutions of the party must necessarily be substituted for those of the government or vice versa. It does mean, however, that both sets of institutions can be looked at afresh as integral parts of a single constitutional system.[90]

Nevertheless a distinction is drawn between the role of N.E.C. and the National Assembly. The N.E.C. is concerned with the formulation of broad lines of policy. 'It is the soul and conscience of the party.' At its meetings the basic assumptions of government policy are frankly questioned and exhaustively debated. The National Assembly, on the other hand, is primarily concerned with the more detailed task of *giving effect to government policy through appropriate legislative measures and exercising vigilant control over all aspects of government expenditure.*[91]

The other central organs of the party are the Central Committee, the 'cabinet', the electoral conference and the disciplinary committee, which have less important functions.[92] Of these only the Central Committee has any effective political role. It consists of the senior officers of the party, together with such persons as may be appointed by the President of the party; several of its members are cabinet ministers, and this fact is given, among others, as a reason for the relative unimportance of the Central Committee – 'there are no members who are powerful purely by reason of their standing in the Party'.[93]

At the local level the organs of the party and government meet in the same office. The Regional Commissioners are regional secretaries of TANU.[94] Also, since 1965, the District Councils include members of the district executive committee of TANU who are *ex-officio* members of the council. The same is true of town councils and municipalities where there is a separate TANU organization.[95]

In spite of the intermingling of personnel, however, the organs of party and state have been kept distinct, performing distinct functions. To that extent, the potential role of the party organs as means of control over the executive may be enhanced.[96]

Some observers consider that the thrust of the changes in Tanzania is clearly in the direction of effective control of the party over government, both in its contact with the people and in its power over the government. It is also suggested that the emphasis laid on institutions of control over the government indicates that the problems of government in a one-party state were perceived by the leaders of Tanzania, and in particular by the President and the Presidential Commission. The establishment of a Permanent Commission of Enquiry is another example which supports the view that the Tanzanian Government and party leaders have made conscious efforts to prevent the emergence of a self-perpetuating oligarchy, by a one-party system in which the government accepts certain controls over itself without equating control with opposition and opposition with treason.[97]

The nature and extent of the party's function as both a motor force and as a brake on government will depend as much on the central party organs as on the party organs in the regions, which in Tanzania show strength and vitality. President Nyerere perceived the importance of strengthening the grass roots. He relinquished his government leadership in January 1962 in order to reorganize and reorient the party for the new struggle for economic development, and he has constantly insisted on the need for the party to keep itself in touch with the grass-roots of the movement and the ordinary peasant.[98] This is further illustrated by the decision of the Tanzanian Government in 1966 to launch a university student service project designed to keep the new *élite* in touch with the general public and with the reality of the nation's life.

We must now turn to the structure of the Arab Socialist Union. It must be borne in mind that the structure of the Egyptian state after 1952 reflects the peculiar way in which it was created, which has an important bearing on the structure of the party. First of all, it was from the outset linked with Nasser and his military colleagues, who brought about the revolution. The membership of the Arab Socialist Union was envisaged as comprising the peasants, the armed forces, the workers, the intellectuals, and the national capitalists. As Nasser claimed, the organization of the Arab Socialist Union would bring to light a new vanguard – 'the nation has invested in me far greater authority than my functions as President of the Republic warrant. I shall put this authority at the service of this vanguard'. But what kind of vanguard was it?

As regards membership qualifications these corresponded roughly to universal suffrage: proof of citizenship, age limit (18), absence of criminal record, acceptance of the charter, and written application. The basic unit of the Union is the village or an equivalent grouping such as a factory. The next level is that of the town, district, or public corporation, composed of more than one basic unit. Then comes the level of *markaz* – a municipal and police unit. After that there is the county level, and finally the national level.

The basic units elect their councils. These basic units also send delegates to elect the members of the councils immediately above them. Similarly the *markaz* delegates elect the county councils.

The supreme organ of the Union is the General National Congress which consists of all members of the councils, right down to the basic unit. It has a six-year term and it meets once a year. The General National Congress elects a General Committee to carry out its work between its meetings. The General Committee in turn selects from among its members the Higher Executive Committee of not more than twenty-six persons.

There was also a Presidency Council which dealt with all matters pertaining to the power of the President of the Republic. Its members were chosen from the Higher Executive Committee of the Congress of the Arab Socialist Union. Nasser's comment on its function is significant, : 'I stated at the National Congress that we would apply the system of collective leadership. There will be a President of the Republic but meanwhile there will be a Presidency Council for all the functions included in the constitution. There will also be a Prime Minister, and a Council of Ministers. We shall all thus work in a collective system. . . . The Presidency Council will represent the supreme authority of the State. The executive council will represent the executive and administrative powers of the state.'[99]

He also explained that the creation of the Presidency Council, which was regarded as a voluntary limitation of his powers, was designed to relieve him of many administrative responsibilities of government and thus enable him to apply himself more fully to the establishment and proper functioning of the Arab Socialist Union.

This emphasis laid on 'party work' by President Nasser can be explained partly by the origin of the Nasserite revolution which needed popular legitimation; and partly by a desire to place the achievements of that revolution on a restructured political, social, and economic basis. The ideology of Arab Socialism was linked with this task. One may with advantage trace its development, in order to see its position and role in a proper perspective.

The power of a military régime cannot bear much fruit in terms of obtaining popular response and participation in economic and social development unless it is properly founded on such a base.

> The same arts that did gain
> A power, must it maintain[100]

This advice needs to be qualified in modern times, where the values of universal participation in government through a political party give the party specific legitimacy. The military régime cannot act as custodian of such legitimacy unless it makes genuine efforts to establish the party on a civilian base. Nor can the military rule as a caste, apart from the society in which it is engaged in politics, as we discuss below. The term 'politics' is here used in a wider sense, embracing the direction and supervision of public life and the interaction involved therein, and not merely in the limited sense of the activities geared to gaining or maintaining power.

The leaders of the Revolution of 1952 were initially faced with the task of the conquest and consolidation of power and the liberation of Egypt (a) from a much abused feudal régime and (b) from foreign domination. The first stage was achieved by 1956 and was influenced by these objectives.

Later, having achieved their first set of objectives, the leaders turned to the task of giving their political revolution an economic and social content. In a word, they began a search for a specific ideology. They introduced a series of measures which culminated in the nationalization decrees of the summer and autumn of 1961, as if testing the particular socialist ideology which they developed by stages. The year 1961 was marked also by a series of crises, including the break-up of the union with Syria. The civilian intellectuals of Egypt at the time seemed to have withdrawn their 'participation', refusing to provide the régime with its ideology.[101] The régime was therefore left to its own intellectual resources to rationalize the progress of the revolution, giving it specific ideology and direction.

Thus, in the spring of 1962, a conference that called itself the National Congress of the Popular Forces of Egypt met to deliberate on the National Charter, which was proclaimed in June of that year. The National Union, which had been formed previously as a makeshift body to rally support for the régime, was now dissolved and replaced by a new one – a party system. Thus the Arab Socialist Union was born.

Mohammed Hassanein Heikal, the editor of the semi-official daily, *Al-Ahram*, defined the role of the military within the framework of a 'new sociopolitical theory': the popular revolutionary movement can only lean on the army to reach the goal of the revolution. And again, echoing Nasser he wrote, 'We do not want politicians within the army. But the entire army constitutes a force within the national politics'.[102] This explains the comprehensive membership of the Arab Socialist Union including, as it does, the entire armed forces. The experiment is all the more fascinating because it is so unlike the majority of other cases in which a political party, headed by men who are also heads of the government, attempts to politicize the army. Here we have army leaders who have a monopoly of governmental power creating a political party which embraces the army. But the experiment had its peculiar precautionary devices: the Arab Socialist Union divided its military cadres into two categories:

(a) The officers who are involved actively in political life.
(b) The officers who continue their military careers.

The first category had to abandon their uniforms and all the prerogatives of military rank. On the other hand they were given key posts in the state apparatus: in the higher diplomatic service as presidents, directors, and members of the administrative councils of state organs, as ministers and under-secretaries of state; and as directors-general and directors of different ministries. They filled almost all the higher ranks, were made directors of the security services and were given a significant proportion of directive functions in cultural domains, in information, in the Press, radio and television. The second category remained in the army.

In this way the 'free officers' had control over the apparatus of government. The supreme organ of the state, the Presidency, was in the hands of one of them – albeit a universally accepted national figure. The key posts in the government, such as the Ministries of War, and of the Interior, were in their hands.

The government of Sikki Soliman, who was a colonel and engineer, contained four Vice-Presidents in the Council of Ministers, of whom three were high-ranking officers of the army (Abdel-Mohsen Aboul-Noun, Mahmoud Younes and Sarwat Okaska); the fourth, Dr. Mohmoud Fawzi (Foreign Affairs), though a civilian, was harnessed to a military man as the Minister of Foreign Affairs, i.e. Mahmoud Riad. Half the members of the Council of Ministers of the Soliman Government were high-ranking military officers. And, as already noted, through the first category of (former) army officers, all the centres of executive decision-making of any importance were controlled by the military.[103]

Nevertheless, the President of the Republic, though originally a 'free officer', became President by a popular mandate. Moreover, he is the President of the Arab Socialist Union, part of whose membership consisted of the army. Even though some key posts in this party are held by the military–political cadres (above all in the executive committee), the execution of the decisions made by the party leadership depends on the goodwill and co-operation of civilian cadres of activists and on the membership which it controls. The mere (mechanical) control of the instruments of power by former military cadres is not sufficient, if the Arab Socialist Union, as a party based on the people, is to have any meaning, and if the government is to secure popular response and participation in its programme of development.

Ultimately the success of the experiment will depend on how far the politico-military leaders will go in creating a genuine, popularly based, party which has effective means of action and control, to mobilize the people round an accepted leadership and government, and to exercise control over that government. The Arab Socialist Union is still a movement – a coalition of forces – and not a party. As Anour Abdel-Malek has put it: 'the popular masses in whose name actions are taken are outside the power of political decision'; and he adds that the resistance by the new class of politico-military technocrats is the source of the political problems of Egypt.

Some General Conclusions

This account of some of the political parties and their relation to the executive has been made on the basis of a belief that the cases discussed are representative. But it is realized that there are always local peculiarities which complicate the picture.[104] With this caveat, we must now generalize briefly on some of the problems which may arise in the system of a one-party state with a dominant executive. If it is true that the strong-executive presidential system of government has been harnessed in a one-party state, it is equally true that it is beset with problems. We can only outline some of the most important of them.

To begin with, in many cases the system was created for and by the national leaders who supposedly embodied the aspirations of their people. One result of this was that the party in some cases became an instrument of personal power in the hands of the leaders. The formal written texts of the constitutions which allocated powers and responsibilities were modified by the fact of the existence and the power-dynamics of the one-party system. Ghana, Malawi, and the Ivory Coast, are examples, as we have seen. It is conceivable that some aspects of this problem exist in all one-party systems, from the nature of things – the absence of opposition, the hierarchic and authoritative structure of the party, the monopoly of government-cum-party power of the leaders and so on.

There are other problems which are connected with this and which flow from it. They may be summed up in the words: popular response, participation, and control, in connection with government policy and action. The power of the state, great as it is, has its inherent limitations. The control of force, money, and jobs, is crucial as a factor in motivating people's conduct, but it is not sufficient to motivate them to required directions all the time or to the extent required. Even the best organized party machines are not in themselves enough. It is now apparent, for example, that popular participation in party activities is not as great as it was in pre-independence or immediately post-independence days. The most effective mass mobilizations in post-independence Africa have been in the states which were faced with the threat of a departing colonial power, as in Guinea and Mali. Admittedly in

Guinea and Mali the revolutionary mystique of the role of the masses and the Jacobin–Marxist tradition of the legitimacy of the 'convention' which the parties in those two countries inherited helped the emergence of strong mass parties.

But the revolutionary *élan* of a party normally weakens with the achievement of some of the initial objectives – be it the removal of the foreign threat or other more positive aims. This may be expected to happen in these countries unless drastic measures are taken that can engage the energies, interest, and support of the masses, and the party is revitalized as a key centre of decision-making.

The initial enthusiasm for participation in mass movements cannot be maintained at the same level for long periods. For one thing, people's private lives make prior demands on their time and energy. This is true at the level of the party leaders and activists. Indeed, in their case, it is not their private lives alone, but government work that may make prior claims. In the post-independence period most governments needed all the qualified men they could muster. The parties inevitably suffered as the governments took the cream of their leadership. Government work precludes full-time party work, so that even though these former party cadres may still be members, the party work has to be carried out by other members of lesser prestige.

The proper test of an organization is its responsiveness to the needs of the members, and the degree to which those involved in it actually and directly participate in decision-making. The two are related; the behaviour of the leadership in relation to popular needs and desires determines the nature and degree of popular responsiveness to government policy and action. The continued experimentation in Tanzania indicates that this is possible within the one party, with the important proviso that the leaders must not only be devoted to encouraging participation, but must be seen to be doing so. There also must evolve rules and institutional devices for nurturing the control of the executive by the party.

In this connection the example of the Arusha Declaration and the rules restricting the ownership rights of TANU leaders is a salutary one, and worthy of imitation elsewhere in Africa. A respected leadership can obtain a popular response very easily. And a responsive public, willingly participating, is an essential instrument in the implementation of plans. Popular participation, organized through the mechanism of a well-structured party, is also an effective means of ensuring control. The exercise of governmental power in a development context can thus be more effective when the chief executive is at the same time the chief of the party and in a position to set the party machine in motion for such participation.

What of the control over governments? A system of one-party government is most likely to succeed in serving a useful purpose in the long run only if it is subjected to proper controls. Traditionally, in Western systems, control over the executive has come from two spheres: the legislature and the judiciary. The doctrine of the separation of powers was the source of this.

Legally, control means the power to supervise the exercise of certain functions within a given situation as defined by law; its operation is restricted. Politically, Parliament could bring pressure to bear on the government either in relation to the totality of its policy or on certain specific actions. In Africa, the scope of both these means of control is restricted, if not non-existent. Parliamentary control can indeed be exerted through budgetary means and through a debate on the best means of implementing certain proposed policies, but the control of the executive in Africa must be sought elsewhere.[105]

In the one-party state it must be sought within the party itself. But is this possible? In this connection two facts must be reiterated: (i) the best among the militants of the party are in the government, and (ii) the top leadership of the party and government are the same people. This tends to subordinate party to government; and, in terms of the potentialities of the party for control this trend has not been encouraging. In the absence of properly developed institutions and practices to that effect, a great deal must depend on the integrity and foresight of the leaders. Mali was an exception in having a majority of members of the party Political Bureau who were not members of the government. In the other cases, even where the notion of 'self-criticism' is advocated, it cannot exercise an effective controlling function in the absence of a body of people who are placed institutionally in a position where they can pass objective judgements on the government as frequently as possible. The party congress meets too infrequently to fulfil this purpose, and is too unwieldy. It is the Political Bureau (or Executive Committee) of the party which must therefore do this.

The Tanzanian leaders have shown an awareness of the dangers of the one-party system. The relationship of the TANU National Executive Committee to the National Assembly and their defined roles are signs that a controlling role is envisaged for the party.

One of the terms of reference which President Nyerere gave the Presidential Commission on the establishment of a democratic one-party state was the following:

What should be the organs of the party through which –
(a) National policy is formulated.
(b) The people's will constantly finds expression.
(c) Changes can be brought about through peaceful means.
(d) Corruption or abuse of power overcome?[104]

It is clear that in Tanzania the answer has been to make the party an organ of control as well as of policy formulation. One of the practical applications of the self-examination to which the Tanzanian leaders have subjected themselves is the novel electoral practice in which two members of TANU contest an election in the same constituency.[105] If one can rely on historical precedents it is possible that other African states will adopt similar attitudes in order to revitalize the single party, particularly in view of the shadow of the *coup d'état.*

It must also be remembered that in the circumstances of the strong neo-presidential systems of Africa, the President can share a 'confessional' role with the party, as its head. He cannot do this on the basis of a claim to a monopoly of ideological 'truth', if the one party is to be 'democratic'. He can do it as the nation's leader. He is Head of State and party chief as well as chief executive. As Head of State he embodies the national will, and as party chief he has a party machine at his disposal to activate that will.

Constitutionally he has the power to initiate policy and to propose laws to render the policies concrete. But his national and party leadership charge him with a responsibility to subject government policy and action to some necessary questioning. The party National Bureau, of which he is President, even when it consists of a majority of ministers, can afford him a legitimate and effective forum to do this. At the same time a wise leadership would pay due attention to the establishment and development of an independent mechanism of control. Tanzania's Permanent Commission of Enquiry is one such mechanism which may prove that a conscious attempt has been made which may spur other or complementary experiments. It is on such conscious self-examination that the success of the one-party system may depend.

NOTES

1. Art. 7.
2. Aristide Zolberg, *One-party Government in the Ivory Coast*, Princeton U.P., 1964, pp. 261–3; cf. also Law pp. 59–118, *Journal Officiel*, 1 Sept. 1959, Arts. 1, 2 and 7 cited therein.
3. cf. Seydou Madani Sy, *Recherches sur l'exercice du pouvoir politique en Afrique Noire*, Paris, 1965, p. 144.
4. e.g. (1) Ruth Schachter, 'Single-party systems in West Africa', *American Political Science Review* 55 (June 1961) pp. 297–307; (2) Marilin Kilson, 'Authoritarianism and single-party tendencies in African politics', *World Politics* 15 (Jan. 1963) pp. 262–94; (3) Immanuel Wallerstein, *Africa: The Politics of Independence*, New York, Random House, 1961, pp. 85–102, 163–67; (4) Frank G. Snyder, *One-party government in Mali* (Yale U.P. 1965); (5) John A. Ballard, 'The Evolution of Single-party systems in French Equatorial Africa' – Institute of African Studies, University of Ife, Ibadan Branch, Ibadan – Seminar paper 1963/64/8.
5. e.g. Ruth Schachter, op. cit. On African political parties in general, cf. Thomas Hodgkin, *African Political Parties*, Penguin, Harmondsworth, 1960.
6. e.g. M. Kilson, op. cit.
7. e.g. I. Wallerstein, op. cit.
8. The constitutional talks held in London in the autumn of 1963, on the eve of independence were marked by such divergence of views; and the constitution worked out at that conference contained some of the most elaborately cumbersome provisions on 'regional' and 'minority' rights. The KANU government substantially modified these after independence. President Kenyatta, expressing satisfaction on this matter, said: 'Our greatest triumph as a party and as a nation came with the voluntary dissolution of KADU'; *East African Standard* 12 March 1966.
9. e.g. Congo, Gabon, and Chad, cf. J. A. Ballard, op. cit., p. 2.
10. *Annual Report of the African Bureau* (London), April 1962–March 1963, pp. 5–6.
11. cf. *Encounter*, August 1965, p. 3 and December 1965, p. 51, 'Beyond African Dictatorship'; cf. also Arthur Lewis, *Politics in West Africa*, London 1965, pp. 17–63.
12. cf. Julius K. Nyerere, *Democracy and the Party System*, Dar-es-Salaam, 1962.
13. cf. Nyerere, op. cit., pp. 4–5.
14. ibid.
15. ibid.
16. For a theoretical justification of the one-party systems along Marxist lines cf. Madeira Keita, 'Le Parti Unique, en Afrique Noire', *Présence Africaine*, XXX (February–March 1960) pp. 3–27.
17. cf. A. Zolberg, op. cit., p. 264, and also footnote 48 on p. 264.
18. cf. Clark Kerr, *Unions and Union Leaders of their own choosing*, Centre for the study of Democratic Institutions, Santa Barbara, California, p. 12.
19. Jomo Kenyatta, op. cit.

20. e.g. the assassination attempts on Nkrumah in 1962.
21. cf. Colin Legum, 'Is Africa falling apart', *Observer*, 27 February 1966.
22. An interview with some Guinea officials has revealed to me that President Sékou Touré used the party organization to secure the consent of the party when he decided to invite Kwame Nkrumah to share the headship of the Guinea state.
23. cf. V. W. Turner's definition of ritual as a mechanism which periodically converts the obligatory into the desirable: in *Closed Systems and Open Minds*, p. 32.
24. cf. Seydou Madani Sy, op. cit., pp. 167–202.
25. Sy, op. cit., p. 148; cf. also generally Thomas Hodgkin, op. cit.
26. His policy was in harmony with that of France.
27. cf. Millicent, 'Forces et idées forces . . .' p. 56 cited by Sy, op. cit., p. 147.
28. cf. Sy, op. cit., p. 148.
29. cf. Ph. Yace (Secretary-General of P.D.C.I.) in *Fraternité*, No. 119, August 1961, p. 7.
30. President Sékou Touré is the Secretary-General.
31. One of the six must be a woman. The national Bureau must also have at least two women members. cf. Sy, op. cit., pp. 156–7.
32. cf. Art. b. statutes.
33. cf. Internal regulation of the party, Travaux du VIe congrès de l'U.S.R.D.A. p. 2.
34. In the Sixth Congress it was the political secretary, Mr. Idrissa Diarra, who presented the main report. cf. VIe Congrès de l'U.S.R.D.A. Bamaka, les 10–12 Septembre 1962, pp. 13–140.
35. cf. Sy, op. cit., pp. 264–5.
36. cf. A. Zolberg, op. cit., p. 151.
37. cf. Sy, op. cit., p. 170.
38. cf. A. Zolberg, op. cit., pp. 272–4.
39. Gonidec quoted by Sy, op. cit., p. 111.
40. cf. *Fraternité* No. 87, 16 December 1960, p. 2.
41. cf. Sy, op. cit., p. 165.
42. The Congress passes resolutions on the basis of propositions contained in the report presented by the Secretary-General, who, as chief executive, would give a government orientation to his report – cf. Sékou Touré, *'La Révolution Guinéenne et le progrès social'*, VI (edition special) Conakry s.d. (1963).
43. op. cit.
44. Report to the Fifth Congress, p. 1.
45. The Presidents of the technical commissions in 1965 were all cabinet ministers.
46. This post was for many years occupied by Mr. Leon Maka who was the President of the National Assembly. The relation of the executive, the party and Parliament was thus neatly tied up under the control of the Secretary-General.
47. cf. Horoya, No. 296, 10 August 1963, p. 1; cf. also Sy, op. cit., p. 179.
48. cf. VIe Congrès de l'U.S.R.D.A., 'Résolution économique et sociale' in *l'Essor* No. 170, September 1962, pp. 1–3.
49. In Guinea, the Political Bureau, by contrast, is largely dominated by members of the government.

50. cf. Sy, op. cit., pp. 190–1.
51. As No. 31 P.G.R.M. cf. Sy, op. cit., pp. 191–2.
52. cf. Sy, op. cit., pp. 193–4.
53. cf. Sy, op. cit., pp. 180–1, 194.
54. *Ghana Government White Paper on Regional Constitutional Commission*, 1958.
55. cf. Dennis Austin, *Politics in Ghana, 1946–1960*, London and New York, O.U.P. 1964, p. 364.
56. cf. Henry L. Bretton, *The Rise and Fall of Kwame Nkrumah – A Study of Personal Rule in Africa*, Pall Mall Press, London 1967, p. 46.
57. ibid. This assertion is not elucidated by illustrations.
58. cf. H. Chipembere, 'Dr. Banda's Opposition in Exile', *The Guardian*, 7 July 1966. 'I was myself an enthusiastic advocate of it (one-party government) until two years ago, when as a result of experience within Malawi and observations of trends in other African states the system's susceptibility to abuse became clear.' The author was a minister in Dr. Banda's cabinet until 1965.
59. This consists of green-shirted youths who form a movement that was originally modelled on the youth movement of Ghana, also known as Young Pioneers and associated with the C.P.P.
60. In 1966 there were 1,163 trained Young Pioneers, cf. *Yorkshire Post*, 6 January 1966.
61. *South African Financial Gazette*, 3 June 1966. This paper describes Banda as 'Realist Banda'.
62. R. B. Fitch and M. Oppenheimer, *Ghana: End of an illusion*, Monthly Review Press, New York and London, 1966, p. 73.
63. ibid., p. 77.
64. cf. Dennis Austin, op. cit., p. 335.
65. Their marches and rallies, which numbered tens of thousands, apparently gave a shock to the government and forced C.P.P. ministers to drive their cars down the side streets of Accra; cf. Fitch and Oppenheimer, op. cit., p. 79.
66. ibid.
67. Clause 2, Section 1 of the Preventive Detention Act, 1958.
68. Under it the executive could remove from circulation without publicity any person regarded as being a threat to the 'security of the state'. It has been claimed that up to 2,000 people were detained between 1957 and 1966.
69. cf. H. L. Bretton, op. cit., p. 48.
70. cf. Chapter 8 on the Ghana coup.
71. cf. *Report of the presidential commission on the establishment of a democratic one-party state*, Dar-es-Salaam, 1965.
72. The Commission acknowledges the usefulness of this report, cf. p. 7.
73. Report of the Commission, op. cit., p. 15.
74. cf. Chapter 8 below.
75. cf. Mohamed Ali Rifaat, 'The Egyptian Experiment', 15 December, Paper 33rd Study Session – International Institute of Differing Civilisations – Palermo 23–27 September 1963, p. 3.
76. cf. J. K. Nyerere, op. cit., pp. 24–5.
77. cf. Statuts de *L'Union Progressiste Sénégalaise*, Article 5, *Societé communautaire*.

78. Habib Bourguiba, 'The Tunisian way', *Foreign Affairs*, April 1966, pp. 480–8.
79. 'The Arusha Declaration and TANU's policy on socialism and self-reliance', Dar-es-Salaam, 1967, Part 4.
80. ibid.
81. ibid., Part 5.C.
82. ibid., Part 5.A.
83. ibid.
84. ibid., Part 2(a), (d).
85. cf. J. P. W. B. McAuslan and Y. P. Ghai, 'Constitutional Innovation and Political Stability in Tanzania: A Preliminary Assessment'. *Journal of Modern African Studies 4*, 4 (1–1967) pp. 497–515.
86. TANU Const. E.2.
87. Its membership is estimated as between 400 and 450 persons, cf. McAuslan *et al.*, op. cit.
88. cf. Report of Commission, op. cit., p. 29.
89. ibid.
90. op. cit., p. 16.
91. ibid. (italics supplied).
92. cf. TANU Const. E.5, 7, 36.
93. cf. McAuslan *et al.*, op. cit., p. 485.
94. Regional secretaries are *ex officio* members of the N.E.C.
95. cf. The Report of Commission, op. cit., p. 25.
96. It is hoped that the 1972 decentralization decisions will ensure this.
97. cf. McAuslan *et al.*, op. cit.
98. ibid.
99. cf. Mohamed Ali Rifaat, op. cit., p. 9.
100. Andrew Marvell, 'An Horatian Ode upon Cromwell's Return from Ireland'.
101. cf. Anouar Abdel Malek, 'Le rôle de l'armée dans la vie politique', in R. All, '*Revue française d'études politiques africaines*', February 1967, No. 14, pp. 58–73.
102. *Al-Ahram*, 23–27 July 1962.
103. A. A. Malek, op. cit., pp. 69–70.
104. The focus is on the neo-presidential régimes. The role of parties in other régimes has been touched upon in the appropriate chapters.
105. On the various possible means of control in the Tanzanian one-party state cf. McAuslan *et al.*, op. cit.; cf. also Wjatz and Prezeworski – 'Control without opposition', in Vol. I of *Government and Opposition*, January 1966, pp. 227–39.
106. Report of Commission, op. cit., p. 4.
107. The election following the electoral change produced some startling results; one important cabinet minister, Mr. Bomani, the then Minister of Commerce, was defeated along with several junior ministers.

6

The Role of the Civil Service
in Neo-Presidentialism

A. The Nature and Role of the Civil Service

The civil service is part of the executive. A common definition of
the civil service derived from metropolitan models is that it is a
service comprising all servants of the state, other than holders of
political or judicial offices, who are employed in a civil capacity and
whose remuneration is paid out of moneys voted by Parliament.[1]

> A. L. Adu, following the spirit of this definition, has written:
> as a servant of the State the civil servant's first loyalty is to the
> State. Since the government is charged by popular choice with
> the control and administration of the affairs of the state the
> civil servant's loyalty is to the government of the day and he
> should appropriately feel a positive and consistent responsibility
> to prosecute the interests of the government as his employer.
> Usually the focal point of the civil servant's loyalty is the head
> of the state.[2]

Clearly, the role of the servant, here expressed, was conceived in
the context of a two-party or multi-party system of the metropolitan kind. The use of the phrase 'the government of the day' alone
suggests this. Yet, at the time of the publication of A. L. Adu's
book, the one-party state was already almost universal in Africa.
Although reading of his book reveals that he was aware of this,
he did not redefine the peculiar role of the civil service in neo-
presidential systems.

In Tanzania, the presidential commission on the establishment of a democratic one-party state had reported in the same year. Its recommendation on the civil service reflects the approach of most African states and is, therefore, worth quoting once more. It reported:

> The political neutrality of civil servants and members of the military and para-military forces is no doubt an essential feature of any system in which more than one political party is allowed. In a one-party state, however, the idea of political neutrality has no meaning and only serves to exclude a substantial group of sensible and patriotic citizens from participating in public affairs.[3]

President Nyerere had written in a similar vein earlier. In his view also the logic of the one-party state makes it absurd to exclude 'a whole group of most intelligent and able members of the community from participating in the discussion of policy simply because they happen to be civil servants'.[4] This view is shared by most African leaders.

THE CIVIL SERVICE UNDER THE COLONIAL SYSTEM

In the colonial situation, the role of the civil servant as administrator was important in at least two respects: (i) he was instrumental in carrying out the centrally directed colonial policy and the executive decisions made under it; and (ii) he was also important in helping the formulation or revision of that policy. The second role was crucial during the early period of colonial rule when there was comparatively little information on local conditions, and the district officer or the *commandant de cercle* was a pioneer researcher, occasionally preceded only by missionaries. To the local inhabitants he was the obvious symbol of the colonial power.[5] He was part of the colonial civil service along with the higher officers of that service.[6]

The structure of the colonial civil service had two central features. Firstly, it was hierarchically organized with some room for the ventilation of popular opinion or grievances, but *not for popular control*. Everyone was appointed by a higher authority over whom the African people had no control or influence. Therefore the power of the District Officer was absolute in the eyes of the local population. He, and the colonial civil service of which he was a part, was the government.

Secondly, the structure was based on paternalism and a degree of decentralized authority which left much discretion and initiative to the District Officer. At the top, in the colonial capital, there was the Governor and his secretariat. The District Officer was generally responsible for maintaining law and order and was the representative of the government, with co-ordinating functions in relation to the field representatives of technical departments in his province or district. He also had either judicial power or the duty of inspecting 'native courts'.

Again, at the apex, the role of the top civil servant (the Principal Secretary, sometimes called the Colonial Secretary) was not seen as purely administrative. The Colonial Secretary, the Governor's principal assistant, in the early days transacted business by corresponding with the District Officers or Residents. With the increase of economic and social activities, a Financial Secretary was added, and the two, together with other departmental heads, would sit in the Governor's Executive Council and in the Legislative Council to discuss and formulate policy.

In some territories civil servants were even appointed as 'ministers' responsible for the supervision of departments and for answering questions about their activities in the Legislative Assembly. And in the last days before independence African (non-official) members were appointed as ministers, while civil servants responsible to them became Permanent Secretaries.

The history of the civil service during the colonial period is as important in explaining the attitude of Africans to its role as are the exigencies which created the one-party state. It has been said, with reason, that the executive nature of the colonial civil service made its Africanization, and in particular the Africanization of the higher posts, an attractive symbol of status.[7] This is the 'status-symbol' argument, but it is by no means the only important one. Africans had lived under the impact of decisions of District Officers and Colonial Secretaries which had deeply affected their lives. Any demand for political rights therefore necessarily involved a demand for the Africanization of the civil service. This coincided with the material and other allurements which the administrative services had for prospective candidates, thus whetting personal as much as political appetites.[8]

B. Africanization of the Civil Service

The advocacy of a policy of Africanization of the colonial civil service was started some years before the independence movements got under way. Initially colonial educational policy did not have room for a planned African take-over of the civil service, any more than it had a calendar for African political independence.[9] Eventually the policy changed, and more attention was paid to the training of Africans for responsible posts in the administration. But the delayed start meant that for several years after independence many key posts were to remain in expatriate hands. Africanization as a policy of replacement of expatriate officers involved a heavy financial burden in training administrative and technical staff.

The shortage of qualified manpower was acute in some states. In Malawi, for example, the government service required some 430 officers with university degrees or professional qualifications, and only thirty-three Malawians had such qualifications in 1960, with some more in training, most of whom have since assumed posts. It was estimated that only 120 would be available by 1971, at the rate of educational progress of the time.[10] Nor was Malawi an exception, though the magnitude of its qualified manpower shortage is not representative of the majority of African states.

Ghana, in 1958, still had thirty-one per cent expatriates in its civil service. This represented a rapid decrease in the proportion since 1952.[11] Even so, it was a slow process when seen against the pressure for rapid Africanization.

The colonial educational policy had been geared to a different administration, an administration which was primarily concerned with the maintenance of law and order. The 'successors', however, would spend most of their time in administering development programmes which in many respects required a different type of educational background and training. As it has been maintained elsewhere, 'the objective of the former colonial service was to provide good government rather than exciting government. It brought integrity and impartiality, efficiency and loyalty to the tasks of preserving law and order and obviating disorder. But to meet the exciting – if somewhat impracticable [sic] – aspirations of the new African ministers a completely different and more dynamic outlook was called for.'[12]

Nevertheless, educational policies with standards and other requirements taken over from the metropolitan universities were adopted by the new colleges which sprouted in various parts of Africa. Those Africans who were trained abroad may be presumed to have imbibed the spirit of the university education they received in the metropolitan universities. One of the results of adopting or following the requirements of the Universities of

London or Paris, for example, was that far fewer graduates were forthcoming to meet demands. It was with this in mind that the Adu Committee on the localization of the Malawi civil service recommended that Malawians should not be expected to pass the standard of examination set by the British.[13] The general feeling was that there was too much emphasis on literary subjects, too little on technical subjects.[14]

The criticism of the heritage of an inappropriate education policy is not limited to Anglophone Africa; the French heritage was subjected to similar criticism by African leaders and by some Frenchmen. President Sékou Touré, for example, complained that too much emphasis was placed on formal education and diplomas.[15] The top officials in the French colonial civil service, who could be posted in any French territory, were required to have a university degree. The middle group, who could be posted to any one of the territories under one administrative group (e.g. A.O.F., A.F.F.) were required to have secondary education. The last group, those in the local cadre, who could only be employed within one territory, had primary education. But French colonial educational policy had been such that by 1954 there were only 88 Africans out of 1,327 civil servants of the middle categories in the A.E.F. group of territories.[16]

The École William Ponty near Dakar produced teachers and some doctors, many of whom were to be the leaders of the political parties and to emerge as heads of the new states.[17] Many Members of Parliament and local assemblies are also former teachers. In this respect the French policy of permitting civil servants to be eligible for election produced some interesting results. The exodus of former African teachers and medical officers from the civil service to take part in politics just before independence, had an impact on the civil service itself and its position in government. The newly elected African deputies made their influence felt both on the educational system and on the position of Africans in the government services. They demanded equal status for Africans and Frenchmen in these services, and they spoke with the authority of experience.[18]

As for the ex-Belgian territories, the Congo tragedy would probably have been averted were it not for the Belgian educational policy, and the policy of decolonization, which came too late. Programmes of Africanization started only eighteen months before independence, and there were only three university graduates when independence was declared.[19]

POLITICIZATION OF THE CIVIL SERVICE

The Africanization of the civil service was connected with its politicization in one important respect. The accelerated replacement of expatriate civil servants by Africans was accompanied by an identification, on the part of these African civil servants, with the political ideas and sentiments of the nationalist movement, which voiced the needs and aspirations of the masses. This in turn affected the structure and function of the civil service and the minister–civil service relationship. The colonial pattern of the Governor and his secretariat sitting at the apex of the administration was replaced by a ministerial system with a cabinet co-ordinating the various ministries headed by ministers.[20]

In short, the civil service changed from being the main machinery of colonial government to being the executive arm of responsible government. The senior civil servants became the administrative staff of ministries charged with advising and assisting ministers in carrying out their responsibilities.

This constituted a fundamental change in the nature of the civil service – its responsibilities and tenure, in particular. The civil servants serving the ministers became answerable to them and came under their general administrative control. Above all it meant a change of attitude on the part of the civil servant as to the nature of his function – a change from the bureaucrat's faith in his patriarchal vocation to direct the destinies of politically 'immature' or 'incompetent' people to an acceptance of the popular will as represented by an elected government and as interpreted by the minister concerned.

This did not mean that civil servants in the new system were not involved in the formulation of policy. Indeed one of the features of politicization in the new systems under one-party governments is the fact that civil servants can be members of the party and through their membership influence or help to formulate policy. As the recommendations on this subject of the Presidential Commission of Tanzania put it, the idea of political neutrality in a one-party system is meaningless. In reality, of course, the colonial civil servants were not unfamiliar with one-party government; was not the colonial régime an ever-present one-party government, after all? The difference lies in the basis of the government, in the direction and orientation of policy, and in the allocation of resources. Also, now there was the party man, who, as Milton Obote put it, was ready to bring the grievances of the people before the administrator, who must show a greater awareness of them.[21]

Under the French system there has been less emphasis in the division between the civil service and 'political' office. No Public Service Commissions existed in the French colonial civil service. In the former British territories, on the other hand, Public Service Commissions had been established to undertake recruitment to the government services and to advise on promotion. With the grant of internal self-government the commissions suddenly acquired a more executive character. The object of this change, as it had been pointed by R. Symonds, was 'to protect the position of British civil servants against the African ministers'.[22] But this eleventh-hour attempt at complete insulation of the civil service was counter-productive. For one thing, it placed what was sometimes construed as an 'insulting limitation' on the authority of the new African Prime Minister, thus causing much irritation. Then again, when considered against its colonial background and the new tasks which the African governments set for themselves, it was bound to be regarded as an impediment. So, in most cases, the function of the commissions in respect of the appointment of the most senior civil servants was put on an advisory footing again after independence. And even in cases where the commission was required to be consulted by the executive on the appointment of Permanent Secretaries, as was the case in Kenya, its members learnt only through the radio on independence day that the expatriates had been replaced in those posts. Again in Malawi, the first candidates selected for training as administrative officers were chosen not by the public service commission but by a committee of ministers.[23]

This was quite understandable in view of the temper of African politics around independence days. But, as matters stood, there was the problem of replacement and the lurking fear that there might be disruption of government work in case of mass withdrawal of expatriate civil servants who disagreed with some of the government policies. The experience of Guinea and Mali was instructive. The complete withdrawal of French administrative and technical aid from these two countries affected the economic and social development plans of their governments. These and other political factors compelled a reappraisal of the role of the civil service and its relation to the party and the government.

C. The Civil Service within the Machinery of Government

The civil service, as part of the executive branch of government, operates to implement policies. The effectiveness of the government, therefore, largely depends on its proper functioning. This means a proper orientation, that is to say, being in tune with the policy of the government, and it means efficiency, and what A. L. Adu has called 'ability to respond in practical terms to its (the government's) policy decisions'.[24] What does all this mean in practice?

First of all it must be remembered that the civil service consists of administrative and technical experts – of economists, statisticians, agronomists, engineers, public administrators, accountants, health officers, etc. The expertise of these people and the experience of many among them makes them indispensable instruments of policy. It also means that they participate in devising policy. The policy of a party (any party) as expressed by its Congresses, and National Executive Committees (or Bureaux) can only be expressed in generalized forms, on certain fundamentals, some of which also need the help of 'experts' to formulate them.[25] When one is considering the detailed technicalities and the implications involved it is the 'experts' who decide.[26] 'Policy decisions' made to the exclusion of such people are amateurish at best and shots in the dark at worst. At all events, 'policy' should not be taken to mean only that which is formulated or which is in the party resolution, or in the statute book. Every administrative act worth its name involves a policy decision. Ultimately, therefore, administrative decisions concern policy.

It is no wonder, then, that the reputation or fate of a government may depend on the performance of the civil service. This explains the sensitivity of African governments to the attitude of civil servants towards their régimes, and their concern to ensure that attitudes and orientations in the civil service are in accord with the philosophy underlying the government's policies. It also explains and justifies the need for executive control over the appointment of senior civil servants. As stated previously, the chief executive appoints senior civil servants, in most cases on his own initiative and without any requirement of mandatory consultation.

The Public Service Commissions have reverted to their

pre-independence advisory character, and with good reason. The senior civil servants are the ministers' principal assistants in directing and supervising the implementation of policy. This, as we have said, necessarily involves them in sharing 'policy decisions'. This is not peculiar to Africa. It is a matter for reflection, for instance, that the Royal Commission on the British Civil Service (1929/31) defined 'administrative work' as 'that which is concerned with policy, with the revision of existing practice or current regulations and decisions and with the general administration and control of the departments of the public service'.

This is not particularly remarkable for those who know the ins and outs of the 'corridors of power' of Whitehall. But to the enthusiasts of the 'apolitical' civil service it serves as a reminder that in practice minister and civil servant work hand in hand as part of an integral machine, even in a two-party system. The Queen's Government could not go on otherwise.

1. THE SENIOR POSTS

The highest post in the civil service in most Anglophone states is that of the secretary to the cabinet who is head of the civil service. He is sometimes called the chief secretary to the President or Prime Minister, as the case may be. The rough equivalent in Francophone African states is the *secrétaire-général du gouvernement*, who is directly responsible to the President.

Such a special functional relationship with the President seems to be dictated by the nature of neo-presidentialism. Both the secretary to the cabinet and his Francophone equivalent supervise the cabinet secretariat and are in charge of the preparation and timely transmission of the agenda to ministers, as part of their function. In general the President of the Republic is loath to go over the heads of his ministers to consult with civil servants. But the secretary to the cabinet (or the Secretary-General of the government) is there partly to act as a point of contact with the civil service. It is also interesting that in some Francophone states such as the Congo he must be a member of the party.[27] In some states, such as Tanzania and Congo, the present secretary to the cabinet is a member of the National Executive Committee of the party (and also of Parliament in the case of Tanzania).

The secretary of the cabinet occupies a central position in the minister–civil servant relation. His work as head of the cabinet secretariat and as head of the civil service, which involves him, among other things, in attendance at cabinet meetings, provides the key to the machinery of co-ordination and consultation which is so essential in government. He is the custodian of cabinet records, which contain important decisions and serve as a personal reminder to the President, who must follow up decisions and see to their implementation. His function of drawing up the agenda gives the cabinet secretary initiative for choosing priorities, the importance of which he is in a position to impress upon the President, e.g. proposals for legislation to be discussed, which his office helps to prepare and circulate in advance. The legislative activities of the ministers are thus indirectly controlled by such initiative, and in the ministers' jockeying for a place on the agenda, the President's decision can lean heavily on the impartial position of the Secretary-General of the government, thus making the ministers dependent on the latter, which lends weight to the office.

The cabinet secretary can provide continuity in cabinet procedures and practice within the limits of whatever change of general policy might be introduced by new ministers. If he is a member of the party's Executive Committee he can also create patterns of relationship between party policy, government decision, and consistent administrative action through the civil service, in order to carry out the policy and decision. In this capacity he would, of course, be acting under the general direction of the President of the Republic whose constitutional position requires him to undertake such supervision. But the harmony which must exist between party policy, government decision, and administrative action, can be maintained to a large extent through the good offices of the cabinet secretary.

The development of such a harmonious relationship, or of a set of consistent practices on such matters, is, of course, not in itself evidence of efficiency. The functional significance of such patterns of relationships, in a developmental context, depends on other factors as well. It depends, for instance, on the effective demands which are made on those involved in the relationship and in particular on the cabinet and the civil service. Such demands can be made by the President as a Head of State, by the party and by the Parliament. The response to such demands may be reviewed or decided upon by the cabinet or the President as chief executive. If the question concerns some financial, economic, or social project, normally the cabinet has inter-ministerial committees to deal with details of a decision made by the cabinet. Such committees, which depend on informal personal relationships, have proved to

H

be effective in carrying out policy or in preparing one. But cabinet or cabinet-committee effectiveness will depend on sub-cabinet administrative efficiency. It also depends on clearly defined departmental functions and consistent practices built on these functions. This is the more necessary in states where frequent cabinet reshuffles occur.

Each minister is assisted by the next most senior civil servant, namely the Permanent Secretary (sometimes called principal secretary). Each Permanent Secretary of a ministry is responsible for advising the minister on departmental policy, for ensuring the implementation of such policies and for personally administering the services of the ministry on behalf of the minister. He is generally responsible to the public accounts committee of Parliament for ensuring that the expenditure under the votes of the ministry is incurred in accordance with standing instructions and with the legislation on appropriations. The staff of the ministry under the Permanent Secretary are: one or more deputy permanent secretaries, other senior administrative officers usually with the rank of 'under-secretary', principal assistant secretary, and assistant secretary.[28] Then there are the usual supporting junior executives, clerical, secretarial and subordinate staff.

In Francophone African states the civil servant at the level of the Permanent Secretary performs similar functions. The general practice is to have two such persons: (i) the *directeur du cabinet* who is in charge of general policy matters concerning the ministry; and (ii) the *chef du cabinet* in charge of administrative matters, including questions on personnel and accounts.[29] They have under them similar supporting staff.

Normally each ministry is organized into functional divisions and sections to handle subjects covering the departments under the ministry with a view to administering the ministry with maximum economy and efficiency. The volume of work determines the numbers of each rank of civil servant employed in each ministry, though this has not prevented a Parkinsonian proliferation of positions.[30]

The Permanent Secretary, as administrative head of the ministry, co-ordinates all the divisions within it. He is responsible for seeing that all the professional, technical, and administrative skill is put to best use in a co-ordinated manner at the stages both of deliberation on policy and of implementation. He must devise mechanisms for consultation and processing opinions for the purpose of making integrated proposals of policy ready for decision or action by the minister. He must also direct and control, with skill and diplomacy, all direct access by other top civil servants to the minister for advice, when there is a need for this. Such direct communication with the minister is always essential in order to ensure the best first-hand professional and technical advice. But it can also be overdone, causing a waste of time, and the skill and judgement of the Permanent Secretary is required to ensure proper use of it. As a general rule, however, the minister's door must be kept open to top professional and technical advisers or heads of departments, for otherwise resentment may be caused which could affect efficiency and good will.[31]

It must also be said that machinery for consultation is not limited to each ministry. There are many instances of inter-departmental *ad hoc* committees consisting of the permanent secretaries of various ministries. The operation is informal and often cordial, and therefore likely to increase co-ordination of decision and implementation of policy and thus avoid waste or duplication. Such machinery for co-ordination at sub-cabinet level, apart from its obvious advantages, can also strengthen the civil service as a unified apparatus of the government, with a permanent head.

2. RECRUITMENT AND TERMS OF SERVICE

An efficient civil service depends on the quality of its members. This in turn depends on certain conditions, the most important of which is that there must be certain objective criteria, which determine recruitment to and advancement in the service. There must be fixed and easily ascertainable rules for the selection, appointment, promotion, discipline, and retirement, of civil servants. This ensures the attraction of talent and the efficiency as well as the stability of the service. Individual merit and public interest should at all times prevail and external influence, patronage, and nepotism, should be eliminated.

The normal machinery which has been adopted to fulfil this task is the Public Service Commission, called Civil Service Commission in some states.[32] The Commission is charged with the responsibility for advising (in most cases) on the appointment of the higher ranks of the civil service, and for making appointments and transfers, and taking disciplinary action concerning civil servants below the rank of permanent secretary. The Commission usually acts in consultation with the head of the ministry in respect of the higher posts. It is also normal practice for the Commission to delegate power to the heads of the ministries in respect of the lower posts. In the early days, when the commission was vested with executive powers, some confusion and delay was caused in many cases. The delegation of power to the heads of ministries was therefore considered to be a necessary step to obviate such difficulties. This resulted partly in a certain amount of disappointment with an institution which many were trained to see as a guarantee against possible arbitrariness. But there can be no doubt that some delegation of power was necessary.[33]

The possibility of arbitrary decision may be met by certain institutional safeguards with built-in mechanisms which operate more or less automatically and thus inhibit or minimize arbitrariness. For example, Article 23 of the Ivory Coast Civil Service Law provides that each year all civil servants must obtain a numbered card followed by a general appraisal indicating a professional evaluation. This makes external influence or manipulation somewhat difficult, and may perhaps be regarded as a sort of mechanical compensation for the absence of a public service commission. There are, of course, personnel committees in each ministry or department that must give their opinion on the annual list of proposals for promotion which is prepared by each division of the ministry.[34]

The status of the Public Service Commissions sometimes varies. In Ghana (under the Nkrumahist Constitution) and in Tanzania, for example, although the appointment and promotion of public servants was vested in the President by the constitution and legislation, the Commission had power delegated to it to act executively over certain classes of posts, except the highest and the lowest posts. In other states the Commission enjoys executive powers over appointment, promotion, and discipline, in respect of all posts except those of the Permanent Secretary and comparable or higher posts.

Apart from direct concern with recruitment, promotion, and discipline, it is also part of the function of the Commission to adjudicate in disputes arising from the civil service regulations on these subjects. The Commission interprets the civil service regulations. Normally the chairman of the Commission is appointed on a full time basis. The other members are full time, appointed for a fixed term of years, with security of tenure.

Objective methods of recruitment to, and advancement in, the civil service create the necessary incentives which can properly motivate the individual civil servant to make his maximum contribution. Exhortation for service, for more effort, for integrity and hard work, are of course necessary. But they cannot be a substitute for objective criteria and fixed standards. The executive and the party can play a controlling role in modifying these criteria for reasons of declared public interest. But this must be done explicitly and according to law. The system based on merit has legal backing not only in the sense of sanctions but in sociological terms. The publication of competitive examinations and results in official gazettes, and the glare of publicity, can help to resolve problems of patronage.

Executive control in the appointment and tenure of the top civil servants should be sufficient to ensure the implementation of party and government policy. Below that, attempts at wanton interference can only harm the working of the civil service and reduce performance, and hence ultimately harm the party and government policy. It will lead to a crisis of confidence which is dangerous in the long run. This does not, of course, exclude the role of the party as recorder of public sentiments and grievances which can be aired through proper channels.

The party–civil service relation is bound to be a delicate one for many years until institutional mechanisms are developed. But it is at least plausible to say that in a one-party system which makes membership of the party open to civil servants there is less reason for attempts at manipulation of the civil servants by party officials than under a multi-party system. If attempts at manipulation are made they must be presumed to be made on a personal, family, or factional basis, which is conceivable under any other system.

In fact the preoccupation seems to be in the reverse: a fear that membership of the party might induce civil servants to enter into active politics by seeking election to the national assembly and thus cause a decline in efficiency. As a remedy for this, it was recommended in Tanzania that civil servants should only be eligible for membership of the National Assembly if nominated by the President, but not otherwise. It was also recommended that the President should have power to nominate a limited number of civil servants to membership of Local Assemblies, and that civil servants should not be otherwise eligible for membership of Local Assemblies.[35]

As a result, civil servants in Tanzania are encouraged to join TANU but their political activity in the sense of seeking election is heavily circumscribed. Some civil servants have resigned their posts to contest seats in the general election.[36]

As for regional and district administrators, many states took over the colonial system and retained the services of District Officers as civil servants. In the case of the Francophone states the more centralized and direct system of administration of French colonial administration made the continued use of civil servants as District Officers easier. In most of these states the civil servants remained as the central government's representatives in the district with a change of name.[37] In some Anglophone states such as Tanzania the top civil servants were appointed as Regional Commissioners, a post regarded as political.

D. Government Policy and the Civil Service

The civil service as the executive arm of government is an integral part of the executive and as such assists in the formulation, direction, supervision, and control of policy. In a multi-party system there is generally a rule which enjoins civil servants to serve all governments of whatever complexion with equal loyalty and efficiency. It is a matter for doubt whether a government with radical policies can expect unquestioned loyalty and efficiency from a civil servant opposed to those policies. But this is conceivable also in a one-party system. The civil service, being daily concerned with administration according to certain established rules and practices, tends to be 'conservative', and 'radical' policies tend to disturb some of its established beliefs and practices. Equally true, however, is the need for machinery for the formulation and implementation of policies. In a word, the bureaucracy is a necessary evil.

It may be stated as a general rule that the new African governments have not met with opposition from the civil service as a distinct bureaucratic class. Nevertheless, the quality of its composition and the crucial nature of its function makes the civil service a vital sector in government. It is necessary to devise institutional machinery for the effective supervision and control of the civil service in its working as executant of government policy.

1. FORMULATION

The qualifications of civil servants and their involvement in the implementation of policy compels the participation of their higher ranks in the formulation of policy, which could include the planning of overall government policy. It may be reiterated here that in most African states the responsibility for the conception, direction, and supervision of government policy belongs to the President. However, the President cannot properly discharge this responsibility by himself. The cabinet is there to assist him, and the civil service is one of the pillars on which both the President and the cabinet rest.[38] Any planning (and especially economic planning) presupposes a searching and detailed study of the (economic and social) needs and resources of the country. Geophysical, demographic and other data have to be known and specified, plus the available means – equipment, transport, etc. Only such basic studies will permit the production of a plan. This presupposes an administration adapted to development, which includes an adequate flow of information from the various ministries, and a central co-ordinating ministry or office of planning. All these offices also need adequate and professionally competent staff.

To the extent that planning means formulation the broad outlines of policy on the general direction the country should take; and in so far as it involves decisions on priorities in development, on the allocation of resources and adopting controls to ensure the best use of resources, the executive has the major responsibility for decisions. The party Congress and its National Executive Committee provide the executive with the platform for hammering out the general principles which will guide policy and action.

The executive must take the initiative in working out programmes and proposing legislation for the implementation of the general policy. For this purpose it relies on the fund of expertise and experience which is concentrated in the civil service. This means that there must be a close relationship between the executive and the civil service and between goals and actions.

One economist has put it thus:

If a close relationship is to exist between national goals as expressed by politicians and economic programmes as expressed in the plans, close interaction is essential between political leaders and planners (whether expatriate or national). The relationship needs to be two way: planners to do their job must insist (1) that they should be supplied with a clearly stated set of socio-political goals, for example the desired levels of employment, consumption, the national versus the foreign share of economic activity, the economic role of the public sector, and the minimum progress to be made in each front within the proposed period; and (2) that politicians should examine, first, the broad alternative strategies for the economy, as a whole and its various sectors and, later, the more detailed plan drafts, to ensure that these do, in fact, interpret their goals correctly. Planners, on their side, need to accept the desired socio-political framework as given, and to shape economic policy towards its attainment; they should also make clear the costs, especially where the two goals – for example, a high rate of growth of output and a rapid buying out of foreign interests – are basically competitive, so that more of one means less of the other.[39]

The political aspect of national planning efforts should not be divorced from the technical aspects. 'It is not only useless but counter-productive to challenge the basic goals and aspirations – as opposed to specific projects – which cause a government to commission a development plan.'[40] In fact a clear-cut political climate of opinion well organized and oriented towards the attainment of economic development is a prerequisite.

By and large, the new African states decided to organize their economic and social development on the basis of long-term plans. Plans which must involve decisions on priorities and general direction of development cannot be worked out purely on technical criteria; or, in other words, they cannot be the work of technocrats only, independent of general policy. Technocrats can and must help to collect, collate, analyse, and classify data, in order to facilitate choices about priorities, and to draft the plan accordingly. But, to paraphrase René Dumont, it is impossible to construct an apolitical plan.[41] Ivory-tower plans must be discarded because they stand little chance of success.[42]

It is generally agreed that the only sort of plans which can effect a 'take off' are those which involve the total engagement of a government and its people in action based on deliberate choice and in a readiness to make certain sacrifices. This will need a set of clearly defined sociopolitical goals and an unreserved commitment to their attainment. In the absence of such objectives and commitment plans, and the exercise of executive power based on them, would entail waste of human and material resources. Many African governments have professed socialism as a unifying ideology to guide them in setting out their sociopolitical goals. But, as we have seen, different interpretations of socialism are given, and in some cases it is no more than a catch phrase.

Socialism, in so far as it is related to a national plan, is generally understood, and proclaimed by many African governments, to imply that the government must give priority to the satisfaction of the most urgent needs of the great mass of the population. 'As against the massive importation of motor cars, it would prefer buses and lorries; refusing sumptuous palaces, it would build a great number of schools and small dispensaries. It would not sacrifice the primary and professional education to the peasant masses to the very high (degree) of education of a small oligarchy, destined to increase the privileged caste. It would seek to remedy the shortage of protein for the poor, instead of importing luxury foodstuff for the rich. . . . Each one of these propositions determines a series of orientations essential for development.'[43] Very few governments can claim to have stuck to such propositions.

Studies of the early plans of some African states have shown that they suffer from a lack of clearly defined objectives, in relation to basic ideological commitments. Some of these plans have also suffered from over-optimism and too great a dependence on foreign aid; while most of them suffered from a lack of co-ordination.[44] It has been found in Tanzania, for example, that the planning secretariat was left with a far broader and less specific set of goals to translate into economic policy, as a result of a lack of detailed proposals in the Five Year Plan for Economic and Social Development (1964–69). The secretariat therefore proceeded to offer basic alternative choices to the government both at a general and a specific level. This meant that they induced further thinking on a set of detailed sociopolitical aims and an economic plan for their attainment. In other words much of the sociopolitical programme which was worked out postdated the plan and did not stem from a party ideology. As a result there was a very low level of national consciousness of the plan and of its relevance to national aspirations, for example in the lower ranks of the civil service, the party, and the party related mass movements.[45]

Co-ordination is a key to the success of a plan, and it gives more meaning and better efficacy to individual executive decision at every level. The importance of co-ordination impinges not only on the various stages of implementation, but also arises at the pre-planning stage. Indeed, the latter has a bearing on the former to a great extent. Thus in the Nigerian National Development Plan (1962–68) there were four (later five) plans, one for each regional government and one for the Federation, which were not fully co-ordinated on paper, and even less so in regard to organization and implementation. It appears that the plan was worked out by a limited number of expatriate economists, 'working virtually in a vacuum so far as detailed direction or consultation with political leaders went, and with only peripheral advisory contact with Nigerian civil servants and planners'.[46]

In Kenya, the Development Plan (1964–70) was prepared in great haste without sufficient detail, owing to the urgency felt for the need for such a plan by 1964, and the political events which overtook it.[47]

The balance between industry and agriculture is one of the subjects on which economists debate. A hastily conceived plan is bound to upset such balance, and its enforcement would be met with failure.[48]

No development plan, however well conceived, can replace the will to develop. Behind such a plan there must be a well-organized and mobilized population. The need for universal education is an obvious one. But over and above that there is a need for a politically educated and motivated population. In pre-independence years this was easily achieved in the face of the colonial ruler. Post-independence years have required mobilization for development. If the civil service can be termed 'development administration', then 'development politics' is an appropriate term to characterize the role of the masses in such a context and their relation to the government. The executive and the party officials have a great task in inspiring the public with a will to develop, and sustaining this will. It is not an easy task, but it is imperative, given the need and the logic of the political system adopted by these states.

The party congresses and the meetings of the party executive committees can set the broad sociopolitical goals, and the party apparatus can help the government administrative machinery in providing the means for policy appraisals, for searching examination of public attitudes, and for indicating problems and suggesting solutions. Thus party, executive, and civil service, can find a meeting point. One of the advantages of systems which permit civil servants to be party members is that they enable civil servants to avoid making ivory-tower proposals. They can give them an opportunity to feel the pulse, as it were, of public opinion, through direct participation at party meetings. If this could involve duplication of effort it can also be remedied through the avoidance fo isolation, which could be fatal. Serious errors and waste can be avoided if proper use is made of the one-party system. Senior civil servants can participate in the formulation of policy not only at the ministry level but also within the party organs, and thus bring the benefit of their knowledge and experience to bear on the formulation of general policies.

The direct participation of civil servants can also help to avoid three-cornered tussles (party–executive–civil service) or tugs of war (party–civil service), in that each would be involved in a common decision which creates unity in shared responsibility. Such unity is one of the conditions for the successful implementation of a plan. It would also be a safeguard against the development of a gap between a privileged salariat and the general population.[49] But this is easier said than done. It would need a dynamic and dedicated leadership, at party, government, and civil service levels. Present trends are not encouraging. More governments will have to promote projects with the general welfare of the public in mind, and to that end reduce administrative expenditure, especially higher salaries, before they can inspire the masses, and maintain their confidence and will to develop.[50] The role of the party in this respect can be crucial as a standard bearer and controlling agency.

As for the relation between the ministers and the civil servants, it has been maintained that a convention must develop whereby the minister should seek the advice of his staff on all policy matters. As the political head of his ministry he expounds the policy and the manifesto of the political party. The Permanent Secretary and his team should know which policy or programme will work and which will not. They should be in a position to make policy proposals in line with the minister's broad policy, for consideration by him.[51] The argument proceeds from an assumption of a multi-party system. Its validity is none the less applicable to any system. Even though the final decision in regard to the ministry rests with the minister, a proper understanding of the nature of his role and that of his principal assistant and his team would compel him to seek their advice constantly before making his decisions. Policy decisions undertaken in disregard of such eminently necessary steps are bound to be faulty or inadequate.

The experience of the past few years suggests, however, that the real problems in the executive–civil service relation lie in the implementation of policies, plans, and programmes, more than in their formulation.

2. IMPLEMENTATION

Once broad principles and goals have been formulated in resolutions, national plans, and laws, the executive has again to rely on the bureaucracy to translate them into action. This process includes, *inter alia*, interpreting plans and laws and making decisions accordingly; constant evaluation of plans on the basis of results and problems encountered; drafting memoranda, proposing solutions and action by the minister, who in turn, would take the necessary decision or take the matter to the cabinet.

The shortage of trained manpower is keenly felt in this as in all aspects of the administration in most African states. The top positions in the planning offices of several governments are mainly staffed by expatriates, and there are several of these in planning units and other technical departments of many ministries. Obviously the employment of highly paid expatriates, necessary as it is, must be concentrated in a few places. After independence the continuation of expatriates in such posts, or the lending of expatriates to fill them, was not favoured unless found to be absolutely necessary. Experience since then has shown that the young Africans, educated during the post-colonial period and given the right training in theory and practice, make better civil servants.

Shortage of trained and ideologically committed manpower has a bearing on the present inquiry because (i) it can inhibit the action of the executive in carrying out certain policies, or even in formulating what they, or their parties, believe to be the right policies, and (ii) it affects the quality of the administration's performance in carrying out government plans and programmes.

Again, professional qualification, even where it is available, is not sufficient. Dedication, commitment, and honesty, are needed; in addition to training, and where a limited number of qualified people is available, the choice of the government in making appointments to key posts becomes limited, with the resultant possible danger of producing a smug or even corrupt bureau-technocratic salariat.

All this has some serious implications for government policy and action. For example, one of the obstacles to the implementation of the 1964–69 Five-Year Plan in Tanzania was the shortage of skilled personnel, which meant that some of the projects could not be started, while others were delayed.[52] Development projects in Mali and Guinea were hampered by similar shortages. Shortage of capital, equipment, and organizational experience, are of course equally keenly felt. In the face of such shortages, when audacious plans are made and meet with failure the result often is a tendency, on the part of the bureaucracy, to harangue the masses through the party about the need for greater effort and to issue them with orders which they do not really understand.

The shortage of trained young extension workers to go and live with the masses and explain to them the purpose of the plans, tempts the party and civil service hierarchy to issue orders, as was characteristic of colonial bureaucracy. But this cannot create a fruitful dialogue and contribute to development. The masses can be aroused to face the fundamental changes which development implies by being faced with the *fait accompli* of experimental projects (directed by technicians and agriculturalists) which they can see. The party can then help in mobilizing them to a sustained interest in the efforts for change along the new lines demonstrated to them.

A bureaucracy issuing orders from the comfort of city life, remote from the reality of the peasant life, cannot be an agency for change. Yet, decentralization of its power would presuppose (i) that there are competent people at the periphery to engage in the direction of development, and (ii) that the periphery is always loyal to the central government,[53] which is not always the case, especially where certain traditional forces have been left intact.

The recognition of the problem of shortage of trained manpower and allied problems, and the need to attend to them urgently, is one of the essential conditions for the progress of a country. Shortage of trained people implies a limitation on government decisions in all directions. It would limit the value of avowed socialist policies in, for example, the nationalization of privately owned industries, as this presupposes the existence of a qualified executive, administrative, and financial staff capable of directing the nationalized bodies with efficiency. Dependence on expatriate staff imposes limitations on government action or options in carrying out certain policies with which some expatriate staff may not be in agreement.

3. DIRECTION AND CO-ORDINATION

Government involves policy making as well as direction and co-ordination in the execution of such policy. One of the implications of a neo-presidential system is that the President must assume more responsibility in the direction and co-ordination of policy, as he does in its formulation. The question of devising suitable machinery for the proper discharge of that responsibility is therefore an important one.

The usual machinery of the cabinet, of cabinet committees, cabinet secretariat, and the civil service can be utilized, of course. But undue dependence on the normal cabinet system would be unsuitable for an executive presidency. It would defeat the basic philosophy behind the constitutional structure of an executive presidency, which imposes responsibility on the President to carry out these tasks, as it would transfer that responsibility to the cabinet.

A cabinet system has its own laws of dynamics which diffuses power – power that has been concentrated in the case of an executive President for a definite purpose. In a cabinet system each minister has equal status and autonomous control over the affairs of his ministry. And, in the British type of administrative and institutional structure, the Treasury enjoys a dominance through an emphasis on budgetary and short-term financial problems. But the administration and politics of development which underlies the executive presidential system compels a departure from the classical cabinet system.

Development administration presupposes development planning, the objective of which is a decision-making process in which government decisions which bear upon the development of the country are taken with reference to an integrated and comprehensive plan and according to an agreed and internally consistent set of national priorities.[54]

The most common machinery which has been adopted to help direct and co-ordinate developmental decision-making is a Ministry of Development Planning (sometimes called the National Plan). This ministry is usually responsible for preparing a national plan in consultation with other ministries and other units. The whole process is then co-ordinated at a higher level, usually through a Cabinet Planning Commission presided over by the President or by a minister delegated by him.

The Ministry of Development Planning reports to the Planning Commission, a procedure which should normally obviate difficulties of co-ordination. But experience in the past few years has shown that this machinery of co-ordination and direction does not always work satisfactorily. Evidently, there must be attached to the office of the President, a staff of experts to advise and help him prepare the necessary directives to be sent out to ministries and other units, in order to overcome the difficulties caused by conflicts between departments. The dangers of scattered implementation have been seen in several African planning efforts, leaving the general policy contained in the plan as a set of isolated programmes which are amended *ad hoc* by the Ministry of Finance and by other ministries.[55]

In such circumstances executive decisions lose meaning, being subject to the hazards of uncontrolled events. As a student of the subject has put it:

> important projects and inter-relationships are dropped without re-estimating the overall impact; policies crucial to development are modified or dropped for inadequate reasons.[56]

And, it may be added, a great deal of energy is sometimes wasted in clashes and recriminations. An example will serve to illustrate the type of issues involved in such a conflict.

Usually the conflict occurs between the Ministry of Development Planning, on the one hand, and the Ministry of Finance and such other Ministries as Education and Agriculture, on the other. For example, in Tanzania the Ministry of Development Planning (created in 1963 and abolished in 1964) was involved in clashes with the Ministry of Finance over the allocation of resources and assumptions as to the rate of growth. The ministry was involved in clashes with the Ministry of Education over the expansion of primary schools, and with the Ministry of Agriculture (plus that of Finance) over policy on rural development. The conflict with the Ministry of Agriculture illustrates a weakness in the machinery of co-ordination as well as in the direction of basic policy. The conflict involved a difference of approach to agricultural development. The Ministry of Development Planning preferred a dramatic change in rural life through a major effort to plan the co-ordinated cultivation of agricultural holdings and by gathering farmers into Ujamaa villages where resources could be more easily provided for them. The Ministry of Agriculture, on the other hand, stressed agricultural extension, with the emphasis on agricultural productivity, without involving major efforts to transform the social and cultural life of the rural areas.[57]

Disagreements like this prove the point that in the absence of a clearly defined policy, and a machinery of direction and co-ordination directly issuing from the President's office, there is a tendency for the planning ministry to press its own views strongly on a number of important matters which lie within the jurisdiction and professional competence of other ministries. The resistance encountered from such other ministries is, in such circumstances, understandable. For they have within them (especially in the Ministry of Finance) a greater concentration of professional, administrative, and technical staff able to cope with matters falling within their competence. Clearly more definite planning procedures and effective reporting systems and co-ordination by the office of the President are necessary.

In some states such experiences have been used to revise the machinery of direction and co-ordination in the process of decision. The Tanzanian experience is again instructive, because of the boldness and frequency with which structural changes have been made to correct defects. The Ministry of Development Planning was abolished in 1964 and replaced by a Directorate of Development Planning which would function within the President's office. But the President appointed three Ministers of State in charge of planning, and delegated extensive powers to them and to the Directorate, authorizing them to give directives to individual ministries. This act constituted a definite break from the cabinet system; each minister could now be given directives about his ministry in accordance with the plan.

The arrangement did not prove a success, however, for reasons which need not detain us here.[58] But it is interesting to note that, apart from the inadequacy of staff and the lack of a flow of information and progress reports, among the contributory causes was the fact that the three ministers did not use their delegated powers. They did not issue any directives; they never consulted regularly together. In short, there was not the unity, vigour, and single-minded drive which ought to characterize such an office. It was inevitable that the Ministry of Finance in particular would reassert its authority in such situations, with the result that development administration would be replaced by *ad hoc* and unintegrated decision-making.[59]

The position of the civil service in such situations is significant. The Directorate of Planning, which is the link with the civil service, made an effort to assert itself at the civil service level, but met with equal failure.[60] For in a situation of clashes and disunity at the ministerial level the civil servants in each ministry normally back their ministers. Indeed in many instances the civil servants recapture lost initiative and formulate, post-haste, new *ad hoc* policies and supply their ministers with such policies as ammunition in the 'battle' with the development ministry or directorate.

The shortage of trained people to check on the appropriateness of *ad hoc* policies and to arbitrate between conflicting proposals can leave the President's office captive to such happenings. A co-ordinated decision-making process implies a continuous follow-up through an effective reporting system, and a panel of experts to appraise the progress reports and to prepare further orders or directives. Shortage of qualified and experienced staff to assist the President in this task will inevitably make him dependent on the civil service in the individual ministries, as was the case in Tanzania, for example.

Now, in the ordinary administrative process this need not entail any problem. Each Permanent Secretary is expected to prepare a policy proposal for his minister concerning his ministry. Further-more, such a preparation normally involves a consideration of the implications of the policy. Whether this originates at the initiative of the minister or the Permanent Secretary, the relevant chiefs of departments or divisions, who live with the problems, will have helped in the preparation. Presidential dependence on the civil service in the ordinary administrative process is therefore perfectly reasonable. The machinery of the cabinet, its committees and the cabinet secretariat can also be used, and is used. For this purpose A. L. Adu recommends that:

> there should be periodical and regular conferences between ministers and their staffs for the discussion and consideration of major problems, or even for the purpose of talking generally about the general programmes of the particular ministries. There should also be occasional meetings between the president or prime minister and permanent secretaries and heads of departments, so that the overall government policy can be understood against the background of discussion with the highest authority in the land and also that the president or prime minister may come to hear the views of the top level officials concerned with the operational policies and get to know them and their worth.[61]

This is no doubt useful. None the less there must be central planning with machinery which ensures that all policy proposals are assessed in relation to the plan and in terms of its basic economic priorities. This machinery, whatever its form and name, must be under the firm control of the President, and must be staffed adequately with highly qualified people, experienced in all the necessary subjects. The machinery of the civil service and of the cabinet secretariat can be used additionally for co-ordination. But it must be subordinated to a central directing and co-ordinating office attached to that of the President. The experience of the past few years and the logic of the whole system demands this.

This is not merely a matter of theory; it concerns practical matters relating to the attainment of national goals. Failure in direction and co-ordination results in a lack of unified effort and dynamism. This is reflected at the top ministerial and civil service level as much as at the local level. Experience has demonstrated that such failure makes it difficult even for enthusiastic local officials to know how best to organize local effort for the attainment of national goals. The absence of clear directives with immediate and specific targets at the local level results in the dissipation of momentum; and public opinion, which is initially mobilized through the publication of the plan and the publicity given to it, can easily grow sceptical about the government. The office of the President is eminently suited to give the necessary corrective to such defects. Through his presidency of the National Executive Committee of the party, the President can issue the necessary directives to the party for the mobilization of public opinion and effort. But before public opening and effort can be mobilized he must have at his disposal policy proposals worked out on the basis of periodic research and accurate information supplied to his office from various ministries and other units through an effective reporting machinery, and assessed by a panel of experts. This can avoid waste and facilitate the efficient implementation of policy.

The need for such an integrated decision-making process, although more urgent in developing countries, is not peculiar to them. In some developed states where the civil service operates according to well-established procedures, it has been pointed out that 'wrong advice' has been given by officials to ministers, from time to time, notably on economics and finance.[62] The relationship between ministers and civil servants in Britain has been said to favour a civil service dominance; and this through no weakness of the ministers, but rather as a result of the power structure of the civil service which comes from a hierarchical organization, the permanent position of civil servants, the veil of secrecy which separates the present from the past, and the control by civil servants of the processing and selection of information. The magnitude of such power, it is maintained, makes it essentially political power.

The minister–civil servant relationship in Africa is somewhat different at the moment, with the balance in favour of the minister. The one-party state, which permits longer tenure of office by the minister, is one cause. Another is the fact that many African ministers possess individual qualities and experience which compel them to intervene more and dominate their civil service, which is not yet a hierarchically organized and disciplined 'union', as it is in Britain, for example. There are no established 'corridors of power' – no fine gradation of officialdom. Not yet. The one-party system is not conducive to the growth of such power. But, as recent studies of the bureaucracy in developing countries have suggested, in a world where bureaucratic centralization and the acquisition of power is the general tendency, the bureaucracy can very easily become strong enough to challenge or resist the challenge of other institutions of the state such as the party. Its monopoly (or near monopoly) of administrative and technical skill facilitates this development, and may, in time, make its control by other institutions the more difficult.

The problem of control in this area will be felt more, as government plans and programmes become more and more complex and the bureaucracy assumes more control over their implementation. The controlling role of the Party, of the legislature, of the President, and of other institutions such as commissions of enquiry, will then demand closer attention. Indeed in some countries there are signs of attempts by the civil service to assert its domination in the society by structuring privileges to itself and pre-empting any basic changes which threaten its becoming a major economic accumulator.[63]

NOTES

1. cf.: e.g. the definition of the Ghana civil service in A. L. Adu, *The Civil Service in New African States*, Allen & Unwin 1965, p. 24. cf. also, definition of *fonctionnaire* (civil servant) in the Ivory Coast public service law, Loi No. 64–488, 21 December 1964, as 'a person who is appointed to permanent employment, who is a rightful holder of a grade (*titularisée*) in the administrative hierarchy of the central administration of the state' (Art. 1). This law excludes judges (*magistrats de l'ordre judiciaire*) and military personnel from the definition of a *fonctionnaire* (Art. 1, last paragraph).
2. ibid.

3. *Report of Commission on the establishment of a democratic one-party State*, Dar-es-Salaam, 1965, p. 24.
4. Julius K. Nyerere, *Democracy and the Party System*, Dar-es-Salaam, 1962, p. 26.
5. cf. Richard Symonds, *The British and their successors*, London, Faber, 1966, pp. 149–51.
6. In the earlier years the Governor was usually, if not always, a colonial civil servant; ibid.
7. cf. R. Symonds, op. cit., p. 150.
8. In India, interestingly enough, the policy of the Congress Party led by Mahatma Gandhi was for many years one of hostility to the Indian civil service, as a colonial instrument. Gandhi's philosophy of 'Purna Swaraj', which advocated village democracy, did not look with favour upon a hierarchically-organized and authoritarian administrative machine. cf. V. Subramaniam, 'Evolution of minister-civil servant relations in India' in Vol. I *Journal of Commonwealth Political Studies* (1961–63), pp. 223–32.
9. cf. Kenneth Younger, *The Public Service in the new States*, London U.P., 1960, Parts II, III and IV, and R. Symonds, op. cit., pp. 149–70 and pp. 211–26.
10. cf. Report of the Localisation Committee (Adu Report), Zomba, 1960, p. 22.
11. In 1952 the ratio was in the reverse, with twenty-nine per cent Africans in the civil service. Then, there were only 544 Africans to 1,322 expatriates, whereas in 1958 there were 1,984 Africans to 880 expatriates. In other words, 1,440 more Africans were employed in six years: cf. K. Younger, op. cit., p. 33.
12. John Fletcher-Cooke, 'Parliament, Executive and civil service', in *Parliament as an Export*, Alan Burns (ed), loc. cit., p. 158.
13. cf. *Report* . . . op. cit.
14. cf. K. O. Dike, Paper at Nigerian Seminar on manpower problems, Lagos 1964. This is the feeling expressed at various conferences in education in Africa.
15. cf. Sékou Touré, *La Guinée et l'émancipation Africaine*, Paris, 1959, pp. 125 and 168.
16. cf. R. Symonds, op. cit., pp. 212–3. The author quotes a former education director of French West Africa (A.O.F.) as saying: 'the danger is never to teach too little; it is to teach too much.'
17. cf. S. M. Sy, *Recherches sur l'exercice du pouvoir politique en Afrique Noire*, Paris, 1965, Annexe II pp. 210–13. This 'annexe' shows an interesting proportion of former Ponty 'old boys' in the governments of the Ivory Coast, Guinea, and Mali.
18. Thus intensive Africanization started after the *Loi-Cadre* (1956), which enabled the African voice to be heard more clearly and loudly than before. Since independence the French Government has provided substantial assistance in various forms, including direct scholarship grants and technical and financial assistance to the governments.
19. i.e. apart from the 400 Congolese trained as priests. cf. R. Symonds, op. cit., p. 223.

20. This is, of course, subject to the changes brought about by the presidential systems which modify the role of the cabinet.
21. In a speech to a public administration seminar at Makerere College, n.d.
22. op. cit., p. 257.
23. ibid.
24. cf. A. L. Adu, *The Civil Service in New African States,* loc. cit., pp. 25–6.
25. There may be such 'experts' present at party executive committees as members. But the fund of expertise found in the civil service is of a different order of magnitude, owing to the number of the people possessing it and the administrative apparatus at their disposal.
26. Technocracy and meritocracy are words which are bandied about, sometimes in derision. But in modern public administration technocrats count for much.
27. Information gathered through interviews with embassy officials. In the Congo the Secretary-General of the government has the rank of minister; cf. *Statut général de la fonction publique du Congo,* Loi No. 1562.
28. Titles sometimes vary; the above are typical: cf. A. L. Adu, op. cit., pp. 171–3.
29. cf. e.g. The Ivory Coast, Loi No. 64–488 of 21 December 1961; and Mauritania, Loi No. 64–7 of 24 April 1961.
30. In the Ivory Coast there are five major categories in the civil service – A, B, C, D, and E. There are fifty corps in category A; forty-one in B; thirty-nine in C; twenty-two in D; and eight in E (*corps transitoire*). Each category has its *corps des fonctionnaires* who are subject to the same status, e.g. teachers. Within each corps there are grades, and within each grade there are échelons. More government work means an expansion of sections to be staffed by people falling into any one of these classifications of position.
31. A. L. Adu proposes this as a considered opinion, on the basis of his experience as a permanent secretary in Ghana, cf. op. cit., pp. 175–6.
32. This is limited to Anglophone states.
33. Based on personal experience of the author as head of a department and confirmed by exchange of views with other African department heads.
34. They are called *commissions administratives paritaires* in the Francophone states, which also have a Ministry for the Public Service (*Fonction Publique*).
35. cf. *Report of commission,* op. cit., p. 24.
36. cf. McAuslan *et al,* op. cit. (p. 187, note 85). Mr. C. Y. Mgonja, for example, resigned his civil service post to contest an election, won, and was made Minister of Community Development and National Culture; and he was not a professional party man. ibid.
37. The name *Préfet* replaced the colonial name *commandant de cercle*; cf. Robert Delavignette, 'Des commandants Français au préfets Africains', *Revue Française d'études politiques Africaines* No. 2 (February 1966), pp. 30–40.
38. The other pillar being the party.
39. Reginald H. Green, 'Four African Development Plans: Ghana, Kenya, Nigeria and Tanzania' in the *Journal of Modern African Studies,* 3, 2 (1965) pp. 249–79, at p. 252.

40. ibid.
41. René Dumont, *L'Afrique noire est mal partie*, Paris, 1962, p. 96.
42. There is a story current among African *élite* circles which recounts the meeting between a shepherd watching a flock of sheep, and a city man who went on a picnic. The latter asked the shepherd why he let the wool on his sheep grow so long; why did he not cut it and take it to market? Whereupon the shepherd answered, horrified: 'What! and spoil the five year plan!? The trouble with you city people, is that you don't practise what you preach!'
43. R. Dumont, op. cit., p. 98.
44. R. H. Green, op. cit., pp. 253–62; and R. C. Pratt, 'The administration of economic planning in a newly independent state: the Tanzanian experience 1963–1966', in *Journal of Commonwealth Political Studies*, Vol. V, No. 1, March 1967, pp. 51–8.
45. cf. R. H. Green, op. cit., pp. 253–4.
46. ibid. The 'bottleneck' of foreign advisers was ironed out in the subsequent post-Civil War plan.
47. ibid, pp. 259–60.
48. On the experience of other countries on the balance between industry and agriculture. cf. R. Dumont, op. cit., pp. 122–5.
49. One of the disturbing phenomena in these societies is the gap between the salary scale of high-ranking civil servants (and ministers) and the lowest civil servants and workers.
50. Some governments have been overthrown by army *coups* when they proposed a reduction of salaries, e.g. in the Upper Volta, the government of Maurice Yaméogo. The personal fortunes of Yaméogo and some of his colleagues were thought to be considerable, which reduced the value of the proposals for reduction of salaries.
51. cf. A. L. Adu, op. cit., p. 180.
52. cf. *First Year Progress Report on the Implementation of the Five-Year Development Plan (Public Sector)*, 1 July 1964 to 30 June 1965, Dar-es-Salaam.
53. Tanzania in 1972 has come up with a policy statement that sixty per cent of all personnel and funds of the central government will be administered at the periphery. This is an experiment worth watching.
54. cf. Pratt, op. cit., p. 39.
55. cf. R. H. Green, op. cit., p. 270.
56. ibid.
57. cf. Pratt, op. cit., pp. 45–6.
58. For a further account of the reasons, cf. Pratt, op. cit., pp. 52–6.
59. The triumvirate of planning Ministers was replaced by a new Ministry of Economic Affairs and Development Planning.
60. *See* Pratt, loc. cit.
61. A. L. Adu, op. cit., pp. 233–4.
62. cf. Peter Shore, *Entitled to Know*, MacGibbon & Kee, London, 1966.
63. *See* Kenneth Prewitt: 'The Functional Justification of Inequality and the Ndegwa Report: Shaping an Ideology', East African Universities Social Science Council Eighth Annual Conference, 19–23 December 1972, Nairobi, Kenya, for an extensive discussion.

PART III

The Advent of Military Rule—
Crisis of Neo-Presidentialism

7

Structure of Military Intervention

A. Causes of Intervention in General

Between June 1965 and January 1967 governments were changed by violent means in ten out of thirty-eight independent African states. As a result, Algeria, Burundi, Central African Republic, Zaire, Dahomey, Ghana, Nigeria, Togo, and Upper Volta, have been ruled by military men who assumed office after the forceful overthrow of the previous régimes. The Sudan returned after a military rule lasting six years to an uneasy civilian rule, which operated under a transitional constitution providing for a peculiar kind of collegial executive, only to be subsequently ousted by another military régime. (*See* page 233.)

Why have the military made such a thrust in politics? Before we try to answer this question it will be helpful to make some remarks on the phenomenon of armed intervention in civil government in general. Civil government rests on authority, legitimated by various mechanisms, which secure the habitual obedience of the people. Whether the government is a monarchy which governs through prescriptive right or a presidential régime based on popular mandate it commands authority because there is a general acceptance of its legitimacy. Legitimacy is a difficult concept. But, to the extent that one can generalize about any concept, it may be stated that the power of the government acquires legitimacy because of a general recognition either (i) that it is there to protect and serve; or (ii) that it is capable of manipulating organized coercion to maintain itself; or (iii) because of a combination of both factors. Indeed there is a link between physical power as monopolized by the government and the popular view as to its legitimacy, because its use or abuse has a social context. Either as a historical fact or as a postulate of reason it is assumed by political theorists that at some time men delegated their own responsibility, in regard to themselves and their families, to some amongst them to exercise it for a certain end. This delegated responsibility became power in the hands of its holders, and the postulated or actual delegation laid the foundation of legitimacy. A psychological basis was needed for this legitimacy, and it came in the form of the requirement that the power holder must be fit to exercise it. A sort of 'comprehensive insurance' invariably followed, purporting to ascertain that power is in good hands, and this took religious form, sometimes by investing the person who held it with sanctity. This explains the origin of divinity associated with absolute rulers.[1]

Legitimacy may be said to exist when a general habit of obedience has been established for a sufficiently long time. This is how the concept is linked in the minds and conduct of people, and it is conditioned historically, psychologically, economically and socially. And, as already explained in a previous chapter, in modern societies the mass media count for much; and coercion must be conceived less in terms of physical force, and more in terms of the manipulation of the values and sentiments accepted by the society. A large part of the use of state institutions is designed to achieve control without the resort to brute force. Even the administration of justice, in the final analysis, is the subtle dispensation of coercive power, as the Swedish school of jurisprudence has demonstrated.[2]

But all this assumes a state of things in which the government has the backing of a significant portion of the population or of critical sections of it, which enables it to exercise its authority. Where a serious break occurs in the habit of obedience, for some reason, resulting in a revolt, the mechanisms of peaceful persuasion give way to physical coercion to suppress the revolt. A government which loses general popular support cannot indefinitely use armed force to maintain itself in office. This in fact is one way of inviting armed intervention in politics. For when a government becomes too dependent on the armed forces and makes use of them too much or too frequently the armed forces tend to end by seizing control of the government on their own behalf.

The paths of military men to the high magistracy of the state are strewn with the human débris caused by the order of corrupt, ambitious or desperate political masters. This, as much as individual ambition, explains the advent of the Caesars of which history is full. The Caesars' victory laurels are a prelude to their crowns. But the undue dependence on the military caused by their frequent use as repressive agents is not the only situation which leads to direct military involvement in politics. Nor are all military *coups* led by reluctant heroes.

In the Middle East, the military have taken upon themselves the task of leading, or providing the impetus for, radical change. Latin America has given the world an image of a continent in which power-hungry army officers have deposed governments and each other with astounding rapidity, frequently leaving their nations easy prey to the caprice of whoever happened to have control of any section of the armed forces.

Military involvement in politics has been associated by some with underdevelopment; it has been explained as 'a response to the difficulties which the new states have encountered in their efforts to establish themselves as modern sovereignties'.[3] Its discipline and organization and its effective chain of command make the military machine well suited to cope with situations of crisis where a general breakdown of law and order is involved. But this is not enough to explain the political behaviour of military men and in particular their intervention in civil government, totally or substantially replacing constituted authority.

Among the factors which are crucial in determining the political behaviour of the military are the educational background and professional ethos of the officers, the historical background of the army, in some cases including its reputation and role during the colonial period, and in many countries the ethnic balance of officers and soldiers.[4] Some of these factors influence the political attitude of officers in the long run, while considerations of salary increase, career advancement, and conditions of service, are the most likely causes of mutinies. There can be no one single factor or one type of condition applicable to every case – which makes military *coups* likely. A combination of two or more factors may be present, though one factor may trigger off the actual event. A major decision or blunder by the government may do this. Or the *coup* may be the result of cumulative acts or omissions of the government. Whatever the final reason given, the motivation for the *coup* may be found in the corporate interest of the army as an interest group; or some regional, ethnic, or personal self-interest of significant leaders may be involved; or it may be actuated by genuine concern for the national interest. Any one of these interests, even the national interest, may also be dovetailed with a class interest or with foreign interests, or with both.[5]

Whatever its motive, the capacity of the army to overthrow a government seems to depend more on its cohesiveness and on surprise, rather than on its size or fire-power, as events in several African states have shown. We shall see that this factor of cohesiveness is adversely affected in some cases where inter-ethnic or inter-regional differences reach the ranks of the army itself, as in Nigeria. There, the danger is not limited to disputes between army officers alone, but may affect the unity of the state. The capacity to overthrow governments is one thing. It is quite another matter to govern better or to prepare a better government. The bayonet is no substitute for the ballot box in this matter, though the ballot box is itself no substitute for the fulfilment of popular expectations and for bread and butter. But it is clear from the history of the army's intervention in politics that its readiness to intervene is not always matched by modesty as to its ability to cope with complex situations. What it will do in the face of such problems will depend on various factors, including the original cause of intervention, the post-intervention situation, and the quality of the military leaders in question.

In Africa the infancy of political institutions inherited or established at the moment of independence, and the manifold problems which the new states face, have made them vulnerable and attractive to military intervention. The ecstasy of the national birth was followed by growing pains. The search for a form of government consonant with the needs and aspirations of a continent in the process of change meets danger signs at every twist and turn. The movement for independence, and in many cases the sudden and dramatic gain of sovereignty, had raised high hopes in the peoples of the liberated territories. Party programmes, election manifestoes, mobilization campaigns, and songs of freedom,[6] all worked to heighten this sense of expectation. Promises had been made whose fulfilment eludes many leaders. The 'revolution of rising expectations' came face to face with disappointment and frustration, aggravated, in a number of instances, by disenchantment with politicians and the spectacle of corruption, waste, and an ever-widening gap between the few rich and the countless poor. As Edward Shils has written:

In almost every aspect of their social structures the societies in which the new states must be based are characterised by a gap.

It is a gap between the few very rich and the mass of the poor, between the educated and the uneducated, between the townsman and the villager, between the modern and the traditional, between the rulers and the ruled. Almost every feature of the social structure of the new states conspires to separate the ordinary people from their government. This is a fundamental fact of life of the new states.[7]

Developing nations have to develop fast enough to catch up with increasing demands. Education is universally recognized as the key to development, and a large proportion of direly needed financial resources have to be allocated to education. Yet for decades to come[8] the supply of educated manpower needed cannot catch up with the demand. In the meantime there is a rising population of unemployed or underemployed school leavers. These and the many school failures add more yeast to ferment the unrest. The growth of trades unions and co-operatives has also raised problems which have to be solved by governments. The trades unions, together with youth and women's organizations, were linked with the movements for independence.[9] After independence the object of complaint is no longer a foreign ruler. Anti-government strikes or demonstrations are now seen in quite a different light. The intolerant attitude of governments to such problems is sometimes understandable. But whether their explanations can convince unemployed or disaffected men and women is a different matter.

In the cultural, economic, social, and political cross-currents in the life of these nations, one fact is primary. The increase of food production is less than the increase in population.[10] Meanwhile, the harder the African works the less the reward, in some cases.[11] The rich nations get richer and the poor nations poorer. This is the most crucial problem to be faced by the generation of the post-independence period. The implication of the gap, which Edward Shils has so very well expressed, is where there may not have existed – or not to a significant extent. Taken in a global context, this could create a small national bourgeoisie financially linked with the capitalists of the developed world. On the other hand there will be the vast mass of peasantry, which has been described as the true proletariat of this century.[12]

In the background there is the whole process of modernization with its inexorable logic of economic and social change, and the transformation of the value system which this change implies.

The modern (educated) *élite* is at once a result and an agent of this modernization process. This *élite* generally ranges itself against traditional ideas and forces. Even when some members of the *élite* affirm the past of their country they must stress its adaptibility to present needs. There is an ambivalence in their attitude to some of their past heritage. The most crucial aspect of this ambivalence is seen in ethnic ties and in particular in the dependence of some political leaders on such ties for support. This continues mistrust and cleavage.

At the governmental level this also gives rise to instability. The chief executive's role, originally cast as captain or steward, becomes one of referee or conciliator. And any signs of partiality are signals of danger, as enhancing the feeling of mistrust and undermining confidence in the national leadership. The outer national symbols of unity can easily be discredited in societies where localism is dominant, as it is in all Africa. In such societies the loyalties of the ordinary man are confined to a narrow local range. This situation favours the emergence of leaders who appear to serve these parochial interests. Where parochial interests are fostered or advocated, and the national interest dictates that they cannot be satisfied, strife is created. Again, this hinders the development of stable and coherent nationwide parties, and, by creating mistrust, it creates a crisis of confidence in which one section of the population feels dominated or exploited by another section. This in turn weakens the effectiveness of government.[13]

Now the army – even in its barracks – is not separate from society. The general ills of the society affect it, as they affect other units. It has been said that the standards given them by their training are crucial in determining the behaviour of military officers. In particular it has been pointed out that commissioned officers feel that these standards are affronted when the state which they serve flounders and the civilian politicians 'make a mess of things'.[14] All the pronouncements uttered by army *coup* leaders lend support to such view. One is impressed by the puritanical tenor which seeks to revive 'moral standards or to abolish corruption'.[15] Some of these pronouncements are, of course, rationalizations. But it is generally true to say that an important aspect of the training of the military is a spirit of discipline which influences its political outlook. The life of the army, which emphasizes austerity, also contributes to a general puritanical outlook in politics. Again, in the underdeveloped world studies have shown that the army 'tends to recruit into its officer ranks the brightest and most ambitious young men of the small towns and country-side . . . who are aware of distance separating them from the rich and the political *élite*'.[16] As most of these come from poor families, it is suggested that class structure affects the conduct of the military *vis-à-vis* the political order.[17] No detailed study of this has been made in Africa. The policies of recruitment may vary from place to place. For instance, in the Sudan there was a period when young people who failed to attain required standards of entry into the institutions of higher learning in the Sudan were recruited into the army. The same must be true of many states which needed to form their officer corps with some haste in the post-independence periods. This was no doubt the case where the pace of Africanization in the army had to be forced in accordance with general policies of Africanization. Or again, take the case of Ethiopia, where some among the brightest students were chosen for the military academy for the first few years. But it is not possible to draw any conclusions on the importance of this particular kind of policy for the political formation of these young officers.[18]

Much has been made of the fact that in most African states the army is a colonial creation and therefore its behaviour must follow the criteria underlying the professional ethics laid down by the colonial army. Among these is the fact that the army must be apolitical. The symbols which separate the soldier from the civilian are more noticeable, it is argued, in the case of the African who stands out against an African background.[19] But the fact remains that those uniformed members of an organized body called 'the army' are also members (*a*) of a modernizing *élite* and (*b*) of ethnic groups; and that the influences of these two factors impinge on them and their activities. To give a simple illustration: A is a lieutenant in the army of state X. He comes from ethnic group P and is educated. At one level of relationship he is subject to the impact of modernist ideas and values by virtue of his education and membership of an officer corps which shares similar ideas and values. He meets his colleagues in his work and at the officers' mess. He also meets, at the mess or elsewhere, educated civilian members of the bureaucracy, of the party, and of other institutions like the universities.[20] Among the issues discussed are political, social, and economic issues of topical nature. Some go deeper and analyse issues, putting them in a larger and deeper perspective. Inevitably the latest political scandals or crisis, and titbits of gossip come up. Inevitably also there are always people in such a group (as in any other group) whose particular background and intellectual make-up will force them to put such questions in an ideological perspective.[21] The conduct of politicians will stand condemned by such people not because (or not only because) it constitutes an affront to narrowly conceived standards imbibed during professional training, but (also) because it deviates from new value-systems which require a basic policy orientation and an honest and unflinching pursuit of such policy. This latter may roughly be called social justice, as the concept represents the modernist aspirations in its sociopolitical aspect. It will be seen that our army officer is not restricted by the narrow confines of professional ethics.

At another level, our lieutenant meets his relatives: parents, brothers, sisters, cousins, aunts, uncles, nephews – and it must be remembered that the ties of the extended family in Africa are strong and demanding. It is a fallacy to think that an African officer will remain separate because of his training, uniform, and all the paraphernalia that go with an army life. To be sure, this cannot be underestimated; army training, drill, and discipline, is a strong cohesive factor. But it does not insulate the soldier from the daily influences of the more vital social contacts in the African context.[22] Col. Afrifa, who subscribes to the view that the army must be kept out of politics, nevertheless writes:

> I know that in Ghana people normally underrate the intelligence of the soldier. This has a long tradition. The British army did not at first attract the most able of our men. To our people, therefore, it seemed that only the failures in our society joined the army, that only the ones who did not go to school, or were not able to till the land, or were disobedient to their elders, put on the white man's uniform. A new army had however grown in Ghana, an army of men who were no longer failures but part of a great country that had won freedom from British rule. *An army that has come to identify itself with the aspirations of the people. An army that shared their sufferings, their joys and their hopes for the future.*[23]

After making some laudatory remarks about the British army tradition, Afrifa goes on to say that the Ghana army had among its ranks men who 'had begun to ask questions about our country, about Kwame Nkrumah, about the Convention Peoples Party and its intentions'.[24] In short, the army did not see its place limited to the barracks or to the battlefield.

Thus the professional ethic which was developed in different systems over a long period of time, and which subsumes other sociopolitical bases, cannot act as a barrier against military intervention in the politics of African states. As already stated, the motives may vary from place to place and they may be rationalized. The military men may also declare, as they always do, that they will stay in power for a short period, long enough to 'clear the mess'. But few of the leaders of military *coups* have returned to the barracks of their own free will. Some observers have even gone to the extent of solemnly declaring that 'Africa has entered the era of pronuciamentos'.[25] The great number of *coups* and the quick succession of events certainly lends credence to such assertions. And there is some evidence in the post-*coup* behaviour of the military executives which suggests that they have come to stay for some time. Whether more civilian heads will fall is a matter for conjecture. One thing is certain; violence begets violence, and to every *coup* there may be a counter-*coup*.

The professional ethics and the apolitical role which they assume do, of course, have implications, looked at from the angle of the military men as a corporate group. While such corporate existence cannot ward off the impact of factors mentioned in the foregoing paragraphs, it does create a certain pattern of 'interest' which responds to certain threats. Keeping politics out of the army and the army separate from politics, as Major-General Alexander has called it,[26] was one of the lessons which was sedulously inculcated in the armies of Europe and hence in the colonial army. It is a lesson which can easily be recalled and invoked by army leaders when they feel civilian politicians are encroaching on what they consider to be their preserve. One of the consequences of what has elsewhere been called the politics of mobilization, where the primacy of politics is asserted, may be a sharp reaction by the army where it feels its corporate existence is being threatened. This comes out clearly from the writings or utterances of some of the *coup* leaders.[27]

Attention needs to be paid to the question of the relationship of the political party and of the armed forces, particularly in one-party states. Since the chief executive provides the meeting point between these two factors, the problem is central to the whole subject of the executive.

We will now present some case-studies of military *coups* in Africa. Then we will examine the structure of the military executive in some of these states.

B. The Military Coups in Africa

1. THE FIRST STAGE

(a) Egypt

The first *coup d'état* in modern Africa took place in Egypt, in July 1952, when the monarchical régime of King Farouk was overthrown. The Egyptian *coup* was a military *coup* in its execution, but in terms of its conception and impact it was a revolution which abolished an old order – and with it the sense of humiliation suffered by the Egyptian people in centuries of alien rule. It ushered in a new era of social and political life in a way comparable to the French and Russian Revolutions. Its difference from those revolutions lies in the fact that the Egyptian Revolution was bloodless. It is clear that Nasser and his fellow Free Officers conceived of a swift bloodless *coup* as a way of securing control of the state apparatus before proceeding to sweep the Egyptian stables – an act which the officers were determined to carry out from the very beginning.[28] Nasser and his fellow 'Free Officers' had planned the *coup* for more than seven years in secret against heavy odds. As one observer has reported: 'they had a clear idea of what they wanted to destroy in Egypt – the monarchy, the power of the landlords, foreign influence and the corruption of political life – and they had a vision of the kind of society they wished to become. But they had had very little time to consider the political techniques needed to make the vision a reality.'[29]

In Egypt it took over ten years for President Nasser to produce the celebrated National Charter which was the basis of the constitution under which the National Assembly and later the President were elected. The length of the period may be partly explained by the nature of the change, which in the case of Egypt was fundamental.

In any appraisal of the behaviour of the military régime the nature of the changes they brought about and the sense of mission they espoused must be taken into consideration. By the behaviour of the military is meant here the speed and degree of demilitarization, or alternately a greater role played by the army in the political life of the nation.

In Egypt after the *coup*, Nasser and his fellow Free Officers had two alternatives before them. One was to go back to the barracks hoping that with the removal of King Farouk, all would go well. The other was to stay in power and govern the country themselves. Their mission, however, was more than the removal of a corrupt king and his court. As long as Egypt's social system remained unchanged nothing would change.

The Wafd Party, which had begun with promise earlier, had become hollow and discredited. So the new leaders were left with the second course, which they followed relentlessly. This had appeared to them as the only solution long before the *coup*, and every one of their subsequent acts confirm this – including the climax of the revolution, namely the National Charter, and the transformation of the military régime into a constitutional authority.

(b) *The Sudan*

The next military *coup* in Africa took place in the Sudan, where General Ibrahim Abbhoud intervened in November 1958 to put an end to the inter-party strife which had paralysed the Sudan Government since its independence two years previously.

The first political party was formed in 1938 when the Graduates Congress of the educated Sudanese was founded. But religious and ethnic factions reappeared when elections took place. These factions, which had been buried in the common struggle for independence before 1956, reappeared soon after, dominating politics in the national Parliament.[30] In spite of their modernity and national aspirations, the leadership depended for support on tribal groups, with the result that different combinations of coalition government proved unstable. The economic problems caused by poor cotton crops and the falling price of cotton in the world market added to the crisis.

Abbhoud's intervention was made at the request of Abdallah Khalil, the Prime Minister, in the hope that his party (the Umma) could come back to power after the soldiers had dealt with the opposition. This was not generally known when he took over, and the public seemed to have been pleased because parliamentary government had done nothing but foster strife and division. The military junta did not declare any ideology, but they laid stress on the 'reintroduction of moral values in the national politics' and appealed to the public over the heads of political parties and politicians.[31] They also declared an intention to go back to their barracks which added to the general satisfaction.

As it happened Abbhoud and his men were in no particular

hurry to go back to the barracks. Their Egyptian counterparts were still in power, they must have felt, so why should they hand over power to civilian politicians who were still divided? The military régime was itself divided and engaged in an internal power struggle during the first twelve months. There were abortive counter-*coups* which were caused by personal rivalries. In the last of these attempted counter-*coups*, five young officers were sentenced to death and executed. The executions came as a great shock to the Sudanese people, who began to question what an observer has called 'the legitimacy of the army'.[32] It appears that a legitimacy had been assumed for the army on an understanding that it would put 'the house in order' and then withdraw to its barracks. But as the régime started showing its real nature by suppressing basic liberties and declaring a state of emergency, a current of dissatisfaction arose among politically conscious Sudanese. The Press was censored and all political parties and demonstrations were banned. Some political leaders protested, petitioning for the return to parliamentary government. For this they were detained in a remote southern town.

General Abbhoud and his Supreme Council of the Armed Forces, composed of twelve members and himself as chairman, ruled the Sudan for six years. The Supreme Council nominated a Council of Ministers and took over the whole bureaucratic machine, inserting military personnel for general supervision and control. The close involvement of the military in the administration laid it open to charges of corruption, which added more fuel to the fire of civilian resentment. However, when the régime was swept out of power, the burning issue which acted as a critical factor in precipitating the revolt was the question of the Southern Sudan. General Abbhoud's régime was overthrown in October 1964.[33] This revolt had the quality – unique in Africa – of being the first in which a military régime was overthrown by a civilian uprising. For that reason alone something more must be said about it.

It is ironic that a military régime was overthrown on a question involving law and order. The Southern Sudan was in a state of rebellion, which the military régime was unable to quell. The problem was political but had been transformed into a military one during Abbhoud's reign; and it was natural that when a military régime failed to solve a military problem, such failure sealed its doom. What is the good of the military, after all, if they cannot put down a rebellion? With political meetings banned and leaders in detention, it was left to university students to offer solutions. The students of the University of Khartoum proceeded to do this by holding a conference on the problem of the south. But their efforts were frustrated by obstruction from the police. A clash between students and police took place, followed by a large-scale demonstration staged by the whole student body and some members of the staff. Again, this met with police resistance and further clashes took place, resulting in the death of two students. The situation became charged with deep emotion which was demonstrated by the huge turn-out at the funeral of the two students killed by the police.[34] A general strike was called by a revolutionary committee set up in the university and the response was swift and total. The whole country was paralysed, causing a shortage of vital supplies such as food. General Abbhoud saw the hopelessness of the situation, gave in, and agreed to hand over power to a caretaker government, until an election was held and a new government formed.[35] The election took place later, and the Umma party formed a civilian government.

The elements that had brought about the October Revolution of 1964 were elbowed out by the older conservative parties, who did not or could not solve the Southern problem. By early 1969 large-scale civil war engulfed the Southern Sudan. The stage was thus set for another army take-over which took place on May 25, 1969, under the leadership of General Nimeiry. President Nimeiry took an imaginative view of the Southern question, recognizing as he did the historical, cultural and geographical differences between North and South and the right of the Southern people to develop their own cultures and to enjoy administrative autonomy within a united Sudan. [35a].

A new constitution has just come out modelled on the Egyptian constitution. The party – the Sudan Socialist Union – is also modelled on the Arab Socialist Union. The influence of the Nasserite revolution is evident. Nimeiry's prestige has been enhanced by his ability to solve the Southern problem and his continuation and that of his system will depend principally on the ultimate solution of the outstanding issues regarding the South.

2. THE NEW TRENDS

The next military *coup*, and one which set a new trend in post-independence Africa, took place in Algeria, in June 1965.[36] The Algerian *coup d'état* of June 1965 marks a turning point in African politics in the post-independence era, in the same way (though in an opposite sense) that in Ghana the Nkrumahist Constitution of 1960 was a turning point in neo-presidentialism. The Algerian *coup* set an example for the political behaviour of the army in Africa which could be interpreted as a response to situations where neo-presidentialism had either overreached itself or was not able or willing to cope with critical problems. We will consider some of the significant factors and events leading to the *coup* in Algeria, and follow it up with similar reflections on the *coups* in Zaire, Nigeria, Ghana, Togo, and elsewhere. Togo will serve as an example for the other Francophone states which have undergone *coups* (i.e. Dahomey, Central African Republic, and Upper Volta), as it had certain features which are representative of the others. Also the short accounts already given of the Sudan revolt and the first Uganda *coup* will be sufficient for our present purpose.[37]

(a) Algeria

President Ahmed Ben Bella was deposed by Colonel Houari Boumedienne, his Minister of Defence and one-time ally in the struggle against Youssouf Ben Khedda for the Algerian leadership. The *coup* was achieved by turning a military exercise into an operation, thus averting suspicion and catching the government unaware, and securing all strategic points by surprise.[38]

The pretext given by the putschists for their take-over was that President Ben Bella had set up a dictatorial régime. The previous cabinet was substantially retained though it was reshuffled.

The event created strong reactions among students and other organized bodies who staged protest demonstrations in Algiers and other big cities, and were involved in clashes with the military. These lasted for over a week. Soon afterwards a resistance movement was formed, calling itself 'l'Organisation de la Résistance Populaire' (OR.P.). Some months later another opposition group emerged under the name of 'l'Organisation Clandestine de la Révolution Algérienne' (O.C.R.A.). O.C.R.A. stated that it was against military dictatorship and in favour of the establishment of constitutional legality.[39]

The fate of Ben Bella and his presidential régime is linked with the fate of the F.L.N. (Front de Libération Nationale) which we need to consider in order to get a clearer perspective of the event. The F.L.N. was, by its origin, a political movement which served as the embodiment and the driving force of the Algerian struggle for independence between 1954 and 1962. It was a movement forged in a struggle – in armed combat against superior military power. Through united by this common factor, its leadership was none the less composed of some disparate elements, ranging from moderate liberals like Ferhat Abbas and Ben Khedda, who were middle class professional men, to Mohammed Bouddiaf and Ben Bella himself, who were militant left-wing Socialists. Nor was the internal division limited to the ideological plane. Ben Bella and Boudiaf were locked in personal rivalry and animosity. The Arab–Berber division was also an element present, though it was kept in the background. The F.L.N. was thus not a political party, mono-lithic and disciplined in the Leninist tradition. It was a liberation movement. With the achievement of independence in June 1962, the F.L.N. lost much of its drive and sense of direction. The tensions which had been subordinated to the common goal during the struggle began to break out. The division emerged during the Tripoli meeting of the F.L.N. National Council (C.N.R,A.) in June 1962. Nevertheless the F.L.N. survived the tension and emerged with a general programme which came to be regarded as its guide to political action.

The essential elements of the Tripoli programme were (i) that the armed combat should give way to an ideological combat and peaceful reconstruction of the Algerian nation along Socialist lines; (ii) this task of peaceful reconstruction would embrace every Algerian, irrespective of class origin; and the Algerian cul-ture would be 'revolutionary, national and scientific'; (iii) the leadership would foster an agrarian revolution involving modern-ization of farming and giving land to those who worked in it; (iv) the F.L.N. would sponsor the nationalization of credit, foreign trade, mineral resources, and energy resources; the F.L.N. would also direct programmes for the realization of social aspira-tions, including the improvement of the standard of living, elimina-tion of illiteracy, emancipation of women, etc.; (v) in foreign affairs the F.L.N. would be in the forefront, assisting liberation movements, fighting against imperialism and for Arab and African unity. The Tripoli programme was slightly modified by the Charter of Algiers which was issued at the end of the first post-independence Congress of the F.L.N. (held 16–21 April 1964). The notable additions were (i) an emphasis on the doctrines of Islam and (ii) the introduction of the idea of *auto-gestion* (workers' management) of farms.

It was understood that the F.L.N. would establish further guidelines of policy and maintain control over the government by assuring that the head of the government and the majority of the ministers were its members. The inference from this was that the cabinet would be responsible to the Political Bureau of the party. These were the general policies with which all agreed. But the organization of the F.L.N. left much to be desired.

Ben Bella was aware of the weakness of the F.L.N.; and he and his group conceived its role in terms of a party machine run by the Political Bureau, which would continue to be responsible to the C.N.R.A. (Conseil National de la révolution Algérienne). He would be head of this party, which would be separate from the government. The government would be elected by the National Assembly, but since the party would nominate candidates to the Assembly, it would control the government. This conception of the role of the F.L.N. was given constitutional expression under the Constitution of 1963. The Constitution provided that the F.L.N. was the only party in the state.[40] The right to designate candidates for the National Assembly and for the presidency of the Republic were entrusted to the F.L.N.[41] The F.L.N. was empowered to define national policy, inspire the actions of the state, and control the National Assembly and the government.[42]

But the constitution had apparently enshrined a myth. In the process of attempting to create a disciplined party with unquestioned leadership Ben Bella had alienated many of the most important leaders who commanded large followings, like Mohammed Boudiaf, Krim Bel Kacem, Ait Ahmed, Mohammed Khider, and Rabah Bitat. The moderates like Ben Khedda and Ferhat Abbas had left earlier. These leaders, many of whom were founding members of the F.L.N., quit one by one either through resignation or dismissal, leaving the F.L.N. to be filled by less qualified and more opportunistic members.[43]

This state of affairs created more confusion than confidence among a war-weary and jobless mass of Algerians. Then there was the A.L.N. (Armée de Libération Nationale). The A.L.N. had been the military arm of the F.L.N. during the struggle. It was trained and organized mainly outside Algeria and, during the struggle, operated from the neighbouring states, in consort with the Willayas (the military districts) which operated guerrilla war within Algeria throughout the struggle. But the A.L.N., which was better trained and organized, emerged towards the latter days of the struggle as a tightly knit professional army.

Meanwhile, with the mass exodus of French settlers, vacancies had suddenly materialized in the government service, which came to be filled by Algerians. The external army (as opposed to the internal guerrilla movement), was reasonably well off in terms of salary and related matters. The new civil bureaucracy also had stepped into a new and comfortable life. In short, a new class was born into a new way of life, which the army and civil bureaucracy shared. As these new centres of power and interest emerged, a divided and debilitated F.L.N. could no longer attract any significant following. Ben Bella still enjoyed popularity among the masses but, in the absence of a vigorous party, his call could not get any meaningful responses. In the face of unresolved economic problems, and particularly unemployment, some of his policies (especially his foreign policy) were viewed with growing scepticism by the army.

Strains had appeared between Ben Bella and Boumedienne which must have had a cumulative effect on the decision about the *coup d'état*. Boumedienne wished the army to have a more direct role in the formulation and execution of policy.[44] This could mean that, even assuming that Ben Bella had succeeded in cementing a united F.L.N. leadership in the framework of a newly defined role of the F.L.N. as a political party, the army would eventually have wished to intervene in politics. On the other hand, such a demand may have been made because of the division among the F.L.N. leadership. Whichever reason is the more likely, Ben Bella had clearly left his position and that of his civilian régime vulnerable by his undue dependence on Boumedienne, particularly at a time when he was 'purging' the F.L.N. leadership. Boumedienne watched the F.L.N. leaders – the *chefs historiques* among them – leave the F.L.N. one by one, and Ben Bella became increasingly isolated.

Ben Bella realized this and had gambled on Boumedienne's loyalty and 'safeness'. It was a gamble that could perhaps have paid off had he acted swiftly and struck the right target first. He started his purge of Boumedienne by peripheral attacks. In October 1963 he had appointed Colonel Zbiri as chief of staff of A.L.N. while Boumedienne was visiting the Soviet Union. In 1964 he himself assumed control of the Ministry of the Interior, precipitating the resignation of Ahmed Medeghri, a Boumedienne supporter. He then announced plans to form a people's militia, and to reshuffle the cabinet. And then by the end of that year (1964) he told a confidant that he would remove Abdel Aziz Bouteflika, Minister of Foreign Affairs and the most influential protégé of Boumedienne.[45] The announcement of a cabinet reshuffle shows Ben Bella's position to be threatened from another front, that of his cabinet colleagues. The decision to create a militia was clearly designed to redress the balance against the A.L.N.; but it was obviously a serious tactical mistake, whatever its substantive merit. All in all it was an unhappy position. By then Ben Bella may have seen evidence of Boumedienne's political ambition. He took steps to reconcile himself with the opposition created by his former comrades-at-arms, notably with the F.F.S. (*Front de Forces Socialistes*) led by Ait Ahmed, whom he had kept alive by commuting a death sentence passed on him for armed rebellion to a life sentence. The military wanted Ait Ahmed's execution.

But the motivation of the Algerian *coup* cannot be explained simply in terms of personal ambitions. It contains several of the other elements mentioned before: personal, corporate, and national interest, the last, of course, as interpreted by the army, and by Boumedienne in particular.

The history of the struggle for liberation and the massive social and economic disruption which it brought about undoubtedly increased the magnitude of the problems faced by Ben Bella's government. The failure of the F.L.N. as an effective party was emphasized, if not caused, by Ben Bella's style of leadership. His flamboyance and charisma appealed to many, and his foreign policy initiatives, in particular his advocacy of more military and other help to African liberation movements, endeared him to millions.[46] But this was evidently not favoured by his military high command. It is conceivable, of course, that the army stepped in partly at any rate to provide the supreme corporate leadership which the F.L.N. failed to do. Clearly the party system of the F.L.N. and its relation to the government was found wanting. Some observers have viewed this failure against a more complex background: 'the rise and decline of the F.L.N. mirrors the painful process of social change in Algeria as well as the dislocations, contradictions and incompatibilities which more than seven years of conflict with France have produced.'[47]

The response of the population to the military régime was

ambiguous. Politically conscious sections were initially dissatisfied with army rule, as can be seen from constant threats of strikes and arrests. The underground also persists, as shown by the assassination of Mohammed Khider, and the series of ministerial resignations.[48]

Boumedienne's régime, on the other hand, seems determined to obtain a popular basis of support, as witness the time and effort it spent in preparing and organizing the municipal elections of February 1967.[49] It is also making determined efforts to improve the economic condition of the country. These are legitimate activities of government, and are not in themselves proof of the future intention of the leaders, one way or the other. On the other hand, the address Boumedienne delivered before the assembly of the 675 presidents of the municipal bodies elected in 1967 was one index of his intentions. He declared, notably, that 'the elections should not be considered as a political action designed for foreign consumption'.[50] In the same address he announced the rejection of the constitutional structure of the previous régime including presidential election, election to the National Legislature and referendum, because [sic] these had served to consolidate 'une certaine forme de pouvoir personnel, une certaine tendance déviationiste'.[51] The address contained attacks on the policy of the previous régime, claiming that the Socialism which the new régime was following was one based on 'authentic norms', with 'realism and seriousness', and without any 'forms of demagogy and all facile attempts to gain popular favour'.[52] Boumedienne could also be accused of attempting to gain popular favour, now. But the essential point is whether some material improvement in the economic situation will be achieved. The extent of the problem is recognized by the government. The official daily, *El Moujahid,* has reported as follows:

> The Algerian economy is incapable of responding to the essential needs of the population: employment and food (*consommation*)... in relation to the total active population less than one person in four is more or less employed. It is in this sense that it can be said that work is an exception in Algeria.

Figures show that out of a rural population of 7,000,000 which has an active population of between 1,200,000 and 1,300,000 only 250,000 are permanently employed. The rest are unemployed or underemployed.[53]

The problem is acute, and in the face of this reality the performance of the government will be judged by the number of jobs it creates, and the houses and schools it builds. Ultimately all governments are judged by the fruits of their actions, and their service, which becomes the first task of 'legitimacy' in such situations.

(b) Zaire

General Joseph Mobutu, commander-in-chief of the Congolese army, led a *coup d'état* in November 1965, ousting President Joseph Kasavubu, and his Prime Minister, Evariste Kimba. Mobutu took Kasavubu's place and replaced Kimba[55] by Col. Mulamba, of the A.N.C. (Armée Nationale Congolaise). The rest of the cabinet was retained. Mobutu announced that Parliament and the provincial assemblies would continue to sit and that elections would be suspended for five years, during which time he arrogated power to himself to rule and to prepare a new constitution.

The event was preceded by several weeks of government crisis and a state of partial paralysis of the administrative machinery. Zaire had suffered more upheavals than any other African state, except Nigeria, in the post-independence period. The chief cause is well known: a stubborn refusal of the colonial government to prepare the Zairiens educationally and administratively for independence. This general absence of preparation was aggravated by the vengeful act of mass withdrawal of Belgian colonial officials, at the moment of independence.[56]

Zaire became independent on 30 June 1960, and on 12 July of that year the Force Publique mutinied. One of the highest-ranking Zairiens in this army, was a young sergeant called Joseph Mobutu, who was engaged in civilian work at the time. The Prime Minister, the late Patrice Lumumba, appealed to the United Nations to help restore law and order. Thus began the tragic story of 'independent' Zaire. Katanga later seceded and the intervention of the United Nations became a full scale involvement in a civil war. Mobutu's Zairien army fought throughout the five years of the war, and the final phase of the war to end the secession of Katanga helped create a sense of unity in this army.

After the end of the Katanga secession Tshombe, the Prime Minister of the secessionist government and perpetrator of the secession, was asked by Kasavubu to form a government of Zaire. The motive was clear. It was felt by Kasavubu and his advisers that there would be no permanent peace and no unity in a country like Zaire with three widely separate centres of power (Leopoldville, Stanleyville and Elizabethville),[57] and as long as these places were held by people with differing ideas of national interest. So they decided to use Tshombe as the stick to beat the Stanleyville 'Lumumbists' with. Tshombe accepted the invitation, formed a government and, using white mercenaries, eventually crushed the rebellion. He then decided to form a new party which appeared in February 1965 under the name 'CONACO'. CONACO was, in fact, a projection on to the national arena of his old Katanga party, the CONAKAT. It embraced a coalition of forty-nine other political formations, and relied on the support of traditional elements. At the general election which followed CONACO emerged with the largest number of seats – a fact that threatened to assure Tshombe control of Parliament and eventual election as President of Zaire. When it was known that Tshombe had his eye on the presidential office, Kasavubu declared that he would offer himself for re-election.

A series of events followed in quick succession which showed the conflict between Tshombe and Kasavubu. Election results in three of the provinces were quashed by the Court of Appeal to CONACO's disadvantage. But Tshombe was still strongly placed. Then, in July 1965, Kasavubu gave the Ministry of the Interior to Victor Nendaka, overruling Prime Minister Tshombe's protests. Nendaka had been elected on a CONACO list of candidacy, but quit CONACO, presumably at Kasavubu's suggestion and the offer of a key ministry, and formed an anti-Tshombe front (Front Démocratique Congolais), helped by other politicians. When Parliament met, President Kasavubu asked Tshombe to dismiss his provisional government so that a broader-based government could be formed. Tshombe refused to resign and on 13 October 1965 Kasavubu dismissed him and asked Evariste Kimba to form a new government.[58] The whole episode is full of shifting allegiances and political somersaults. The events that followed after 13 October show parliamentary government at its most farcical. After a long series of consultations, Kimba presented his team for investiture by Parliament on 14 November. Tshombe's strength was demonstrated when Kimba's 'government' was rejected by a vote of 134 against 121 and 7 abstentions.[59]

Kasavubu, who had dismissed Lumumba and been successful, was not one to budge an inch. He asked Kimba to start all over again and form another government. CONACO attacked his decision in a Press release, '. . . . the political Bureau of CONACO', it declared, 'could not tolerate that consultation should be limited, whereas in democracy the parliamentary group which defeats a government is always necessarily called upon to form an alternative government.'[60] This is true enough in principle. But under the then constitution the President was the chief executive and the Prime Minister was appointed and dismissed by him. A campaign of mutual vilification in the Press and radio followed.[61]

Then, on 25 November 1965, the army *coup* took place. The communiqué of the army high command stated that it seized power, 'After having witnessed the failure of the civil authorities, who only thought of their fight for power, neglecting the interests of the country.' This was later elaborated with a view to gaining general popular acceptance.[62]

(c) Nigeria

The Nigerian *coup d'état* took place on 15 January 1966. It was organized by a small group of officers and men led by five majors.[63] The group struck throughout Nigeria with remarkable speed and co-ordination. In the north they killed the powerful Regional Prime Minister, the Sardauna of Sokoto, Sir Ahmadu Bello. In the Western Region they killed the Regional Premier (and ally of the Sardauna), Chief Akintola, and kidnapped the Federal Prime Minister, Sir Abubakar Tafewa Balewa, and his Finance Minister, Chief Festus Okotie-Eboh. The last two were killed later.

It is not clear what the leaders of the first *coup* intended to do once in power. The only broadcast made by Major Nzeogwu from Kaduna radio station spoke of ending tribalism, nepotism, and corruption. The *coup* failed for various reasons. There is evidence to show that General Ironsi, the commander-in-chief of the Nigerian army, was not involved, and that he was in fact on the list of key figures to be eliminated.[64] The General escaped, and in rallying round him a loyalist army, contributed to the failure of 'the *coup* of the majors'. It is also believed that the Federal Prime Minister was kidnapped with a view to forcing him to call on them to form a government. He died while their prisoner, killed by them. Instead the rump cabinet called on General Ironsi to set up a military government, which he did. A few days after that the leader of the northern *coup*, Major Nzeogwu agreed to surrender to the new government.

The *coup d'état* which shook Nigeria had its roots in the ethnic, regional, religious, and personal conflicts which plagued the

Federation. Corruption and thuggery, which were rampant, also no doubt had their part to play in the dissatisfaction that led to the drastic action of the majors. The assassination of the Sardauna of Sokoto and of Chief Akintola provides one clue to the motivation. The Sardauna of Sokoto was probably the most powerful figure in Nigeria. As ruler of the largest region of the Federation and as head of the larger of the coalition parties – the N.P.C. (Northern People's Congress) – that was ruling the Federation, he exerted immense power and influence. In the north, he combined, in his person, traditional autocratic leadership and religious (Muslim) standing. In the west, he connived at, and succeeded in creating a partnership with, Chief Akintola, after the latter had broken away from the Action Group. The Prime Minister of the Federal Government, Sir Abubakar, was the Sardauna's deputy as Head of the N.P.C., and many Nigerians openly claimed that he was his lieutenant in Lagos.

Although a military *coup* was not generally expected in Nigeria, in retrospect, ominous signs of things to come could be seen in the general election of October 1965 in the Western Region. That election was marked by disturbances, leading to loss of life and bitter recriminations in which charges of rigging and intimidation were made. The supporters of Chief Adegbenre (Akintola's rival) were unwilling to accept the verdict returned by the ballot boxes. Many embittered southern Nigerians felt a threat of northern (Muslim) domination, and saw in Akintola a willing tool of the Sardauna's machinations for eventual total control from the north. After the election disturbances of October, the Western Region became the real challenge facing the government of Sir Abubakar Tafewa Balewa. All southern Nigerians (east and west) were united in the sentiments implied in this challenge. The fact that the majority of the officers in the *coup* were Ibos[65] is perhaps one small piece of evidence of the unity against the threat of a powerful northern ruler. Another piece of evidence was the fact that the Sardauna and his ally, Akintola, were the first targets, as already pointed out.

The government of Sir Abubakar Tafewa Balewa itself – a ruling coalition of N.P.C. and N.C.N.C. (National Council for Nigeria and the Cameroons) – had become thoroughly discredited for inefficiency and corruption, particularly among the young. It has been argued by some observers that when the young majors struck on January 1965, they acted politically as the arm of the young.[66] These officers were recruited in the late fifties and early sixties, and were not men who had seen long service in the army. They must be considered among those who least regarded themselves as members of a closed corporate entity (the army), existing independently of the rest of the society. Sociologically, therefore, they belonged to the intelligentsia – civil servants, teachers, graduates, school leavers, etc.[67] If this conclusion is correct – and it is hard to refute, especially in view of the political mood of the time before the *coup* – then it leads to the further conclusion that the *coup* of the majors had a definite political purpose, motivated primarily by the national interest.

The failure of the *coup* saw the installation of General Ironsi, commander of the army, a soldier of long service and with a professional soldier's attitude to politics. He was placed in a position not of his own making, and his army was thin on the ground in a country of Nigeria's size.[68] He therefore had to rely on the civil service for the administration of the country. His top advisers included people like Messrs. F. C. Nwokedi (Permanent Secretary in the Ministry of External Affairs) and A. A. Ayida (Permanent Secretary in the Ministry of Economic Development). General Ironsi set up various committees to review the constitution, the structure of the educational system, the restructuring of the civil service, and future economic development, to mention the most important. The members of these committees were all civil servants and academics. As politicians were associated with a discredited régime, none was included in any of these committees. Indeed a decree had been issued banning all political parties and tribal organizations. The constitution was suspended.

Among the measures proposed by General Ironsi, the Unification Decree announced on 24 May 1966 created the sharpest reaction in the north, where disturbances occurred on 29 May. The background to these disturbances, and the tragic events of July and September 1966 in which thousands were massacred, is not entirely clear. The events of July involved the kidnapping and death of General Ironsi, and the death of many Ibos residing in the north. They also produced a counter-coup which installed Colonel Yakubu Gowon to head a new military government in Ironsi's place. Colonel Gowon was described by publications of the national military government as 'a soldier reluctantly in government' and as a 'thirty-one year old son of a humble Christian evangelist of the Church Missionary Society in Zaria'.[69] The same publication makes reference to factors other than the civil service unification required by the Unification Decree as giving rise to the disturbances. Reference is made to the part played by 'local petty contractors and party functionaries whose livelihood depended solely on political party patronage. . . .' It is claimed that such elements were the hardest hit by the change in the government, especially since those indebted to the Northern Marketing Board and the Northern Nigerian Development Corporation were made to pay up their arrears. They thus resorted to whispering campaigns and incitement.[70]

After the May disturbances an uneasy calm settled on the country. The atmosphere was charged with tension and mutual suspicion, particularly in the army. 'Political' rivalry within the army had assumed larger dimensions. The ethnic-regional factor had asserted itself as predominant, and entered the ranks of the army. It is claimed, for example, that regular channels of communication (on which the efficacy of the chain of command depends) were being by-passed in the transmission of instructions.[71]

In the meantime, after steadily deteriorating relations between the central military government and the Eastern government of Colonel Ojukwu, resulting from the July and September events, attempts were made to settle differences. In the east the problem of displaced Ibos coming mainly from the north was very grave.[72] Then a meeting was held at Aburi to try to solve the problem of the future constitutional structure Nigeria should take – the centre–region relationship, the position of the central government in relation to the regions, the composition and function of the national army, etc. But the Aburi 'agreement' did not resolve the differences – each gave a different interpretation to it, and in particular to the future of the northern soldiers stationed in the south.

Charges and counter-charges of bad faith followed; these were followed by threats of secession or charges of such threats, which were mostly denied but were sometimes confirmed conditionally.[73] Then the Western Region joined in the demand for the withdrawal of northern soldiers from its region. This was soon followed by the secession of the Eastern Region and the declaration of a new state – Biafra. The civil war followed, with the central military government determined to 'crush the rebellion' and with the new state determined to resist. The outcome of the rebellion is now well known. It is another story. Nigeria in the meantime is still governed by the military.

(d) Ghana

In Ghana President Kwame Nkrumah was overthrown by a military *coup* on 24 February 1966, while he was away on a state visit to China. The story of the *coup* has been told by one of the organizers, Colonel Afrifa.[74] According to Afrifa, the *coup* was planned and carried out by turning a test exercise ordered in connection with Rhodesia into a military operation directed against Nkrumah's government. Afrifa explains that from November 1965 (after the Unilateral Declaration of Independence) the Ghana army had been in a high state of readiness to move into Rhodesia at short notice. 'We exploited this situation', he says, 'to deceive the intelligence system.'[75]

The *coup* was master-minded by Colonel (later Major-General) Emanuel Kotoka, who was a brigade commander in the Ghana army. Kotoka and his fellow-conspirators brought the police chief, Inspector-General J. K. Harlley, into the planning. But the execution of the *coup* was carried out by Kotoka's brigade. The vital operation was led by Colonel Afrifa, who secured the radio station. Afrifa recounts how he did this with eight men, while 116 men engaged the presidential guard at Flagstaff House, which lay on the way to the radio station and which could not be secured because the commander of the guard, Colonel Zanerigu, had managed to escape and alert his men. The guard gave in after a fight lasting two days.

Colonel Kotoka announced the *coup d'état* over the radio as follows: 'Fellow citizens of Ghana, I have come to inform you that the military, in co-operation with the Ghana police, have taken over the government of Ghana today. The myth surrounding Nkrumah is broken. Parliament is dissolved and Kwame Nkrumah is dismissed from office. All ministers are also dismissed. The Convention Peoples Party is disbanded with effect from now. It will be illegal for any person to belong to it. . . .'[76] This was followed by other messages. The event was greeted with some demonstration of relief on the part of a considerable section of the Accra population. The composition of those who took part in the joyous demonstration is difficult to establish. But what cannot be disputed is the fact that no civilian resistance expressed itself in any form, which is clear evidence that the People's Party had remained Leninist only in theory but not in practice.

A review of the statements and comments published or uttered on the Ghana radio shows an array of 'reasons' given to justify the overthrow of President Nkrumah and his government. One of the earliest broadcasts following Kotoka's announcement stated: 'The concentration of power in the hands of one man has led to the abuse of individual rights and liberty. Power has been exercised by the former president capriciously. The operation of the laws has been suspended to the advantage of his favourites and he has been running the country as his own personal property.'[77] General Ankrah, Chairman of the National Liberation Council, followed this by a statement of 28 February: '. . . the right of the people to vote at a free general election for their own chosen candidates was reduced to a formal unpractical privilege of sanctioning the election of such candidates as Kwame Nkrumah himself nominated. His love for the arbitrary use of power . . . led him to whittle away gradually the independence of the Judiciary and to suppress academic freedom. . . .'[78] The same broadcast also stated that too much money was spent to maintain a large force of security officers to secure Nkrumah's personal safety. Reference is also made to the establishment of a 'private army' at an annual cost of £5,500,000 as a counterpoise to the Ghana armed forces. And again, there was a charge of 'mismanagement, waste and unwise spending'.

Many more charges and comments followed, and no fewer than fifteen commissions of enquiry were set up to investigate every facet of the activity of Nkrumah's government. Even if one were to question the validity of some of the charges, none the less it can be assumed that those who made these charges believed them to be well-founded. It would be unjustifiable to dismiss them as a mere post-*coup* 'public relations' stunt. For they offer a clue to an understanding of the causes. A final judgement is not possible, or indeed necessary within the scope of the present enquiry.[79]

Many 'reasons' are given as the cause of the *coup* – officially, or by individual commentators. One commentator, reiterating the charges made by General Ankrah, added that candidates were handpicked by Nkrumah and the central committee of the C.P.P. and 'forced down the unwilling throats of the electorate'. He concluded by saying 'the blatant display of this trickery last June (1965) . . . must be accounted one of the direct causes of last week's overthrow of the corrupt régime'.[80]

More 'reasons' are supplied by Colonel Afrifa.[81] The criticisms levelled against the Nkrumah Government, charged as they are with emotional content, cannot be passed unnoted, because they are indices of what went wrong. Afrifa refers, for example, to the suffering of the people on the basis of his own observation. He has written: 'I came from the village, and I know the sufferings of my people. There were instances when even salt was in short supply. Sugar and milk were nowhere to be seen. No drug could be found to cure the sick. . . . Accra is organised in such a way as to give an impression of happiness and affluence; there were new streets and new lights, while vast areas of this country were planted with misery and suffering. . . . I became convinced that Nkrumah had failed the nation. I had not liked the man since he imposed his party on the country. I again resumed my thoughts about a coup.' The penultimate sentence is revealing as to the mixed nature of motivation for a *coup*. It is not possible to say which of the two reasons – i.e. the national shortage, or the imposition of one-party rule – weighed more heavily in the decision about a *coup*. Possibly the two are interrelated. Again, Afrifa complains of the suppression of human rights. In a statement given in an interview to the (London) *Observer*, soon after the *coup*, Afrifa said: 'We've lived in Britain before, and therefore didn't like this dictatorship. There was no freedom of the Press or of the individual – things we know are fundamental human rights.' In the same interview Afrifa also stated that Nkrumah introduced party politics into the army; he went on: 'He took a man with no training as an officer, a Mr. Hassan, appointed him a Brigadier and put him in charge of military intelligence. Here we had a situation in which mess corporals were watching commanding officers and reporting them. What greater insult to our intelligence and patriotism.'[82]

Here, in the last remark, we have a clue to the most important factor which is explained here in terms of pride and patriotism. Undoubtedly no civilian politician has a monopoly of pride or patriotism; the army has its share of both. But behind this there lies a more profound reason – group interest. The reflections of Colonel Afrifa provide invaluable material for a study of the motivation of army officers who lead *coups d'état*. To an independent observer he proves that the motives of a *coup* are not as simple and clear-cut as the first utterances of *coup* leaders try to make out. Afrifa makes reference, for example, to standards learnt at Sandhurst. His views of the role of the army and its relation to the political head and to political parties reveals the influence of his educational background at Sandhurst. But it would be a mistake to attribute his conduct and that of his fellow conspirators solely to an esoteric professionalism imbibed at metropolitan institutions of learning, though these have their share.

Afrifa, in fact, represented a new professional (*élite*) class whose training was influenced by metropolitan institutions and values. This new class has an interest to preserve since they feel that they are entitled to privileges. The C.P.P. and the politicians, leaders of the C.P.P., presented a threat to that interest. The recurrent theme in Afrifa's reflections is the Ghana army as a corporate group whose efficiency, pride, and (above all) integrity, was threatened by political interferences. 'The Ghanaian soldier,' he writes, 'is one of the finest in the world. He is gentle, kind-hearted, sympathetic, and resolute. . . . The material to make the Ghana army formidable is available! We have the men. I always want to remain with the troops; the very sight of them gives me satisfaction. These are the men for whom above all else their country comes first. These are the men who made up the Ghana army during Kwame Nkrumah's régime. Because of bad planning, economic mismanagement and political interference, this army was rendered incapable, ill-equipped, and had virtually been reduced to a rabble.'[83] This wounded professional pride is sometimes mixed with other sentiments. On the subject of Rhodesia, for instance, Afrifa volunteers an opinion thus: 'I personally know that Her Majesty's Government was quite capable of dealing with the Rhodesian situation. I felt that Nkrumah was making too much noise about the whole issue, especially by raising the people's militia and hurling slogans at everybody as if Rhodesia was his concern alone.' He goes on: 'But Nkrumah was a fanatic and it was wrong to take him for granted. We knew he was capable of making decisions of any nature. From concern for my troops I felt it would be criminal and purposeless to lead such an army of excellent soldiers ill-equipped, to fight an unnecessary war.'[84]

He had similar misgivings on the Zaire operation. He complained of interference by politicians, and in particular by Nkrumah, in military matters. 'I started asking myself,' he muses, 'what had gone wrong. We had lost lives in a struggle that was not ours, in a cause that was not ours. I was at the very beginning of my career, and perhaps not well-equipped to grasp the situation. I felt that General Alexander, the commanding officer, was quite capable of handling the situation if only our politicians left him alone.'[85] Yes, indeed, he was not well equipped to grasp the Zaire situation which was not only a military arena, as he saw it, but a political arena involving international power politics.[86]

It is clear that he missed the central point about Zaire and that he did not share the views of his Head of State and those of the African leaders who had the same approach.[87]

It is also clear that these and similar reflections of Afrifa are not those of an officer who saw his duty as 'not to question why, but to do and die'.[88] Admittedly, the Congo experience was frustrating to a person like Afrifa. But that was not in itself sufficient to instil in the mind of a young officer thoughts of a *coup*. It must be seen together with the whole situation in Ghana and with the position of the army and of officers like Afrifa in that situation. Again, the way they saw their position *vis-à-vis* the whole Ghana situation would be influenced by their educational background, as well as by their social background in Ghana.

The situation was complicated by the role of the C.P.P. The C.P.P., which had lost its popularity long before the *coup*, had made attempts to indoctrinate the Ghana army with Nkrumahism, which the army resented. A branch of the party was opened at the Teshi Military Academy for this purpose, and officers were required to join the party. Afrifa explains that he refused to fill in the form 'on the principle that the army must be above politics', and he goes on, 'the army and the police are the custodians of the nation's constitution. If the army was made to identify itself openly with the C.P.P. and its ideology, it was bound to lose its self-respect and independence of outlook.'

In point of fact the role of the army as custodian of the nation's constitution and as being above politics is contradictory in conception. If the army's role is conceived as a custodian of the constitution it cannot be insulated from politics. Officers like Colonel Afrifa 'participate' in politics in spite of what they say about the army's role being above politics. Their 'participation' may be negatively expressed in that they may reject C.P.P. slogans or even serious programmes. As stated before, the general ills of society affect them in one way or another and they react to these positively or negatively. Moreover, if the army's role is seen as custodian of the constitution in the Ghana situation there would have been a built-in rivalry between the army and the President of the Republic who is declared to be the guardian of the constitution. A group which saw its role as custodian of the constitution would inevitably see 'betrayal of trust' written across any political act of the President whenever such act displeased it for some reason or other. There is thus a gap between the position of the army as being above politics and as custodian of the constitution.

It appears that the C.P.P. and Nkrumah himself committed a series of acts which threatened the integrity of the army as a group. The dismissal of General Ankrah, who was popular in the army, is one example. The appointment of Colonel Hassan as director of military intelligence is another. On the interference of the C.P.P. with the army, Afrifa writes: 'the army was virtually at the mercy of the politicians who treated it with arrogance and open contempt.'[89] Again, the creation of the Presidential Guard not only as a counterpoise but as a favoured army unit was deeply resented, as witness these words: 'we were also aware that members of the president's own guard regiment were receiving kingly treatment. Their pay was higher and it was an open fact that they possessed better equipment. The men who had been transferred from the regular army no longer owed any allegiance and loyalty to the chief of defence staff, but to Kwame Nkrumah who had become their commanding officer.'[90] A policy of calculated balance within the armed forces seems to have been the basis of the creation of the Presidential Guard. This created mistrust without achieving its purpose.

However, no division based on ethnic balance was practised. Nor was the 'tribal' question involved as a critical factor in precipitating the Ghana *coup*. Western observers have greatly exaggerated the 'tribal' factor. When the *coup* took place, the first journalistic reaction was that it was an Ashanti *coup*, because Kotoka's brigade was stationed in Kumasi. But, as Afrifa (himself an Ashanti) remarks: 'the description is correct to the extent that the coup was planned in Kumasi by Col. Kotoka, Mr. Harlley and myself. But Col. Kotoka and Mr. Harlley are not Ashantis. The Ashantis and the Ewes, their tribes, are however, traditional allies.'[91]

A far more serious question was Nkrumah's decision to send cadets to Eastern Europe for military training. This was serious from the point of view of a Western-trained officer corps which felt its future position threatened. General Alexander has written that he had warned Nkrumah that this would split the officer corps of the Ghana army into two camps.[92] His opposition to this decision caused Nkrumah on 22 September 1961 to dismiss him and the other British officers who were in the Ghanaian army. It is now known that the Ghanaian officers had been behind General Alexander and that they had been plotting Nkrumah's overthrow since 1961.[93] The Ghanaian officers' support of General Alexander and their bitter condemnation of Nkrumah's decision to send cadets to Eastern Europe should be seen not only in the light of their educational background, but in terms of how they saw it as a threat to the corporate unity of their group. This is not to ignore or underestimate the importance of the other factors, and in particular some of the methods of the C.P.P., including intimidation which at times degenerated into thuggery.

Indeed, the internal problems of Ghana were projected on to the international scene in the minds of the army officers. To some of them Nkrumah's advocacy of African unity and his support of African liberation movements seemed chimerical in the light of Ghanaian problems. The prestige of Nkrumah, which was high in other parts of Africa, had diminished in the eyes of many Ghanaians, which explains the reactions of the post-*coup* period.[94]

Afrifa, for example, condemns Nkrumah's stand on African unity at the O.A.U. summit conferences at Addis Ababa, Cairo, and Accra, and blames him for having taken upon himself 'unilateral military preparations on an issue that affected the whole Continent and the Commonwealth'. He claims that Nkrumah became unpopular among the Ghanaian army because of this, and concludes somewhat vindictively with these fateful words: 'they realised that he was sending them to war without proper equipment and without adequate preparation. *The moment they started complaining I knew that the days of the Convention Peoples Party were numbered.* At this time it became common conversation among the officers and the men that military action against Nkrumah's régime was the only solution.' (Italics supplied.)[95]

The situation in Ghana presents a contrast to the Nigerian situation in several different ways. The contrast is sharpest on the question of ethnic and regional conflict; Nigeria is plagued by such conflict, which was not critical in Ghana. The contrast between these two states existed before the *coups*. Nigeria had a federal structure while Ghana was a unitary state. Nigeria had a multi-party system where Ghana was a one-party state. Nigeria had a bicameral legislature and a dual executive where Ghana had a unicameral national assembly and a military executive. At a different level – at the level of ideas and political orientation – no two states in Africa could have been more opposed than the two, particularly in their external policies. This could be seen on the questions of Zaire and Rhodesia, for example.

From the point of view of the present inquiry, the fact that military *coups* took place in the two countries underlines the point made earlier that there is no one set of circumstances which produces a *coup d'état*. Whatever the form of government, and the nature of grievances which spark off the discontent, it can reasonably be concluded that military intervention will be inevitable unless there is a solid popular base for the policy and action of the government, with a solidly built and viable political infra-structure firmly rooted in the society. The one-party system is one way of creating such a solid base. But where the government had moved further away from the people, the source of its power, depending entirely or chiefly on its state apparatus of control, and where under such circumstances the party becomes discredited as a mere agency of control, more grievances will be created. And military intervention will not only be inevitable in such a situation, but the people, far from resisting, will organize street demonstrations in support of the military. Such appears to have been the case in Ghana. The three days' demonstrations which followed the *coup* may have been organized by the new rulers, but it is hard to explain the reaction of the secretariat of the Ghana Trades Union Congress (which had resisted wage demands for the past three years while food prices increased as much as 400 per cent), which declared its support for the new régime. 'In the name of the workers,' the secretariat greeted 'with greatest satisfaction the deliverance of the country and the end of dictatorship and economic chaos.'[96] Fitch and Oppenheimer have commented on the apathy of the C.P.P. in the face of the *coup* as follows:

> The Convention Peoples Party (C.P.P.) with its two million members and 500,000 militants, all pledged by oath to support Dr. Nkrumah, organised no resistance at all. The C.P.P. had been founded in 1949 when Dr. Nkrumah together with communists and militant nationalists decided that only a mass-based party could carry out the struggle against British colonialism. In 1952, it helped launch the first general strike in sub-Saharan Africa. The strike forced the concessions which brought Dr. Nkrumah from Fort James prison to the position of 'Leader of Government Business' in the first popularly elected parliament in Colonial Africa. Now, after 15 years as Ghana's ruling party the C.P.P. allowed itself to be dissolved by a simple decree announced over the radio. The day after the coup, the generals wound up the affairs of the C.P.P. by simply announcing over radio Ghana: 'All persons who find themselves

in possession of vehicles belonging to the ex-party, the C.P.P., are requested to return them to the nearest police station'.[97]

And that was that, until April 1967, when an attempt was made at a counter-*coup*, by young military officers. The attempt failed, but the young officers killed General Kotoka. Constitutional rule was restored in 1969, but the military were to return in 1972.

(e) Togo

In Togo the army took over power from President Grunitsky on 13 January 1967. The *coup* was led by Lieutenant-Colonel Étienne Eyadema, the chief of staff. President Grunitsky announced his voluntary withdrawal from office, and Colonel Eyadema declared in a proclamation that the army had taken over full responsibility 'in order to stop the political confusion' which he said was creating a 'psychosis of imminent civil war'. The constitution was suspended, the National Assembly dissolved, all political activity was prohibited and a state of emergency declared.

A 'Committee of National Reconciliation'[99] was set up on the following day and Colonel Eyadema promised that this committee would try within three months to create the conditions necessary to enable free elections to be held, and that the army would surrender power to civilians in due course. The committee, which consisted of eight members, included three former members of the previous cabinets under President Grunitsky. It was presided over by Colonel Kleber Dadjo who was in charge of Defence and Foreign Affairs, while one of the former Grunitsky ministers (M. Benoit Malou) was given charge of the key Ministries of Interior, Information, and Press.

The inclusion of civilian ministers of the former régime as well as the manner in which the *coup* was announced and the treatment of members of the former government is enough to suggest that in a certain sense the Togo *coup* had certain original traits. According to Colonel Eyadema, he and the former President had come to an understanding whereby the military took power. Grunitsky was allowed to leave for Dahomey, whence he went to Paris.

The original tussle in the post-independence years started after the first President, Sylvanus Olympio, was murdered by mutinous soldiers on 13 January 1963. During Olympio's rule there had been some trouble, caused mainly by his government's action to invalidate joint opposition attempts to put up candidates at the

1961 presidential elections, and to ban one party, the JUVENTO, and arrest its leaders. Grunitsky, leader of the other main opposition party (the *Union Démocratique des Populations Togolaises*) had gone into exile in Dahomey.

The flashpoint that caused the demise of Olympio and his régime was a mutiny caused by armed forces mainly composed of ex-servicemen who had demanded to be allowed to join the Togolese army. Olympio had refused on the grounds that expansion of the armed forces would impose an intolerable financial burden on the country.[100] On 13 January 1963 an 'insurgency committee' of the armed forces announced that it had requested Grunitsky and Antoine Meatchi (his ally in exile and leader of the *Unions des Chefs et des Populations du Nord*, a body affiliated to Grunitsky's party) to return from exile and form a government. Grunitsky returned to form a provisional civilian government, whose main task was to prepare 'free elections'. The military leaders declined his offer to take office in the cabinet but declared that the civil authority, set up at their request, must be a democratic government 'respecting all freedom of thought, belief and opinion'.

Grunitsky announced that the armed forces would be expanded by the raising of a second infantry company in the immediate future and the formation of a battalion at a later date.[101] He also announced the raising of the ban on the opposition parties imposed by Olympio's government, a general amnesty, and a forty hour week.

On 5 May 1963 Grunitsky was elected President and Antoine Meatchi Vice-President for a five-year term, under a new constitution. This happened after a series of round-table conferences had been held starting in February, between delegates from the four main parties and representatives of the army's 'committee of vigilance'. The parties agreed on 16 April to nominate Grunitsky as sole presidential candidate, with Meatchi as candidate for the vice-presidency. Agreement was reached on a new constitution which was approved by a national referendum at the same time as the presidential election. Elections for the National Assembly were also held concurrently, on the basis of a single 'National Union' list, which had been put forward by the four parties. The allocation of places on the joint list for the national assembly election had led to a dispute between the C.U.T. party (*Comité de l'Unité Togolaise*, i.e. Olympio's party), which claimed the right to half the seats, and its three partners, who insisted that the seats should be divided equally between all four parties. C.U.T. leaders threatened to boycott the election if their demands were not met. They were arrested the following day. Grunitsky presented his new government to the National Assembly on 16 May. He retained the portfolio for Defence and Interior, while the Vice-President retained the portfolio of Finance and the Ministry of Economics and Planning.

Grunitsky's government was subjected to ceaseless attacks from the very beginning. The first issue in which it was seriously taken to task, mainly by the C.U.T. leaders, was its failure to open a judicial enquiry into the former President's death. They pressed their claims further by demanding general elections. Grunitsky answered by imprisoning some of the C.U.T. leaders. The two years (1964–66) of Grunitsky's régime were marked by plots or charges of threatened plots. Early in January 1965, eight military leaders, most of them from the Moba tribe of Northern Togo, were arrested on charges of plotting to overthrow the government.

A mutiny followed in July of the same year. But the most serious attempt took place on 20–21 November 1966, after Grunitsky's régime had faced dissension in the cabinet, and several thousand people demonstrated in the streets of Lomé, the capital. An attempt to seize power by C.U.T. leaders failed when Colonel Eyadema and his army remained loyal to Grunitsky. Grunitsky then dismissed the whole cabinet and formed a new government, and shortly afterwards secured from the National Assembly the abolition of the office of Vice-President.[102]

But a solution to instability and continual strife was nowhere on the horizon. Grunitsky reshuffled his cabinet within the same month, and things had practically come to a standstill when Colonel Eyadema intervened. Eyadema later abandoned the National Conciliation Committee and on 14 April 1967 formed a new government. He dissolved the Committee and himself presided over a new government consisting of four military men and eight civilians. He assumed the presidency and retained the portfolio for Defence, while another military colleague was in charge of Interior. He promised, as they all do, that as soon as peace and reconciliation had been achieved the army would surrender all its power to civilian authority.[103]

Reconciliations, however, were not easy to come by in Togo, as elsewhere in Africa. One of the ironic facts about present-day African politics is that civilian political leaders cannot rise above their differences to unite even in the face of a 'common enemy', which shows that their 'differences' must be *predominantly connected* with, or have a great deal to do with, personal ambition, more than another issue.

(f) Other states

The situation in Dahomey was very similar to that in Togo, before the *coups* took place in both countries. The government of the first President of Dahomey, Hubert Maga, was deposed by the military in 1963 and replaced by another civilian government, with Migan Apithy as President and Ahomadegbe as Prime Minister. After continual friction between these two and their factions, Ahomadegbe dismissed Apithy in November 1965, only to be deposed himself on 2 December by the army under Colonel Soglo, the chief of staff.[104]

The *coup* in Dahomey was followed in quick succession by a *coup* in the Central African Republic (1 January 1966) where the government of David Dacko was overthrown by Colonel Bokassa; and in the Upper Volta (4 January 1966) where the government of Maurice Yameogo was overthrown by Colonel Lamizana. In Burundi, after some cabinet instability, and the murder of two Prime Ministers and the execution of many political leaders for alleged plots in the course of three years, the King (Mwambutsa V) was deposed by his son, nineteen-year-old Prince Charles Ndizoye, with the connivance of the military, on 8 July 1966. The prince acceded to his father's throne under the name of Mwami Ntare V and appointed Captain Michel Micombero, the Minister of Defence, as Prime Minister. On 29 November 1966, Captain Micombero deposed the new King, and he himself assumed presidential powers. This did not come as a surprise, not even, perhaps, to the young King, who was on a state visit to Zaire and who commented with what must surely go down as the understatement of the year, that Captain Micombero was 'discourteous'!

A further drama in Dahomey was the military takeover of 26 October 1972, when the rotating collegial executive was overthrown.

Each military *coup* has its own peculiar traits based on local conditions. But all *coup* leaders, as already stated, charge the governments they have deposed with corruption, inefficiency, nepotism, inability to deal with economic crises, and creating political crises, or with any one of these. In the Togolese situation, for instance, as in the Dahomeyan situation, civilian internecine conflict eclipsed all other factors and facilitated a military takeover.

NOTES

1. The origin of religion has been explained in similar terms; cf. e.g., Bertrand Russell, *Human Knowledge; Scope and its Limits*, London, 1948, Chapter 1.
2. K. Olivecrona, *Law as Fact*, Stevens, London, 1971; cf, also a discussion on this subject in Denis Lloyd's *Introduction to Jurisprudence*, Stevens, London, 1959, pp. 248–57.
3. E. Shils, 'The Military in the Political Development of the New States' in *The Role of the Military in Underdeveloped Countries*, J. J. Johnson (ed), Princeton U.P., 1962, p. 8.
4. cf. W. Gutteridge and N. Brown, *The African Military Balance*, Institute for Strategic Studies, London, 1964.
5. Whether or not there is validity in the allegation that some of the *coups* in Africa, e.g. the Ghana *coup*, have been instigated by the C.I.A., it is clear that the C.I.A. has toppled or otherwise interfered with governments in the past decade; cf. e.g., David Wise and Thomas B. Ross, *Invisible Government*, Random House, New York, 1964.
6. cf. e.g., The Ghana freedom song: 'Ghana, Land of Freedom', 'Voice of the Free, You have Joy for Ever . . .' etc.
7. E. Shils, op. cit., p. 29.
8. cf. Report on African Education, O.A.U. Conference 17–24 March 1964, *O.A.U. Review* Vol. 1, pp. 27–38.
9. cf. T. L. Hodgkin, *African Political Parties*, Penguin, 1961.
10. cf. René Dumont, *L'Afrique noire est mal partie*, Paris, 1965, p. 7. Dumont gives the average rate of growth since 1959 as 1·7 per cent p.a. for food and 2·5 per cent p.a. for population.
11. The world price of cocoa steadily went down until 1966, when there was a sudden rise with the fall of Nkrumah.
12. cf. R. Dumont, op. cit.
13. cf. E. Shils, op. cit., pp. 14–15.
14. ibid, pp. 18–23.
15. For a sample of such pronouncements in the case of the *coups* of 1965–66 in Africa cf. Dennis Austin, 'The Underlying Problems of the Army *Coups d'État* in Africa', *Optima*, June 1966.
16. E. Shils, op. cit., p. 17.
17. ibid.
18. During the colonial period, the colonial powers adopted a policy of recruitment which was designed to preserve an ethnic balance in order to forestall a unified revolt of the African armed forces. Thus the usual policy of the British colonial service was to recruit from among the minority ethnic groups such as the Tiv in Nigeria, and the Wakamba in Kenya for officer posts, while the soldiery was drawn from other ethnic groups; cf. generally, W. Gutteridge and N. Brown, *The African Military Balance*, Institute for Strategic Studies, 1964.
19. cf. W. J. Foltz, 'Psychoanalyse des armées sud-sahariennes', *Revue française d'études politiques Africaines*, February 1967, No. 14, pp. 22–30, at pp. 23–4.
20. For example, in a number of states, many officers attend evening classes in extension courses offered by colleges, and there meet and

discuss with civilian groups on many issues. This is based on private observation and information.

21. Again this is based on personal observation.

22. As one officer put it to one of the authors in the course of an interview, 'there is no such animal as "the army" separate from society. I have relatives and friends outside the army whose daily problems concern me as much as they concern any civilian. What distinguishes the army man from the civilian is that he feels a certain pride in belonging to a body which is the defender of the nation – that is all. But this does not destroy everything else.'

23. A. A. Afrifa, *The Ghana Coup 24th February 1966*, Cass, London, 1966, p. 93.

24. ibid.

25. cf. *Revue française d'études politiques Africaines*, January 1966, No. 1, p. 3.

26. cf. H. T. Alexander, *African Tightrope*, Pall Mall Press, London, 1965.

27. e.g. Colonel A. A. Afrifa's book (op. cit.) is an example of how intricate the question of motive for intervention can be. Afrifa's resentment of 'political' interference in army affairs, personnel, and strategy, comes out in his denunciation of Nkrumah's Congo policy, as he saw it, and in Nkrumah's dismissal of General Ankrah. Acts which a Ghanaian who approved of Nkrumah's Congo policy may have justified, are condemned by an officer who saw them through military spectacles.

28. cf. Gamel Abd-El Nasser, *The Philosophy of the Revolution*, Cairo, 1954.

29. Peter Mansfield, *Nasser's Egypt*, Penguin, London, 1969, p. 43.

30. The main factions were the Ansars (followers of the Mahdi) and the Khatmiyas (followers of Mirghani) cf. B. S. Sharma, 'The Sudan', in *The Politics of Demilitarisation* – collected seminar papers of the University of London Institute of Commonwealth Studies, April–May 1966, pp. 32–40.

31. ibid., p. 33.

32. ibid., p. 34.

33. Many Sudanese fondly refer to the event as 'the October Revolution'.

34. I have it from an eye-witness account that hospital nurses and dressers refused to treat members of the police who were injured during the clash.

35. After four-and-half years, the uneasy civilian rule that followed the Abbhoud régime was itself overthrown by an army *coup* in May 1969.

35a *See* text of speech delivered by President Nimeiry on June 9, 1969. *See also* Mamun A. Yusuf, *Evolution of the Conflict in Southern Sudan*, unpublished paper, May 1973.

36. There had been army mutinies led by non-commissioned officers: (1) in Togo in January 1963, in which the President, Sylvanus Olympio, was killed; (2) in East Africa in January 1964, which were put down with the aid of British troops sent at the request of the governments concerned (i.e. Kenya, Tanganyika, and Uganda). There was also an old-style revolution in Zanzibar which deposed the Sultan in January 1964; and before that there was a revolt in the Congo, in August 1963, organized by the labour unions and radical militant groups, which resulted in the overthrow of the régime of President (Abbé) Fulbert Youlou. Two abortive *coups* must be noted, viz. (*a*) the attempted *coup*

of December 1960 in Ethiopia, and (*b*) the attempted *coup* in Gabon in February 1964 which was suppressed by French troops sent by President de Gaulle at the request of President Leon M'ba.

37. *See* Chapter 2.
38. Some units of the army were out taking part in the film on the battle of Algiers. This avoided suspicion.
39. cf. *Middle East Journal*, Vol. 20, No. 3, autumn 1966, p. 364.
40. Art. 56.
41. Arts. 23 and 34 respectively.
42. Art. 59.
43. cf. W. A. Lewis, 'The Decline of Algeria's F.L.N.', *Middle East Journal*, spring 1966, Vol. 20, No. 2, pp. 161–72.
44. ibid.
45. The confidant turned out to be a secret agent of the Boumedienne group.
46. cf. his speech to the O.A.U. Summit in May 1963, Addis Ababa, where he made an impassioned appeal: 'Let us die a little so that more will be free.'
47. W. A. Lewis, op. cit., p. 161.
48. Bachir Boumaza (Minister of Information), Ali Mahsas (Minister of Agriculture) and Mohammed Smain (Minister of Reconstruction and Housing) resigned and joined O.C.R.A., in the course of 1966.
49. cf. *Le Monde*, February 1967.
50. *Le Monde*, 1 March 1967.
51. ibid.
52. ibid.
53. 12 January 1967.
54. We use the new name of former Congo Leopoldville – Kinshasa. The people are Zairiens.
55. Kimba was later hanged with others on charges of treason, after a trial lasting a few hours – *see* note 58.
56. The Belgians were not alone in this type of conduct. France 'punished' Guinea (and later Mali) by similar withdrawals plus destruction of vital medical and other supplies and documents, when Guinea chose independence in 1958.
57. Now renamed Kinshasa, Kisangani, and Lumumbashi, respectively.
58. Kimba had been one of Tshombe's chief lieutenants during Katanga's two-and-a-half years of secession. As noted above, he was later hanged with others on charges of conspiracy to overthrow the Mobutu régime.
59. cf. B. Kalongi and Z. Kirbidi, 'Elections Force et Parlement 1965', *Études Congolaises*, January–February 1966, pp. 1–5.
60. ibid.
61. It is claimed that Tshombe had tried to seize power by a *coup d'état* in November 1965 aided by an unnamed foreign government. ibid.
62. In a document entitled *De la légalité a la légitimité* appearing under Mobutu's name. It contains certain policy statements which will be examined later.
63. The size is estimated at 200; cf. K. W. J. Post, 'The Nigerian Case', in *The Politics of Demilitarisation*, University of London, Institute of Commonwealth Studies, collected seminar papers, May 1966, p. 55.

64. Post, ibid.; cf. also P. Keatly, *Guardian*, 26/27 January 1966.
65. cf. *Nigeria 1966*, publication of the Federal Republic of Nigeria, Lagos, pp. 5–6.
66. Post, K., op. cit., pp. 57–8.
67. ibid.
68. The size of the army was 9,000 plus 24,000 police in a population of over 50,000,000.
69. *Nigeria 1966*, op. cit., p. 57.
70. ibid., pp. 8–9.
71. ibid., p. 9.
72. It was claimed by the government of the Eastern Region that as many as 1,800,000 Ibos returned to the Region, leaving their property behind.
73. Ojukwu had declared that the Eastern Region would secede only if attacked or blockaded. cf. *West Africa*, 15 April 1967, p. 507.
74. A. A. Afrifa, op. cit.
75. ibid., p. 32.
76. ibid., pp. 34–5.
77. Radio Accra announcement by the army, 24 February 1966.
78. General Ankrah's broadcast, 28 February 1966.
79. For study of some of the historical socioeconomic forces which were at the root of the failure of Nkrumah's régime cf. B. Fitch and M. Oppenheimer: *Ghana: End of an Illusion*, Monthly Review Press, New York and London, 1966.
80. Radio Accra, 1 March 1966.
81. A. A. Afrifa, op. cit.
82. *Observer*, 13 March 1966.
83. A. A. Afrifa, op. cit., p. 103.
84. ibid., p. 105.
85. ibid., pp. 70–1.
86. cf. Nkrumah's book: *Challenge of the Congo*, Nelson, London, 1967.
87. On the question of the role of Ghana in Zaire, it is worth noting that President Nkrumah followed a moderate course between the Casablanca states, who withdrew their troops, and the Monrovia group, which supported the continued presence of the U.N. Nkrumah's (English) commander, General Alexander commended his decision in keeping the Ghana contingent under U.N. command. cf. Alexander, op. cit.
88. 'Their's not to reason why
Their's but to do and die' – Alfred, Lord Tennyson, 'The Charge of the Light Brigade'.
89. op. cit., p. 100.
90. ibid.
91. op. cit., p. 33.
92. Alexander, op. cit., p. 92.
93. cf. Press release No. 4, Ghana Information Service, 1 March 1966. In this publication, the military rulers bitterly condemn Nkrumah's decision to send cadets to the Soviet Union.
94. To my astonishment, not one Ghanaian student that I have talked to in England either immediately after the *coup* or since has raised a voice, even in private conversation, to defend Nkrumah against some

K

THE ADVENT OF MILITARY RULE

of the attacks made by the military régime or by the Western Press.

95. op. cit., p. 105.

96. cf. Fitch and Oppenheimer, op. cit., p. 2.

97. op. cit., pp. 2–3.

98. Not much is known about the details of the attempted counter-*coup*. Two of the leaders, two lieutenants, were executed after a summary trial.

99. The variety of terms used for the committees is of interest. In Nigeria the committee was called the Supreme Military and Federal Executive Council, in Ghana it was called the National Liberation Council; in Sierra Leone it was called the National Reformation Council. In Ghana the committee formed after 1972 *coup* was called the National Redemption Council.

100. The size of the Togolese army then was estimated at 400 men. The ex-servicemen numbered up to 1,000 men.

101. The armed forces at the time of the last *coup* consisted of an army of 1,200 men, a navy of 250 men, a gendarmerie of 1,000, and a police force of about 300.

102. The Vice-President was involved in the dissension, and during Grunitsky's absence had threatened to use his temporary powers as acting President to dismiss the ministers holding opposing views. Grunitsky's reason for the abolition of the office was that 'a two-headed executive was unsuited to Africa'.

103. cf. *Le Monde*, 15 April 1967.

8

Problems of Military Neo-Presidentialism

Some writers make a distinction between military régimes and régimes of military provenance. The latter comprise all régimes that succeed a military intervention, mostly with a civilian government or with a civilian-dominated government. The government of the Fifth Republic of France is classed by these writers as a régime of military provenance.[1] Military régimes, on the other hand, are 'régimes in which the civilian authorities act wholly or in major part under the covert direction of the military leadership, or alternatively, where the military govern directly in their own name'.[2] The régimes in the African states where successful military *coups* have taken place within the past six years come within this definition.

It may be reiterated here that all military régimes start by declaring their transitional nature: that they have come 'to put the house in order', 'to conduct a mopping up operation', and that as soon as peace and stability has been achieved (or whatever mission they have assigned themselves) they will surrender all power to a civilian government. So far, two of the military régimes, Dahomey and Ghana, have surrendered power of their own accord, to civilian governments which were later ousted by other military régimes. In the meantime the military rule several African states. An examination of the structure of the executive under a military régime is therefore relevant to the present study.

1. THE STRUCTURE OF THE MILITARY EXECUTIVE

The characteristic feature of the military executive in Africa is the complete concentration of governmental power in its hands and its direct supervision of critical sectors of the government administration. All military executives are, in essence, the same, whatever variety of extra-military means they use as intruments of control as local conditions may demand. In this chapter we shall examine significant aspects of the military executive through selective examples, and thereby offer some comments on trends and prospects, in general. The three states chosen for the purpose of this chapter are Algeria, Zaire, and Ghana. The fact that these states were former French, Belgian, and British possessions respectively is purely accidental. The reason for the choice is related to the nature of the change brought about by the *coup* in each state: in Algeria, the *coup* leaders declared their opposition to Ben Bella and that they were carrying on the revolution; in Zaire, Mobutu intervened to put an end to endemic political strife without basic constitutional change at the outset, but later made some basic changes. In Ghana, the *coup* leaders set out not only to depose one man and his colleagues, but to bring about a complete reversal of his policies. Ironically, the second military government was to uphold these policies.

Whatever the basic orientation of a military régime, one important fact of psychology impinges upon the organization of power under it: it is or is perceived generally as being more coercive than any civilian régime. The presence of the soldier is felt in all important sectors of public life. Nevertheless the military leaders are conscious of their limitations and invariably persuade some civilian leaders to give them support or to collaborate with them even at the executive level. Their declaration that they would hand over power to civilian rule and their preoccupation with legitimacy may be seen, at best, as a genuine desire to return government to its rightful claimants; i.e. representatives of the people; or at worst, as the compliment reluctantly paid by Might to Right. It is an aspect of the limitations of Might. It is essential to understand this limitation in order to appreciate the structure of military régimes and the actions of their leaders.

(a) Algeria

The proclamation of the Algerian Revolutionary Council vested supreme authority in Algeria in the Revolutionary Council, headed by Colonel Boumedienne after the *coup d'état*. After proclaiming the overthrow of President Ben Bella and his government, the Revolutionary Council persuaded the members of the National Assembly to sign a resolution entrusting to it the powers of the former President. Then, the Council, in its capacity as 'Head of State', passed three decrees (*ordonnances*) published on 13 July 1965, one of which established the organization of the executive power of the military régime.[3]

In the Algerian situation, where the Algerian revolution and its instrument the F.L.N. was not rejected but was recognized as the source of legitimacy, the transfer of power to the Council also meant that the Council replaced the leadership of the F.L.N. The Bureau Politique and the central committee of the F.L.N. disappeared – on the face of it, temporarily. The only higher organ of the party which was left to function was the executive secretariat.[4] The function of the executive secretariat is not one of decision-making but of preparation and execution of decisions taken by the Revolutionary Council (and previously by the Bureau Politique and the Secretary-General). In other words, the Council substituted itself for the Bureau and for the Secretary-General of the F.L.N., in regard to the issuing of orders to the party through the executive secretariat. The Council pays lip service to the primacy of the party, as it did during its meeting held from 15 November to 30 November 1965 in the following terms: 'the party is the first institution of the country, that which exalts and guides the creative power of the people.'[5]

After he had been 'instructed' to form his government, Colonel Boumedienne stated in a broadcast on 5 July that the F.L.N.'s task would be 'to construct and guide, animate and control, and not to conduct or substitute itself for the state'. It is not remarkable that the leader of an army *coup* should be at pains to warn the party against substituting itself for the state, when it is remembered that this was precisely what the army did itself, albeit provisionally. It must thus see in the F.L.N. an alternative source of state authority. The fact of paying lip service to the party as a source of legitimacy is distinguished from its being the source of authority, which is now plainly in the army. It is therefore reasonable to question the authenticity of this tribute to legitimacy, though it is indicative of the limitations of the army as a legitimized power-holder.

Boumedienne's cabinet was announced on 10 July 1965. It was a broad-based civilian government, in contrast to the military dominated Revolutionary Council.[6] The cabinet consisted of nine members of the outgoing cabinet, three former ministers who had resigned from the Ben Bella cabinet (Rabah Bitat, Ahmed Medegri, and Ahmed Kaid), and eight newcomers. Six of the nine members of the former cabinet retained their posts. Boumedienne was chairman of the cabinet as well as of the Revolutionary Council and Minister of Defense. The head of the government is thus also the Head of State. Diplomatic practice since then supports this view; all ambassadors have been received by Boumedienne.

Ordonnance No. 65–182 provided that the government 'holds power necessary for the functioning of the organs of the state and for the life of the nation'[7] by delegation from the Revolutionary Council. It is further provided that 'the measures taken by the government are taken according to the subject matter under the form of *ordonnances* and *décrets*'.[8]

This means that the government has been entrusted with legislative as well as executive powers. *Ordonnance* as used in French constitutional law and under the brief period of constitutional convention in Algeria, is used to signify a legislative instrument. One difficulty here was the interpolation of the phrase 'according to the subject matter' (*selon la matière*). The 1963 Constitution of Algeria, unlike most constitutions of Francophone states, did not provide for a list of legislative matters, as distinguished from regulatory matters. One way out of the difficulty was to state that any matter which, before 10 July 1965, had been dealt with by a law (*une loi*) or by an *ordonnance* was a legislative matter; and any matter otherwise dealt with was regulatory matter.[9] All the *ordonnances* issued by the head of the government (in the Council of Ministers) since 10 July 1965 have been legislative acts.

The government is subordinate to the Revolutionary Council, under whose authority and control it exercises its functions. The total or partial reshuffle of the cabinet is decided by the Council under an *ordonnance* (*par voie d'une ordonnance conciliaire*).[10] The ministers are individually responsible to the head of the government and the cabinet is collectively responsible to the Revolutionary Council. As to individual responsibility, this gives the head of the government power to dismiss a minister individually and thus maintain discipline, although his replacement by another is a matter for the Revolutionary Council to decide.[11] His chairmanship of the Revolutionary Council facilitates his choice of a new minister. This has proved to be practical and is logical in that he is Head of State as well as head of the government.

As to collective responsibility, the position is obviously different from that of a parliamentary system under which there are opposition forces. The role of the Revolutionary Council may be compared more profitably to that of the National Assemblies in African presidential systems. The difference is that in the case of the Revolutionary Council it is presided over by the chief executive himself, which reduces the role of the Council to a 'confessional' or an autocritical one. The principal point of resemblance emerges in respect of the predominant position of the chief executive and in the collaborative relationship between the executive and the National Assembly, which is also the case with the Revolutionary Council and the chief executive's position in it.[12] The 'controlling' role of the F.L.N., to which reference was made in the declaration by Boumedienne on 5 July 1965 does not extend to making the government answerable for any acts or omissions. Under the 1963 Constitution the F.L.N. had the right to do this. But even if that had not been changed, the post-independence F.L.N. had insufficient vitality left to mount a serious challenge to the military régime. Control of the F.L.N. had now passed to the military.

The military régime has been anxious to preserve the continuity of the policy set out in the Tripoli programme and in the Charter of Algiers.[13] The role of the F.L.N. was recast as an instrument of the 'execution of a coherent policy'.[14] But how it is to discharge this responsibility is not stated. On the other hand, two key concepts have been continually projected: (i) the state must be organized on the basis of respect for 'Arab and Islamic values', and (ii) the citizen must be more civic-minded; must develop the cult of the *chose publique*, show seriousness and exert constant effort. Socialism is asserted as part of the historical heritage of the Algerian nation.

All this partly explains the paradox of the F.L.N.'s position in the context of what is indisputably a military régime. It is also clear that the experiment of the Arab Socialist Union in the United Arab Republic was studied with care in Algeria. The Algerian military leaders must realize that a party embracing the masses is ultimately a necessary source of legitimacy and a guarantee of success. Without this, any régime, whatever its successes in other spheres, is doomed to dependence on brute force, which in the end destroys itself. The attempts that are being made to construct state power from the bottom show a preoccupation with the *chose publique*, a desire to build republican institutions.

(b) Zaire

In Zaire, the army under Mobutu took over power in November 1965. The High Command of the *Armée Nationale Congolaise* under General Mobutu issued a thirteen-point proclamation, dated 24 November 1965. President Kasavubu was replaced by General Mobutu, and Colonel Mulamba was appointed Prime Minister. But the institutions of the Republic were otherwise left intact.[15] In the afternoon of the same day both Houses of Parliament recognized General Mobutu's *coup* by approving his investiture by acclamation. The Constitution as a whole was not suspended, but the articles relating to the holding of presidential elections were and the President imposed a 'state of exception' (*état d'urgence*) for five years.[16]

The President also, by decree, extended the jurisdiction of military courts so as to include, *inter alia,* cases of corruption, embezzlement, etc. He placed the police under military control. The drastic nature of the Zairien *coup* was thus beginning to emerge gradually.[17] At the outset the Zairien *coup* had certain traits which distinguished it from the other *coups* that have taken place in Africa. The principal distinguishing feature was its substantial retention of the constitutional order as this existed before 24 November 1965. The continuation of the institutions such as Parliament no doubt helped the military régime to muster some civilian support. The move to obtain a parliamentary resolution recognizing the régime was proof of this. It was also perhaps a measure of the preoccupation with legitimacy. This is borne out by several statements made by President Mobutu and in particular in an official publication under the revealing title *De la légalité à la légitimité.*[18]

President Mobutu appointed Colonel Leonard Mulamba Prime Minister, while he himself retained the Defence portfolio. The Mulamba cabinet, of twenty-one, consisted of CONACO members and of the Congolese Democratic Front. All the provinces except one were represented in the cabinet.[19]

The real nature of Mobutu's military régime began to emerge in the new year. Opening a new session of Parliament on 7 March 1966, President Mobutu declared that henceforth Parliament would not debate decrees issued by him; and a presidential decree appeared on the same day vesting legislative powers in the President.[20] Article 2 of this law provided that all decrees issued by the President would be presented to Parliament, for information, within two months of their signature. Following the *coup* the position had been regulated by a law under which the President could legislate by decree; but any such decree could be annulled by the parliament.[21] Now the President took complete legislative power without any parliamentary veto.[22] President Mobutu explained this move by saying that the parliamentary deputies were not in agreement with some of his government's policies, or as he put it: 'unfortunately some of those who still depended on colonialists did not like our progressiveness. I had therefore to assume legislative power.'[23]

This move towards greater power to rule by decree was perhaps logical in view of the nature of a military régime which had not yet consolidated its power. This is more natural in a country with the political history and geography of Zaire. The move towards an increase in the power of the executive was also reflected in the decision (on 26 October 1966) by which President Mobutu abolished the office of Prime Minister and assumed the post himself. The explanation given by radio Kinshasa was that a divided executive impeded 'fulfilment of the task of national reconstruction'. The cabinet was reduced from twenty-one to seventeen, eight ministers were dropped from the new list, five ministers changed portfolios and four new ministers were appointed.

President Mobutu announced a number of far-reaching measures in the direction of strengthening central authority and also affecting industrial and commercial interests. A decree was issued on 10 April 1967, affecting the territorial, administrative, and political structure of the provinces.[24] The provincial autonomy that had existed hitherto was drastically curtailed. A Governor was appointed by the President for each province, as a representative of the central government directly responsible to the Minister of the Interior and to the other ministers on matters involving their ministries.[25] The provincial assemblies were reduced to provincial councils (to be directly elected) with advisory functions.[26]

Meanwhile a draft constitution was prepared and President Mobutu explained its nature and object in a message to the people given on 7 April 1967. After reminding the Congolese people of the evils of the previous régime, and expressing satisfaction at the progress made since the *coup* and the popular support his régime had received, as manifested in its reception during a recent presidential tour, he stated that the progress of the 'revolution' must obtain a legal foundation. 'The Second Republic', he now declared 'must create a new order, find new centres of power and lay the new foundations necessary for the direction of public affairs.' President Mobutu now began to speak about *La Révolution*, whereas he had hitherto been content to step into Kasavubu's presidential chair without disturbing the constitutional structure. Now he spoke of the Second Republic, and whereas before he spoke of the legitimacy of fact (*légitimité de fait*), he now announced that 'the revolution implies the creation of a new order, the validity of which is founded . . . on a legal order acceptable to the majority. This means that we must transform into law today's fact unanimously admitted by the mass of peasants and urban dwellers.[27] The proposed constitution follows the pattern of neo-presidentialism. There is a military executive, a unicameral National Assembly, and a unitary state. The President is to be elected by universal suffrage and will have extensive powers, including emergency powers[28] and the right to refer a matter for popular referendum in case of a dispute with the National Assembly.[29]

Zaire has travelled a long way since the crisis which followed immediately after independence, as Mobutu's régime proudly claims. The presence of rich mineral resources has made it an area of intrigue at an international level, as witnessed by the crisis of the early sixties and the dispute between the then government and Union Minière in the late sixties. One fact stands out beyond dispute regarding the line of direction followed by Mobutu's régime. Mobutu seems to have been influenced by the idea of a popular movement as a basis for a new party, in spite of the fact that he talked of a two-party system in his message introducing the draft constitution, and subsequent developments including the promulgation of the new constitution on June 24 1967 have led to the consolidation of the one party.

(c) Ghana

The Ghana military régime that replaced Nkrumah was different from the Algerian régime in that it not only abolished the constitutional structure of the previous régime but purported to install an entirely different régime in its place.

On 26 February 1966, two days after the *coup*, a Proclamation was issued by the leaders, establishing the National Liberation Council (N.L.C.) 'for the administration of Ghana and for the matters connected thereto'. The Proclamation, *inter alia*, suspended the Constitution of Ghana, 1960, and all amendments thereto.[30] The National Assembly was dissolved, political parties were banned, and all the members of the previous government were dismissed.

The N.L.C. consisted of eight members including the chairman, General Joseph Ankrah, and the deputy chairman, Police Commissioner Harlley.[31] The members were named by the Proclamation as amended by decree issued later.[32]

The N.L.C. assumed supreme power; legislative and executive powers were vested in it. It was empowered to legislate by decree until a new constitution was promulgated and a new government based thereon was formed.[33] Paragraph 3 (3) of the Proclamation provided that in any case of inconsistency between the existing laws of Ghana, which remained in force, and the provisions of any decree of the N.L.C., the latter should prevail.

Executive power was retained by the N.L.C. But the removal of the whole Nkrumah cabinet had left a vacuum which could not be filled by the N.L.C. itself. Consequently, the N.L.C. passed the Ministers Functions (Delegation) Decree, 1966,[34] authorizing Principal Secretaries to exercise ministerial functions, while the N.L.C. retained supervisory control.

Thus the role of the civil servant assumed great significance immediately after the *coup*. The magnitude of the work and the comparative lack of experience of the army officers in ministerial functions compelled the passing of N.L.C.D. 11, placing civil servants in ministerial positions. It has often been written that civil servants and the military make better 'partners' in view of their professional and organizational approach to matters. Such a belief presumes that civil servants and army officers are apolitical, concerned only with the administrative and technical side of things, which is a questionable assumption.

At any rate, the arrangement in Ghana soon proved unsatisfactory. In spite of N.L.C.D. 11 and the reasons behind it, it was clear that the N.L.C., unlike the Revolutionary Council in Algeria, retained close supervisory and directive links, and soon decided it must assume full executive function. N.L.C.D. 11 was cancelled and the N.L.C. divided up the ministries among its members.[35] The N.L.C. proclamation was amended on 15 November 1966 to include the provision that the N.L.C. might appoint one of its members to exercise any of the executive powers of the state and to take charge, under its direction, of such departments of state as were assigned to him.[36]

The power of appointment and dismissal was in the hands of the N.L.C. in all respects, including judicial and civil service posts. As to judicial appointments, the Judicial Service Act 1960 was amended, reintroducing the Judicial Service Commission which had been abolished previously. The Judicial Service Commission was appointed by the N.L.C. Initially it was to consist of seven members, including the Chief Justice.[37] This was changed later. The Commission later consisted of (i) the Chief Justice, (ii) the other Justices of the Supreme Court, (iii) other judges and magistrates and the judicial secretary, (iv) persons holding posts created under any other enactment, being designated by law as judicial service posts.[38] Judges were to be removable on the advice of the Judicial Service Commission, on the grounds of 'stated misbehaviour or infirmity of body or mind'.[39] The role of the Commission was advisory; the N.L.C. was not bound to act on its advice.

In September and October 1966, the N.L.C. announced a reduction in the number of judges from thirty-six to twenty-nine and sixteen of the former judges, including Mr. Sarkodee-Adoo, the Chief Justice since February 1964, were dismissed. In his place Mr. Akafu-Adoo was sworn in. He had been dismissed by President Nkrumah in February 1964 from his post as Judge of the Supreme Court.

The military régime also dismissed a large number of local magistrates, alleging that they were unqualified, inefficient, or corrupt. Similarly, chiefs dismissed by Nkrumah were restored and 194 paramount chiefs appointed by Nkrumah were reduced to their former status.[40] All this could be interpreted as being part of a purge or a 'mopping up operation' – of removing all vestiges of support for the previous régime, and consolidating the new one.

As to civil service appointments, the Civil Service Commission, which had been abolished, was reintroduced, and the former members of the Commission were reinstated for the remaining parts of their term with effect from the time immediately before the Commission was dissolved.[41] It is indicative of the view taken by the military leaders as to the role of the various institutions under the previous régime (as well as under their own) that they 'purged' the judiciary and dismissed the Members of Parliament, while they left the civil service intact. An observer has written in this regard as follows:

At no point was the civil service purged. . . . The N.L.C. installed officials from the Flagstaff House cabinet secretariat who were known for their ability and were least involved in policy-making under the older regime. (The two most senior holdovers were given respectable but less sensitive positions elsewhere). It also brought in a group of competent advisers from the ministries, who have added to the air of professionalism now evident in policy-making at the top.[42]

The N.L.C. also appointed various committees to advise it in discharging its functions, notably, at the outset, the Political Committee,[43] and the Administrative Committee.[44] The Political Committee was initially presided over by the present Chief Justice, and had twenty-three members, most of whom were prominent opposition leaders such as Dr. Busia (who was deputy chairman) and Mr. Joe Appiah. The Committee also contained representatives of all eight regions of Ghana and of the various interests in the community. Its function was to advise the N.L.C. on any policy decisions made, or enactments passed, since the *coup*. It reported weekly to the N.L.C. in fulfilment of such functions.[45]

The Administrative Committee was appointed to advise the N.L.C. on all matters relating to central and local government administration. It was required to work in close consultation with the Political Committee, advising on the political implications of N.L.C.'s decisions. It could make recommendations in respect of the machinery for the implementation of executive decisions and the general organization of the ministries and departments.

In matters of local government the N.L.C. made some drastic changes. The Local Government (Interim Administration) Decree, 1966 – N.L.C.D. 26, amended the Local Government Act 1961 to allow for the establishment of management committees, which were made up of central and local government personnel. These committees assumed the functions of the local councils elected under the 1961 Act.[46]

The general orientation of the Ghana military régime seemed to be in a direction diametrically opposed to that of the previous government. For example, General Ankrah announced a 'new liberal economy' in which active state participation would be limited to certain key basic projects and the private sector would remain 'the largest sector in terms of number of persons employed and gross output'.[47] In external policy, Dr. Nkrumah's dedication to the struggle for the total liberation of Africa and African unity was to be revised, or, as General Ankrah put it 'would be placed in a proper perspective'.[48]

In internal politics, the N.L.C. began the process of moving towards civilian rule. A constitutional commission was set up and started its work in the summer of 1966. The numerous committees which were set up (some fifteen in all) to purge the old régime and to advise the new one had mostly finished their work by 1968. The principal object of the military régime in setting up these committees was to reconstruct the whole government machinery according to a different philosophy. The constitutional commission was entrusted with the task of devising a constitution wherein power would be divided or distributed to avoid its concentration in the hands of one man. At the same time Kwame Nkrumah's achievement of a unified central administration was continued. Ghana was to continue as a unitary republic and the boundaries of the regions would continue as before the *coup*.[49]

As for the move to civilian rule, the Political Committee was the first step in that direction. The establishment of the constitutional commission to prepare a constitution and the appointment, in 1967, of Civilian Special Commissioners to be in charge of administering the ministries was the definite signal of a policy of demilitarization. The Special Commissioners were given full responsibility for administering the ministries assigned to them, subject to overriding national policy as laid down by the N.L.C. But the portfolios distributed to fourteen Civilian Special Commissioners did not include the key ministries of Defence, which was still headed by General Ankrah; Interior and External Affairs, retained by Mr. Harlley the deputy chairman of the N.L.C.; and Finance, held by Brigadier Afrifa.

A national advisory committee was also established to act as a general 'clearing house' for the Special Commissioners, and all the standing committees, save four, were abolished by 1968. The remaining four were the Economic, Administrative, Logistics, and Expediting Committees. The Ghana régime, in demolishing the previous constitutional and administrative machine, was faced with a complex set of political and administrative problems which compelled the creation of committees and more supervisory machinery. Thus the Expediting Committee was charged with the duty of making frequent and unannounced visits to public offices, of receiving and investigating complaints from any member of the public, and of following up decisions of the N.L.C. and ensuring their due execution.[50]

The Special Commissioners were given more power than the Principal Secretaries had. They were also expected to be more bold and imaginative. The *Ghanaian Times* warned them to 'insulate' themselves against 'the temptation to lean too heavily on the advice of civil servants', and advised them to be prepared 'to analyse critically red-tape ideas and initiate practical policies that are original and suited to our times'. The cautiousness of the military régime was shown not only by its retention of key ministries but also by its decision to establish a national centre for civic education, to be headed by Dr. Busia. Among the tasks of this centre was the important one of mobilizing the citizens behind the régime and for playing an active part in the government of the country, presumably with a view to preparing them for civilian rule.[51]

Ghana has proved to be a country destined to provide lessons to Africa in more than one sense. The National Liberation Council which wrested power from Nkrumah demonstrated that it is not enough to seize power. For one thing, as one observer has put it, 'the leaders of a coup arouse envy and resentment by the very fact of the success of their coup'.[52] Furthermore, the problems which affect civilian governments do not disappear with the advent of the military. 'Manufacturers will not raise the prices they pay to satisfy military rulers. Thus the N.L.C. had to devalue the Cedi (by thirty per cent) and impose import restrictions as any civilian government would have had to do in the face of the rising prices of European manufacturers and unstable cocoa prices.'[53]

The military ruled Ghana by decree for three-and-a-half years, before they decided to transfer power to a civilian government led by Dr. Kofi Busia, who was sworn in as Prime Minister on 3 September 1969. Afrifa, Harlley, and Ocran, the chief of defence staff, were sworn in as members of the Presidential Commission.

Ankrah's resignation in April of the same year on charges of corruption, which were openly admitted, had given poignancy to the plight of the military, who were paralysed by division. A military régime which has lost its cohesiveness is in no position to maintain a hold on the country even in the best of conditions. Thus the emergence of the old politicians and the transfer to a civilian government was inevitable in Ghana in the circumstances. Apart from the economic difficulties, ethnic rivalries and antagonism had reached the ranks of the N.L.C. Afrifa was Busia's supporter, a fellow Ashanti, while Harlley was Gbedemah's supporter – a fellow Ewe. Ocran was on the face of it uncommitted.

This was part of the background of the general elections of

29 August 1969, which returned Dr. Busia's Progressive Party with 105 seats out of the 140 seats of the National Assembly.

The circle was completed when the military staged a *coup* against the government of Dr. Busia. The new régime calls itself the National Redemption Council (N.R.C.). The word Redemption is revealing of the motives and ambitions of the new rulers. It is too early to pass any judgement one way or the other on the status and policy direction of Colonel Acheampong's régime, other than to note its commitment to Nkrumahist ideals in domestic policy.

Conclusion

Political power has its own occupational hazards and self-perpetuation in office is the prescription against such hazard. This is true of one-party as of military régimes. The original purpose can get lost easily in the maze of daily preoccupations. Whether the military set out simply to displace civilian leaders without basic change of structure, as in Algeria, or whether they start to dismantle the whole system, as in Ghana, the problems of disengagement inevitably arise. One authority on the subject has written: 'the key to the difficulties lies in that displacement or substitution implies the displacement of, or substitution for, a particular social and/or political grouping (e.g. Perfectionists, the C.P.P., the landlords, etc.) and is made . . . in the name of a particular military conception of the national interest, which definitionally, is opposed to that of the groups they have ejected and/or replaced.'[54]

Every military régime thus fears the return of the people it has replaced or the reinstatement of the principles and policies it has reversed, as must be the case with most of the military régimes in Africa. Nor is this the main source of threats. There is a real fear of counter-*coups* from within the military itself, for whatever reason or pretext. There may be 'young Turks' who demand more radical politics. Or there may be sympathizers with the previous régime, as was possibly the case in the abortive counter-*coup* in Ghana.

These difficulties determine the post-*coup* behaviour of military leaders. In Ghana the shock of the attempted counter-*coup*, in which the architect of the first *coup* was killed, seemed to drive the régime to make more energetic gestures of demilitarization, as the appointment of the Civilian Special Commissioners showed. Other régimes may be attracted by the example of the Nasserite experiment. If the example of the United Arab Republic is emulated it raises the problem of evolving a genuine political party and an acceptable leadership. The Algerian régime has laid emphasis on local communes as a basis of support. But even there, the F.L.N. acted as a Trojan Horse, without producing much enthusiasm from the population. In countries like Ghana, where the dominant party was proscribed and there was no alternative party, this problem was more acute. In Zaire, President Mobutu's cautious experiment in creating his own party, the M.P.R.C., shows an inclination towards the type of solution adopted in the United Arab Republic. But there is as yet no true foundation for its successful operation. And this is the problem facing most military régimes.

This problem limits the political freedom of the military leaders and causes them to lose initiative and control, drifting to a situation where they finally lose to the politicians. The course of politics in such a situation is not always predictable, but one thing is clear; if they drift and continue to rule without offering much betterment in the condition of life of the people, there will be other *coups* or civilian uprisings.

By taking direct control of government the military have lost their neutrality and political 'innocence', and will now be directly responsible for any mess that is created. In their case success is of special importance. The slightest gossip of corruption or inefficiency is more likely to harm their image than it would a civilian régime, because they have abandoned their neutral position and broken with legality in order to put an end to such evil. They must not only be honest and efficient but they must be seen to be so. It is being used in different forms in the Sudan and in Zaire. Above all they must create the right conditions for disengagement.

The United Arab Republic model is one possibility to be used with the necessary adaptations to suit local conditions. In states where the one-party system was synonymous with misrule and one of the reasons for intervention, the military leaders may be inclined to be prejudiced against such an experiment. But those who have the interest of their nations at heart – and there are many such – should be reminded that whatever mistakes the past régimes made, they must not allow themselves to be driven to make similar mistakes in the opposite direction. The problems need to be re-examined with depth and vision, always bearing in mind the interests of the people. Let there be devices against

L

abuse of power, by all means. But experience has shown that divided power can be ineffective, and a source of disunity and therefore more strife. This would mean more *coups* and counter-*coups*, which would reduce politics on the African continent to a game of musical chairs. The people of Africa, as indeed all other people, do not deserve such a fate.

NOTES

1. cf. S. F. Finer. 'The Military Disengagement from Politics', in *The Politics of Demilitarisation*, op. cit. (p. 258, note 30), pp. 1–10, at p. 1.
2. ibid.
3. cf. *Ordonnances* (1) No. 65–180, of 22 June 1965; (2) No. 65–181, of 22 June 1965; and (3) No. 65–182, of 10 July 1965. The first two were concerned with amnesty and the release of certain categories of prisoners. The third, *Ordonnance* No. 65–182, provided that pending the promulgation of a constitution, the Revolutionary Council was to be the depository of sovereign authority.
4. cf. François Borella, 'Algérie, L'organisation actuelle des pouvoirs', in *Revue Algérienne des sciences juridiques, politiques, et économiques*, December 1965, Nos. 3–4, pp. 29–39, at p. 37.
5. cf. *El Moujahid*, 2 December 1965.
6. Of the twenty-six members of the Council, fifteen were military men. To my knowledge the list of members has not been published.
7. Art. 3.
8. Art. 6. The term 'decree' in English represents the two terms, i.e. *ordonnances* and *décrets*, which are sometimes used interchangeably.
9. F. Borella, has suggested this, op. cit., p. 38.
10. Art. 3, *Ordonnance* No. 65–182. The term *Ordonnance-conciliaire* as used with the suffix *conciliaire* is distinct from one without such a suffix, which originates from the cabinet.
11. cf. F. Borella, op. cit., p. 38.
12. Another comparison has been made with the assembly government (presumably) of the post-revolution era of the French Assembly. cf. F. Borella, op. cit., p. 39.
13. cf. Proclamation of 19 June, and 5 July 1965. *See also* Chapter 7 for a summary of the Tripoli programme.
14. ibid.
15. cf. Paras 1, 3 and 4 of the Proclamation.
16. Under the 1964 Constitution the President was elected for five years by Members of Parliament, by the delegates of Leopoldville, and the Members of the Provincial Assemblies. He was eligible for re-election for one consecutive term – cf. Arts. 55 and 56.
17. cf. A. Rubens, 'La justice militaire', *Revue Juridique du Congo*, January–February–March 1966, No. 1, pp. 3–12.
18. Haut Commissariat à l'Information, Congo, Kinshasha, 1966. Mobutu argues in this document that his régime was invested with a legitimacy of fact, issuing from the power vacuum which existed owing to the political chaos in the previous régime: *Plutot que parler d'une prise du*

pouvoir par l'armée, il faudrait en ce cas saluer la renaissance du pouvoir (p. 13).

19. cf. *Ordonnances* No. 1 of 24 November 1965; No. 2 of 28 November 1965; and No. 10 of 7 December 1965.
20. *Ordonnance* No. 66/92 *bis* of 7 March 1966.
21. *Ordonnance-loi* No. 7 of 30 November 1965.
22. These measures are reminiscent of the colonial system. Under the Belgian *Charte Coloniale* (Art. 22), the central executive had power, by decree, to take measures which fell normally within the domain of law. The *loi fondamentale* of 19 May 1960, which was the basis of the independence Constitution, also retained this power to legislate by decree, with the proviso that Parliament could, within six months, reject the decree.
23. *Le Monde*, 3 September 1966.
24. *Ordonnance* No. 67–177, 10 April 1967.
25. Art. 5. *Ordonnance* 67–177. Before the decree was issued, new governors had been sworn in for the eight new provinces which replaced the former twenty-one. The new governors, who were career civil servants and state employees, were required to serve in provinces other than the place of their origin, a measure designed perhaps to ensure loyalty to the central government, as well as impartiality.
26. Art. 11, ibid.
27. cf. *Études Congolaises*, March–April 1967, pp. 65–92.
28. Art. 54, Draft Constitution. (Art. 21 of new Constitution).
29. Art. 29. Draft Constitution. Mobutu was elected president for seven years by universal direct suffrage pursuant to Art. 21 of the new (1967) constitution. There was a break with the past, a move from the parliamentary system with a dual executive to a military neo-presidential system.
30. Para. 2 of the Proclamation.
31. Its composition was evenly divided between the army and the police.
32. Para. 1, Proclamation, and Decree No. 1 of 1 March 1966.
33. Para. 3 of Proclamation, as amended by Decree No. 1. All the Decrees issued by the N.L.C. will hereafter be referred to as N.L.C.D.
34. N.L.C.D. 11.
35. N.L.C.D. 67 of 25 June 1966. Seventeen ministries were divided among the seven members of the N.L.C., including the vice-chairman, Mr. Harlley, who held the portfolios of Interior, External Affairs, Information and Secretariat of Departments under the N.L.C. Defence was held by General Kotoka, and General Ankrah remained as Chairman, but assumed command of the armed forces upon Kotoka's death.
36. N.L.C.D. 104. Para. 1(a).
37. Judicial Service Act (Amendment) Act, 1966, N.L.C.D. 39.
38. N.L.C.D. 83, 1966.
39. N.L.C.D. 39. Para. 1(5).
40. cf. N.L.C.D. 112.
41. N.L.C.D. 17. Para. 3(2).
42. W. Scott Thomson, 'New Directions in Ghana', in *Africa Report*, November 1966, p. 18.
43. N.L.C.D. 59, 14 June 1966.
44. N.L.C.D. 31.

45. cf. *West Africa*, 25 February 1966.
46. cf. Para. 3 of the Decree.
47. Statement of 12 March 1966.
48. ibid.
49. cf. N.L.C.D. 73.
50. cf. N.L.C.D. 99. Paras. 3(a), (b) and (c).
51. Subsequent events showed that Busia used this centre to campaign for the presidency. He then abolished the centre – presumably so as to block its being used against his presidency.
52. cf. Peter Enahoro, *Africa* No. 10, June 1972.
53. Enahoro, op. cit.
54. S. F. Finer, op. cit., p. 2.

Index